Mixed Plate

Mixed Plate

CHRONICLES OF AN
ALL-AMERICAN COMBO

JO KOY

DEY ST.
An Imprint of WILLIAM MORROW

HarperCollins books may be purchased for educational, business, or sales promotional use. For information, please email the Special Markets Department at SPsales@harpercollins.com.

FIRST EDITION

Designed by Michelle Crowe

Library of Congress Cataloging-in-Publication Data has been applied for.

ISBN 978-0-06-296996-5

21 22 23 24 25 LSC 10 9 8 7 6 5 4 3 2 1

For my son, who made me be a better father,

a better comic, and a better man.

You continue to inspire me every day.

CONTENTS

INTRODUCTION

I was walking down the streets of Manila a few months ago, taking it all in.

One block was like something out of a postcard. This gorgeous park with long winding paths, lawns that were the greenest of green, and huge tropical trees like you'd see in a rain forest.

A couple of blocks later, suddenly it was nothing but skyscrapers, fancy restaurants, high-end shopping, and casinos. The kind of energy you might find in Tokyo, Singapore, or any other rich, major metropolis in the world.

A few blocks after that, and it was like I was in a different universe. Unfinished buildings that were nothing but skeletons, no windows, no siding, no nothing. Shanties built out of scrap metal where people lived and sold souvenirs to the occasional tourists who walked by. Mothers washing their naked kids with buckets of water in the middle of the street.

But no matter who I saw, no matter who I talked to, rich or poor—every single person was smiling. Every one of them was full of life and happy.

I lived here forty years ago. Spent a few years on Clark Air Base with my white all-American dad, my Filipina mom, and my brother and sister. Base life is a far cry from the city, and I was young, just nine or ten, but I still remember coming to Manila to shop on weekends, the streets looking almost the same as they do now. And I've been back to visit a thousand times since then, seeing my family, bringing my son to learn about his roots.

But this time—this time was different.

This time I was here to shoot my third comedy special for Netflix—my third! I wasn't some struggling LA comic who worked three jobs on the side and could barely pay his rent. I was living the American dream.

I sold out massive arenas everywhere I went. I owned a house in the Hollywood Hills. My son was about to graduate from private school. He didn't have to scrounge for spare change to get lunch from a vending machine like I did when I was a kid—he had a fancy debit card to buy fucking filet mignon in his cafeteria!

I used to worry about what other Americans would say when I told them I was Filipino, how they'd respond, how they might judge me. TV networks turned me down over and over again, saying my story was too "ethnic" and white people wouldn't "get it."

Now I was being paid by the biggest platform in entertainment to shoot a special *in* the Philippines *about* the Philippines. I was gonna tell my own mixed-up, mixed-plate story, I was gonna show off my culture to the world—and I was getting rich doing it.

In all the ways I'd ever hoped, I'd made it. And yet, even as I walked down the streets of my childhood with a film crew following along, even as I realized just how much I'd accomplished, deep in my mind I could still hear my mom the very first time I told her I was gonna be a comic.

"*What?* Josep, you want to be a clown? Is that what you're telling me, Josep? *Ha?* You want to make your living being a *clown*??"

Yeah, Mom. A clown. That's what I want to be.

As I built my career, she kept coming at me with those same

doubts, those same questions constantly. Swear to God, to this day she thinks I should get a management job at Macy's so I can lock down some decent benefits.

And that's why I'm writing this book. Because after all this time, all my struggle and sacrifice, my mom still doesn't really understand.

Not just my mom, either. Friends, family, fans—it's hard for people to understand what it means to be successful as a comic, especially when you come from such a different place, such a difficult background.

In a way, it *should be* hard for people to understand. When I get up there onstage in front of a thousand people, I have one goal—to make them laugh. To help them have fun and escape all their problems, even if it's just for a few hours.

I want them to be dazzled by the lights and electrified by the music. I want them to connect with my stories and my voices and my characters. I want them begging for more.

I don't want them to leave my show being like, "Oh man, the depths of your pain and heartache, fuck!" I want them to cheer, "Bro, you killed it! I never laughed so hard in my fucking life!"

I *love* to make people laugh. I live for it. I have since I was a little kid.

But when I tell my jokes about white people not knowing "what I was" when I was little, when I talk about my mom driving me crazy or my sister getting kicked out of our house or my stepdad making cracks about Asians eating rice—as funny as that shit is there's real emotion behind it, too. Real conflict. Real darkness.

I hint at it in my act. If you're paying attention, it's there. And I actually think that that emotional honesty is a big reason why so many people from so many cultures relate to my stories.

But I never really opened up about my mom's constant judgment, about my dad leaving us, about my brother's violent schizophrenia, or about my own struggles to be a good father to my son. I never really opened up about how hard it was growing up as a half-breed Filipino in suburban America. I never really opened up about all the barriers I had to overcome in the racist entertainment industry as I built my career brick by brick and show by show.

I never really opened up—until this book.

Walking through the streets of the Philippines, this place I'd once so briefly called home but which held the key to so much of who I am, it hit me that it was a land of contradictions.

If you stick to one area, you might think it's the most perfect, most pristine country in the world. Push a little farther, go a little deeper, and you find the poverty, the struggle, the pain. But underlying it all there's a joy, a laughter, a loving spirit that can't be broken.

There's something beautiful about that. Something magical. Something universal. Something that always makes me want to come back for more.

I hope you'll find some of that same magic here, in my book. And that you'll be laughing your ass off along the way.

Mixed Plate

1

THE **AMERICAN** WAY

Lumpia

MAKES 30 *LUMPIA*, TO SERVE 8–10 PEOPLE
(IT DEPENDS ON YOUR APPETITE!)

INGREDIENTS

1 tablespoon vegetable oil, plus more for frying
1 pound ground pork or beef
2 garlic cloves, crushed
½ cup onion, medium diced
½ cup minced carrots
½ cup thinly sliced green cabbage
½ cup bamboo shoots
1 teaspoon garlic powder

1 teaspoon ground black pepper
1 teaspoon sea salt
1 teaspoon soy sauce
2 eggs
1 box of pre-prepared *lumpia* wrappers (you can buy these in any Asian grocery; each box usually contains 30 wrappers)
1 cup of dipping sauce (sweet and sour, ketchup, or soy sauce)

INSTRUCTIONS

1. In a wok or large saucepan, heat the vegetable oil over high heat. Add the ground meat and cook, stirring often, until browned, about 5 minutes. Transfer the meat to a strainer/colander to drain the excess oil from the meat and set aside. Drain all but about 1 tablespoon of the grease from the wok. Add the garlic, onion, carrots, cabbage, and bamboo shoots and season with the garlic powder, pepper, salt, and soy sauce. Cook over medium heat, stirring often, until the vegetables are softened, about 7 minutes, then stir in the browned meat. Remove from the heat and let cool for about an hour, or until cool enough to handle.

2. Beat the eggs in a small bowl. Separate the *lumpia* wrappers and lay them on a clean work surface (work in batches, if necessary). Place 1 tablespoon of the cooled *lumpia* filling on a wrapper, placing it toward the end closest to you. Working from the filled end, roll the wrapper tightly away from you to enclose the filling, then fold in the left and right sides and continue rolling. When you get to the

end, use your fingers to brush the edge of the wrapper with the beaten egg to seal the *lumpia*. Lay the assembled *lumpia* flat in a large zip-top plastic bag. Keep the bag closed as you work so the assembled *lumpia* don't dry out. Continue filling the wrappers, separating each *lumpia* with layers of waxed paper so they don't stick together.

3. In a medium saucepan, heat 2 cups vegetable oil over high heat until oil is so hot it sizzles if you add a pinch of filling. Carefully drop 4 or 5 *lumpia* into the hot oil and fry for about 2 minutes, until golden brown on all sides. Using tongs, transfer the *lumpia* to a paper towel to drain and repeat to fry the remaining *lumpia*. Best served hot. Dip it in your choice of sweet and sour sauce, ketchup, or soy sauce, and enjoy!

Mom, everyone else is only taking one ticket!"

"I don't care, Josep! Do you want this TV? Ha? Then fill them *all* out!"

"But Mom—"

"Do it, Josep!"

It was 1982. I was eleven years old, just a kid, barely getting used to life in the States. Only a few months back I had been living in the Philippines, a place thousands of miles away where people were brown like me, pretty much everyone was poor as hell, and our barbecue was so good we put that shit on bamboo swords.

Now here I was, in Tacoma, Washington, my new home, standing in this dazzling, massive JCPenney, surrounded by all this amazing *stuff*—clothes, perfumes, electronics, stereos, TVs, toys. Mountains and mountains of stuff there was *no way* we could afford.

But apparently there was a way besides money that we could get some stuff. The store was having a raffle at 6 p.m., and the grand prize was a massive Sony color TV.

And my mom was going to win that thing, or her kids were going to die trying.

"But Mom," I pleaded, "people are watching!"

"So what!" she said. "Go get more, Josep! Now!"

The blank raffle tickets were stacked on a table in the middle of the store next to a clear barrel. You know the kind, big and plastic with a crank on the side. Fill out your raffle ticket, put it in the barrel, and at the end of the day the raffle master spins it around and pulls out the lucky winner's ticket.

Each person was supposed to enter once. Just one ticket in the barrel. One.

Not us.

My mom is this tiny little four-foot-ten Filipino lady with short hair and gigantic glasses, and man, she didn't give a *shit* about those rules. She still doesn't care about rules. She got us to the mall at 9 a.m., right after it opened, just to hunt for some discount clothes, but as soon as she saw the sign for that raffle she put her little son and teenage daughter to work. All day, grabbing stacks and stacks of tickets off that table, filling them out and stuffing them in the big plastic barrel. We'd finish one stack, turn around, grab another, and start again. "Mom, my hand is sore!" my sister Rowena cried.

"Just write!"

"Mom, I'm losing feeling in my arm!" I pleaded.

"Just write!"

When my mom wasn't looking, I took a three-second break to stretch my aching fingers and gaze upon the prize, perched high on a display in all its glory. There were no flat screens back then, but this baby was about as close as you could get. I'd never seen a TV that big or that beautiful. It was a giant work of plastic art. I wanted that television almost as much as my mom did.

I took a deep breath, gritted my teeth, and kept writing. If my fingertips were bleeding? Fine. If Rowena was getting carpal tunnel at the age of fifteen? Totally cool. As far as we were concerned, that television was worth an amputated limb or two.

Because it wasn't really just about the TV, you know? For us, this was about *America*.

My mom had dreamed of coming to this country and building a life for herself and her family. It was her only dream, her single goal—get to America. Plus, maybe getting a good-paying job with benefits.

Now we were finally here, and we wanted everything it meant to be American. We wanted the expensive new stuff in that mall. We wanted that huge Sony TV—who *cares* if it was made in Japan!—and all the American TV shows in their rich, pixelated reds, yellows, and blues. We wanted *Happy Days* and *Mork & Mindy* and *Laverne & Shirley*.

To me and my family, that culture, that consumerism, that stuff—that was America. We wanted it. Because if we had the stuff, we'd be like our neighbors. We'd be one step closer to fitting in.

There was just one problem. No one here had ever seen anything like me before.

☙

MY MOM AND DAD CAME from opposite ends of the world—in more ways than one.

My dad, John Charles Herbert, was the poster boy for white, traditional America. He came of age in the late 1960s, when the whole country was up in flames. The Vietnam War, civil rights, protests and revolution everywhere, free love and Woodstock, Jimi Hendrix tripping on acid, the whole deal.

But my dad? No free-loving hippie, this guy. This guy was from Buffalo, New York, the whitest of all white towns in the world—white people, white snow, white picket fences, white everything.

I mean, this dude grew up getting *milk* delivered to his *house.* Think about that—actual glass jars of ice-cold milk delivered to his house every morning by a nice, polite white gentleman in a spiffy blue uniform. His life was like a scene from one of Norman Rockwell's wet dreams.

His parents were conservative and Wonder Bread–white, and he looked like the old movie star Robert Conrad. Chiseled jaw, brown-blond hair parted perfectly on the side, and his eyes—oh man, his eyes were so blue, so bright, so piercing. He was a man's man. Old-school. He smoked a carton of cigarettes a day, he ironed and starched all his clothes *including* his T-shirts and shorts, and he'd spend all afternoon changing the oil on his car instead of shelling out twenty-five dollars to get it done in thirty minutes.

So, when my dad graduated from high school in 1965, did he take to the streets and fight the Man? Hell no, he signed up for the Air Force—actually *enlisted* in the military while thousands and thousands of other kids were doing everything they could to avoid the draft—and got shipped right off to Nam.

Then you have my mom, Josephine Magluyan. Born the same year as my dad, but raised in the Philippines, the other side of the globe from Buffalo, New York. Forget about cold bottles of milk on your doorstep; for breakfast she would have milk *fish*—an actual kind of fish that's so popular there it's seriously like the national fish—in this amazing dish called *Daing na Bangus.* Each fish sliced open, marinated in vinegar, and fried golden brown. Delicious. But my dad couldn't have even pronounced that stuff, and he certainly wouldn't eat it.

It's kind of weird to say it, but where my dad was straitlaced and square, when my mom was young she was *cool.* The woman who eventually became the practical, rule-making, tough-loving terror of my childhood—who *to this day* thinks that I should quit this whole standup thing and find a nice steady office job with a dental plan—that same woman used to be hip. Or groovy. Or whatever they called it back in the sixties.

Mom looked like an Asian version of the go-go dancers from *Laugh-In*. She had short hair like she does now, except back then it wasn't poufy mom hair, it was a cute, trendy pixie cut with little curls wrapped around each ear. She even wore those polyester miniskirts with their psychedelic patterns, lime-green swirls, and electric-pink flowers all over the place.

But that's nothing compared to the real mind-blower. Ready for this?

My mom had a job . . . *without a decent benefits package.* Hell, forget about decent—there was no medical, there was no dental, there was no retirement plan.

My mother managed a band. And you know what? I think she kind of enjoyed it.

As no-nonsense as she was later in life, my mom was incredibly talented and charismatic. She loved to entertain, loved to be part of the action, loved to be involved with singing, performing, anything that got her close to a stage. If you got her to a party, she wasn't standing on the sidelines like some prude—she was out on the dance floor, going crazy to the latest Motown song, doing all the hippest new moves. The Loco-Motion, the Mashed Potato, Twist. And when the 1970s hit? Forget about it. She was a *master* of the line dance. My mom is where I get all my talent from, no question.

That's the thing with Filipinos and Filipino culture. Really all third-world cultures. From the day we're born, we all grow up being entertainers, nurturing our passion and our talent. Why? We don't have any choice! We can't afford to go to concerts or shows or even movies. We can barely even buy a decent radio.

So, what do we do? We entertain ourselves.

You want to throw a party? Fine, my son can dance his ass off, and my daughter can sing. And if they can't sing or dance? Fuck it, we'll make them sing and dance anyway—and now we got our comedy.

But once we hit adulthood, right around eighteen, that's when the responsibility clock strikes midnight, all the magic ends, and this little voice starts whispering in our multicultural ears: *No more talent! Talent will not pay the bills! Get a real job!*

That's why no one is better at karaoke than Filipinos, no one. You got all these Filipino nurses running around, checking heart rates and replacing catheters, and when they don't think anyone is looking they're belting out "Don't Stop Believing" to that dude in a coma. Yeah, they want him to keep believing, but mostly they think they can sing better than Steve Perry—or Arnel Pineda, for that matter.

Back in the sixties, in her late teens and early twenties, my mom was riding that talent train.

With the Vietnam War going on, you didn't just have destruction and napalm, you also had a whole bunch of American soldiers who needed to be entertained. Back then, these guys didn't have shit to do—no iPhones or TVs or Facebook, no nothing. So, give them a cover band of good-looking English-speaking Filipinos who sing and dance like the Supremes, performing all their favorite Motown hits, and those soldiers are gonna go ape shit.

And that's exactly what my mom and her friends did. Traveled from base to base, putting on fancy dresses and singing American music for American soldiers. My mom wasn't one of the singers, but she understood business and spoke English very well, so she negotiated all the deals. She was the brains behind the whole operation.

Now put yourself in my dad's shoes.

You're this young, starchy, blue-eyed conservative white dude from upstate New York, where you get your whole milk delivered in glass jars. You've never even *seen* an Asian woman; it's 1969 and here you are in the middle of Saigon, bored out of your mind. You head over to a Filipino music show, and you meet the young, hot Filipina chick managing the band—and your brain just freaks out.

Holy shit! Your eyes are the shape of almonds! Your hair is black! You're always tan and you never even have to lie in the sun! ***And*** *you speak English* ***and*** *you're wearing a sexy pink and purple miniskirt??!!*

I ain't got time to be a racist! Politics can suck a dick!

Of course, his parents back in upstate New York didn't approve. They knew nothing about Asian people, and they definitely didn't have any Asian friends. If they had any exposure to Asians at all, it was from their local Chinese restaurant.

What? Our son is dating one of the Chans who runs Lucky Dragon Kitchen? Is he crazy?

But that wasn't gonna stop my dad—he was young, he was impressionable. And he was in love.

For my mom, who'd always dreamed of moving to America with all its opportunities, my dad represented everything she wanted out of life. He wasn't just *from* America, he looked *like* America. He looked like a movie star, like all the Hollywood leading men she had seen on the posters, and now he was all hers.

Sure, getting American citizenship was more than just a nice little bonus. It was a game-changer. And let's be honest, a lot of the American-Asian marriages you saw back then were nothing but transactions. A young, pretty Asian girl hooking up with a white guy who could get her a passport.

But lucky for me, that's not how it was with my parents. They were both young, both good-looking, both with their whole lives ahead of them. And they were really in love.

They got married in 1970, the year after they met, when they were both just twenty-four.

To prove his commitment, my dad didn't just marry my mom, he legally adopted her two little kids by her previous marriage. My brother, Robert, was seven years old when my parents got married, and my sister Rowena was three.

Their own father had abandoned them, and I gotta hand it to my dad—he really manned up. Think about it. He was out in the world for the first time in his life, barely making any money on military pay. It would've been so easy for him to pass my mom by once he saw she came with extras. But what did he do? He married her and took her Filipino kids as his own. That's some true man shit right there. He was a trailblazer, adopting Asian kids way before Brad Pitt and Angelina Jolie made it cool.

Then there was the biggest game-changer of all. Me, born in 1971, the product of a white conservative military dad and a Filipino mom in go-go boots.

An all-American half-breed.

℧

AT 6 P.M., AFTER HOURS and hours of stuffing raffle tickets into the barrel, my mom, my sister, and I watched the balding JCPenney employee solemnly prepare to pick the winner.

There was a crowd of seventy-five people watching and waiting with us, but honestly? That container must've been 95 percent filled with our tickets. Swear to God we filled out *at least* a thousand of those things.

But still, as I watched Mr. JCPenney stick his arm into the

plastic barrel, part of me couldn't help wondering . . . What if we didn't win?

What if, after all that, after all our cramped fingers and used-up pens, we still didn't win the TV of our dreams? What if we still couldn't fit in?

By this point in her life my mom had left her band days behind. When our family arrived in Washington, she wasn't hitting the clubs looking for young musicians who needed an experienced manager. Hell no! She had a husband and three kids to take care of. Her Filipino instincts had already kicked in: *No more talent! Talent will not pay the bills! Get a real job!*

First thing she did was walk into a bank and apply for a job as a loan officer—which she got, thanks to all her business experience.

That became her dream once we got to America. Earn a decent paycheck, help support her family, and if any money was left over, send it back to our relatives in the Philippines.

The most impractical she got these days was to pin all her hopes for a big new color TV on a department-store raffle. Even then, she wasn't leaving anything to chance. She didn't believe in chance. My mom believed in making her own odds.

"All right now!" JCPenney Guy said as he pulled out a ticket. "We're gonna start out with our third-place prize, a brand-new General Electric toaster oven . . ."

The crowd got quiet. My sister and I crossed our aching fingers—not to win, but to lose. We didn't work our asses off for no damn toaster!

"And the winner is . . ."

He called out a name that wasn't ours, and a skinny, middle-aged blond lady ran up to collect her lame-ass award.

"Congratulations!" JCPenney Guy said, beaming. "And we're

on to our second-place prize, a state-of-the-art boom box by Panasonic!"

Okay, I had to admit that a boom box would be cool . . . but still, it wasn't a TV.

"And our lucky winner is . . ."

This time a dude with a mustache went up to accept with his teenage son. We were in the clear.

My mom, my sister, and I all held hands as JCPenney Guy cranked the handle and spun that plastic barrel one last time.

"This is it," my mom whispered. "This is it!"

He pulled out a ticket and squinted at it. It felt like he was taking forever.

"And the grand-prize winner is . . ."

We held our breath.

"Josie Herbert!"

Holy shit! HOLY SHIT!

He said it! He said our mom's name!

We all screamed, hugging each other and jumping up and down. Everyone looked at us like "Who the fuck are these crazy people?" But we didn't care.

"We did it! We did it!" my sister and I shouted.

"I told you!" my mom yelled. "I told you it would work, didn't I!"

We sprinted up to the raffle table. I looked up at the display TV, glowing like a Technicolor beacon. It was so close I could almost touch it. So close it was as good as ours. So close I—

"Hold on a second!" someone shouted. *"You can't give them the TV! They cheated! They CHEATED!"*

BAM! We stopped in our tracks like we hit a brick wall.

"Excuse me?" JCPenney Guy said confused, looking around for the source of the voice.

We turned, and there she was. The same skinny blond lady who'd won third place, pushing her way through the crowd and looking pissed as hell. I guess she didn't like that toaster after all.

"I saw them!" she said, pointing at us. "They stuffed tons of tickets in there! Tons of them all day long!"

But if that blond lady thought that just because my mom was half her height she would admit defeat or slink away, she was *dead* wrong.

"So?" my mom said sharply. "So what?"

"So, I put in just *one ticket* like everyone else!" the blond lady said, and her face was turning red she was so angry. "Like a normal person!"

The JCPenney Guy cleared his throat nervously. He did *not* want a part of this lady fight.

"What, you think that's my problem?" my mom said, her accent getting stronger the madder she got. "You should have filled out a bunch of tickets like us! Why is this my problem, ha? *Why?*"

"Because—because you're supposed to follow the rules!"

My mom sensed her opponent's hesitation and pressed her advantage.

"Where are your kids, ha?"

"My—what?"

"They should be here, working like mine! Look at them! Look, they can't even feel their hands!"

The lady looked at us and we gave her the saddest puppy-dog eyes we could manage. She was both horrified and *totally* confused.

"That's how life is supposed to be!" my mom yelled. "Everyone working!"

"But—but—" the lady stammered.

"But nothing!" my mom said. "It's a numbers game, toots! Fill out more tickets and increase the odds! Don't blame me because you and your children are lazy!"

The blond lady's righteous indignation was nothing next to my mom's ruthless immigrant logic. Sure, maybe we'd *technically* cheated, but we'd worked *hard* to do it. We'd earned that TV with blood, sweat, time, and torn ligaments. Hell, we would've accepted *all* those prizes if we could—we'd earned those, too! It was the American way, and that's exactly what we were. American, just like everyone else in that mall. Americans who worked for what they got!

That angry lady shrank right in front of my eyes. Practically melted away. Holding her silly little toaster, she turned and vanished in the crowd.

My mom smiled and turned to the cowering JCPenney Guy as if absolutely nothing had happened.

"Could we please have our TV now?"

Looking both embarrassed and incredibly relieved, JCPenney Guy handed her an order slip. All we had to do was take it upstairs to the customer service desk, and they'd give us our big new Sony color TV, boxed up and ready to go.

Simple, right?

If you said yes, you do *not* know my life yet.

෴

GROWING UP ON MILITARY BASES was not easy. Imagine being five years old and knowing that all the friends you meet and grow close to will disappear in five years or less. Your dad gets his transfer order, your family packs up everything, and just like that you have to start all over again in some strange new place. Only to know that you'll have to do it all over again in a few more years.

Not fun.

When I was born in 1971, a year after my parents got married, they'd already been transferred from Vietnam to a base in Misawa, Japan. A couple of years later we were sent to Scott Air Force Base in Illinois. Then we were shipped off to a base in the Philippines, where we stayed until we finally moved to Washington State. All before I was eleven.

Now, I know what you're thinking. "Wait, so you lived in Illinois a few years before you got to Tacoma? I thought you said Tacoma was your first time in America. What gives?"

Because, man. Living on a base in Illinois wasn't really living in America. It was like living in a whole separate world.

Every American base all over the world was built to be completely contained and self-sufficient, so you never had to leave. They tried to stock the stores with cool stuff, but whoever chose all the supplies for the US government must've been the nerdiest person in the country.

Don't get me wrong—a lot of it was great. Like the commissaries—the grocery stores—were full of amazing food, and it was all incredibly cheap, so my mom would stock up. Man, we ate really well.

But the base exchange—the malls? Yeah, not so much.

I'd be begging my mom for the latest pair of Nike Air Jordans, the badass shoes that were red and black with a cool black swoosh right down the side, but at the base the only Nikes would be dad Nikes. All white with a big, lame blue stripe.

"Josep, here are your Air Jordans, right here!" my mom would say.

"Those are *not* Air Jordans, Mom!"

"Oh yeah? They're $19.95. *Those* are Air Jordans."

If I wanted Polo, the base store could do me even better. They had U.S. Polo Association, which looked almost nothing like a real Polo except for the word "Polo."

"Mom, where's the little polo guy on the front?"

"Why you want one little polo, Josep? This shirt is *three giant polos* on your chest, and they're all playing polo together. Three big polos is much better than one little polo. It's math!"

Each base was like a warped, bootleg mirror of America. Designed to remind all the troops *just enough* of the home they left behind while always whispering, "This ain't it."

But there was something else, too. Something I didn't even appreciate at the time. I couldn't, because it was the only reality I knew. On every base, all the other kids looked like me. Not the *same* as me, but mixed up like me. My crew was all mixed, too, blends of every ethnicity under the sun.

It was the Land of the Half-Breeds.

What, you think my dad was the only soldier tempted by the forbidden fruit of a foreign country? Hell no! It's funny—when people talk about the cultural revolution of the sixties, they're almost always talking about the hippies, flower power, "make love not war." You wanna know where the *real* revolution was happening? It was happening in the military.

My dad and mom were at the head of a movement that changed the world. White men, Black men, Latino men, all soldiers, all meeting and falling in love with Asian women and giving birth to a whole new race of people. Korean-Black, Mexican-Chinese, Japanese-white.

People like me.

Physically, I was this funky mix of my parents—a light tan complexion with bright hazel almond-shaped eyes. I kind of looked Asian, but not really. I was stuck in this strange in-between space, not exactly one thing, not exactly another.

But on base, that was the norm. One of my best friends had a German mom and an African-American dad. His skin was a deep brown, his eyes were green, and his hair was so light it was almost blond, and silky soft. And no one said a thing! No one looked at him and said, "What the hell are you, man?" He was just accepted, that was just life.

Racism was burning down the streets of America in the 1960s and '70s, but in my corner of the military we weren't fighting about social change or even talking about social change—we *were* that change. If anything, we would've been shocked by a kid who *wasn't* mixed up like us.

*Wait, what—your skin is white and your hair is brown and your eyes are brown, too? Where the fuck do **you** come from?*

So, I never felt out of place. I always felt like I belonged.

And even though we moved all the time, even though I'd make new friends and form new bonds only to lose them a few years later, I always knew exactly what I'd find when we got to our next base. Another Land of Half-Breeds, full of kids who looked interesting like me.

Then we got transferred to Tacoma.

There, we lived *near* McChord Air Force Base—but we didn't live *on* base. We were in a neighboring suburb called Spanaway, and suddenly we had easy access to malls, restaurants. We were able to go out and claim our place in America. The real America, not the warped funhouse mirror version I was so used to.

Soldiers all over the country were coming home and bringing their half-breed kids with them around that time. You into sports? Tiger Woods isn't just Black; he's half Thai from when his dad was stationed in Thailand. How about music? Apl.de.ap from the Black Eyed Peas was born in the Philippines when his African-American dad was based there. Comedy? Rob Schneider's white grandfather met his wife when he was a soldier in the Philippines, too.

In the 1970s, people like me were coming "back" to a nation we barely knew. And everything changed—for us, and America.

❧

WE WERE STILL GUSHING OVER our huge win when we got to the escalator at JCPenney. We just had to go one floor up, and that grand prize would be *ours*, man. America was an amazing country.

"I'm pretty sure this is the biggest TV that's ever been made, like, anywhere, right, Mom?"

"Can we get HBO now, Mom? Pretty please?"

Standing right above us on the escalator was a little boy and his mother. He couldn't have been more than six years old. He was looking at us, staring.

My mom saw him and waved. She loved little kids, always cooing and waving and pinching cheeks. Honestly, sometimes I felt like she liked other people's kids more than her own.

"Hello there!" she said in her sweetest voice. "How are you?"

He smiled back at her, this funny little smile, and then he reached up to his eyes and pulled them back into little squinty slits. Then he laughed at us like some kind of silly cartoon Asian—and just like that turned back around toward his mother, who of course hadn't noticed a thing.

It probably lasted a couple of seconds. But it felt like hours.

Life on base wasn't Air Jordans and Polo shirts. But there, I'd been sheltered, protected from the outside world. I'd never seen anything like what that boy did before. I could barely even understand what it was. But there was one thing I definitely understood—when that boy laughed, he wasn't laughing *with* us, he was laughing *at* us.

"Mom," I said, looking up at her, "why did he do that?"

"Don't worry, Josep," she said. "He's little. He doesn't know any better."

"But why?"

"It's okay. He doesn't know."

She was in a daze, like she couldn't even process it herself. She just kept saying those words over and over again with a blank look in her eyes.

He doesn't know. He doesn't know.

Only twenty minutes earlier my mom had practically gotten into a full-on fistfight with a lady who'd dared to challenge our hard-won piece of the American consumerist dream. But against a child's blunt, simple racism, this tough-as-nails lady was almost speechless.

My mom really does love little kids. She adores them. So, to have that turned back on her, used against her? It hurt. And when it hurt her, it hurt all of us.

We picked up our new TV from the customer service desk and took it home. The weather outside was horrible. Back on base in the Philippines, it always felt sunny, warm, bright. But here it rained constantly. Always cloudy, always gray. Always an added layer of depression on top of whatever crap life was throwing at us.

The TV took pride of place in our living room. The whole area was filled with this bamboo stuff my mom had brought from the Philippines. Shelves, chairs, tables, you name it. Not because she loved bamboo, but because she got this idea she could sell it once we got to the States. But then life happened, work happened, raising her kids happened. She didn't sell shit. But that meant when we brought that amazing TV home, we had the perfect bamboo TV stand just waiting for it. An authentic Filipino-made throne for our brand-new idol of American consumerism.

Oh man, I loved that TV. I loved all the places in my new country it took me to in big, bold color—so much brighter than Washington. But I started noticing something, too. My Sony was color, but the people on it—they weren't. None of the people I was watching looked like me.

The Fonz was white. Laverne and Shirley were white. Richie Cunningham was so white he practically glowed. Hell, even the one illegal alien, Mork from Ork, was white. The closest thing I found to anyone like me was Pat Morita, who played Arnold on *Happy Days*. Sure, he was Japanese instead of Filipino, but the first time I saw him he blew my mind.

Holy shit! That guy talks just like my uncle!

It wasn't just on TV. I'd feel how different I was all over town. Don't forget—this was the early 1980s. These days mixed people are everywhere. But back then? I could be walking down the sidewalk on another soggy, gloomy afternoon, and some random white person would see me and do a double take.

"What are you?" they'd ask.

"What do you mean?" I'd say, even though I knew exactly what they meant.

"You know . . . Like, what are you?"

And I could see the gears turning in their white-person brains as they tried to process the puzzle I presented. *Okay, so he's kinda light brown . . . And he's got sorta Asian-style eyes . . . But then he's got these bright hazel eyes . . . Ummmm . . .*

"I'm Filipino," I'd say. "Half Filipino."

"Oh!" they'd say, their eyes getting all wide. "Filipino! I just *love* your orange chicken!"

Seriously? No offense to Chinese food, but if you want to stereotype me, at least use some authentic Filipino dishes. I dare any Chinese restaurant to battle my mom's cooking. Bring your chicken lo mein. *Pancit* noodles will destroy you. Egg rolls? *Lumpia* will fuck your shit up. So, if you're going to be racist, at least deliver it with a side of chicken *adobo*. Filipino food is undeniably the best anywhere.

But I'll be honest. As much as those conversations annoyed me, now that I was off-base and in the real world, I was struggling to figure out what I was, too.

I was eleven years old. I wasn't Asian, and I wasn't white. I was living in a new country that was supposed to be mine, but the people here didn't seem to want me, or at least understand me. My roots were spread all over the world, my friends were the half-breeds I'd left behind over and over again, Black-Vietnamese, Mexican-Thai, white-Filipino. It was confusing. Adolescence is a time when every kid feels like a freak. No one feels like they fit in. If everyone is constantly asking you what you are, you feel a million times more awkward.

So, really, what *was* I?

Then I finally figured out the answer, and it was so simple it actually made me laugh out loud.

I was funny.

2

MY GREAT ESCAPE

I got to the cafeteria of my brand-new school and stared at all the lunch tables as they filled up with kids.

Where was I gonna sit?

It seems like such a tiny, stupid question, right? Literally "what bench do I walk in front of and then bend my legs until my butt hits the surface?" Not exactly world peace.

But when it's your first day of the sixth grade at a brand-new school in a brand-new city in a brand-new *country*, it feels even bigger than world peace. And it wasn't even the beginning of the school year, when everyone starts off fresh with a clean slate! The military had shipped us to Tacoma in the middle of the school year, when everyone already knew each other, friendships had already been made, bonds had already been formed.

So, to hell with world peace. It felt like the fate of the whole *universe* rested on my one decision.

The kids at that table look pretty cool, but what happens if I sit next to one of them and he says "Who the fuck are you? We didn't ask you to sit next to us!" Or I could sit at the end of the table, a few spots away from everyone. But what if they're like "What is that dork doing just sitting at the end of the table by himself? What a loser."

And if they don't like me on my first day, maybe no one will like me *on the second day. And if no one likes me on the second day, maybe no one will like me for the rest of the year. And if no one likes me for the rest of the year, maybe no one will like me **ever again**.*

Plus, I was already off to a rough start at Elk Plain Elementary.

Of course, I didn't really look like anyone else—that goes without saying.

But it was worse than that. I was one of the Scarecrows.

That morning when I had got to class, my teacher put me in a group with a few of my classmates. See, she didn't believe in children learning as individuals. She thought we learned better collectively, so the whole class was neatly divided into five-person groups that were meant to last all year long.

Well, guess what? All the cool kids were clumped together in cool-kid groups that were already full. The only group with any space left was one with three sorry stragglers no one really liked. They called themselves the Scarecrows. To this day, I have no idea why.

That's where I was stuck—with the Scarecrows.

By the way, I don't mean they informally called themselves "the Scarecrows" as some kind of inside joke. We actually had a poster with our name on it in front of our desks with these shitty drawings of the four of us, tied up to sticks with straw coming out of our shirts, surrounded by crows. This was our real, official name in the class. Like even the *teacher* called us that.

"Yes?" she'd say if one of us raised our hands. "A question from the Scarecrows?"

Now, don't get me wrong, the three other Scarecrows were nice and all. But let's be honest. They were nerds. They knew they were nerds. I knew they were nerds. Everyone knew they were nerds. I also knew that in no way did I want to be a nerd.

Standing in the cafeteria staring at all those tables, I decided to take the plunge. I spotted a table full of fun, interesting kids from my grade. The kind of kids who played sports. The kind of kids who did cool shit with other kids on the weekend. The kind of kids who definitely were *not* Scarecrows. I took a deep breath, walked over, and sat at the end of the table, a few seats away from the nearest dude.

First thing's first. I pulled out my lunchbox. Or at least the closest thing I had to one.

"Dang!" one of the kids said enviously. "Your mom lets you bring Cool Whip to school??"

Of course my mom didn't let me bring Cool Whip to school. No normal, brand-name lunchbox for me. This Cool Whip container had my food inside. My mother was *always* packing my shit in some old container of Cool Whip or Country Crock. That was like her version of Tupperware. Then she'd write my name on it all big with a Sharpie, like someone else was gonna have a Cool Whip lunchbox.

I gulped.

"No," I said. "There's a surprise inside."

Everyone around me started trading their lunches, but no one wanted to trade for the mystery bucket. My mouth was watering, seeing all these delicious trades go down.

"I'll give you my turkey and cheddar for your peanut butter and jelly!"

"I'll give you my chocolate chip cookies for your Pringles!"

"I'll give you my Coke for that chocolate milk!"

I looked at all of them and spoke up, as brave as I could.

"Does anyone want *munggo*?"

They stared at me like I was crazy.

"No?" I said. "It's my favorite."

The kid at the end, a big blond dude who seemed to be the ringleader, frowned.

"What the fuck is *munggo*?"

I kind of shrugged.

"It's these little brown beans," I said. "And it sits on a bed of rice."

Silence.

"And if you dig deep enough, you might find a shrimp or two."

The kids looked at each other. And I noticed something. They were smiling.

Not smiling because they thought I was acting stupid or looked weird—not like that boy in the mall who made fun of me and my family—but because they thought I was funny. I didn't know anything about standup, I didn't even know something called "improv" existed, but there was something about what I was saying, about my tone, about the way I could take everyone's comments and riff off them, that people had always found funny.

Being funny was my superpower. From as early as I remember, when I was five, six, seven years old, I knew how to make not just other kids laugh but adults, too. I knew how to be clever, how to be smart, how to read my audience. Wherever my parents took me, everyone knew that Jo was gonna be the funny one. I could take anything, even stuff that made me different—my messed-up family and my mixed-up culture, the way we talked and argued, even the food we ate—and use it to make people laugh. I could take my weakness and turn it into a weapon. Instead of being embarrassed, I became unstoppable.

One of the kids sitting closer to me pointed at my lunch.

"What the fuck is that bag of sauce next to it?"

"Fish sauce," I said. "It really accents the flavor of the *munggo*!"

Now they weren't just smiling, they were starting to laugh. I heard someone mumble "accents the flavor?" and crack up a little. I almost had them.

"And do *not* spill it on your shirt," I said. "You'll smell like pussy all day."

Bam. I had them. They *erupted* in laughter. But I wasn't done.

"Bad pussy, I swear. So fucking bad."

Howls of laughter, tears rolling down cheeks, pounding on the table. Sure, I was eating Filipino food—something completely foreign to everyone at that table except me. But swearing and talking big about girls? That was something all sixth-grade boys could relate to. Of course, none of us knew a thing about sex, and cursing was something we'd only just picked up from our older siblings or parents—my mom could put a sailor to shame with the way she talked. But that's exactly why we loved it. It was new, it was fun, it made us feel like men. Pussy talk was universal.

"It really does smell like pussy in here!" someone shouted.

"Yeah, the new kid's mom made him a bucket of pussy for lunch!"

"Put a bunch of pussy in a Cool Whip container!"

"Look at the new kid going at that pussy! He fucking loves it!"

No one traded me for my *munggo* with *patis* fish sauce that day. But it didn't matter. By the time lunch was over, any empty seats next to me had filled up. Everyone had moved over to my end of the table.

∽

BEING FUNNY BECAME MY EVERYTHING. My identity. My way to fit in. My way to cope with problems and deal with my reality.

That reality was my brother, Robert, my mom's son by her first marriage. Robert was eight years older than me, and when I was younger he was my hero, my role model, the best brother a boy could have.

In 1976, long before we moved to Washington, my family was transferred to Scott Air Force Base near Belleville, Illinois. I was five and Robert was thirteen, and as soon as we moved into our new place Robert set up what I thought was the coolest bedroom in the entire state of Illinois.

He had velvet psychedelic posters and black lights that made them glow in the dark. He had lava lamps and the coolest collection of records you've ever seen. Earth, Wind & Fire, Heatwave, Marvin Gaye. And his closet—man, in his closet there were rows and rows of the funkiest, freshest shirts, and boxes and boxes of shoes all lined up. He'd taken my dad's last name of Herbert, and on his door he had a big red sign that said "Herb Superb." Man, I thought that was fresh.

Robert was good-looking, with black hair and these big brown eyes. He looked like Bruce Lee. He played sports, spoke English really well, and all the girls liked him—even the white chicks. Older girls would pick him up in the mornings in their cars and take him to school, and I'd watch from the window in awe.

He taught me how to play basketball, which is a big deal when you're five years old and most older people don't have time for you. He showed me how to pass from my chest, how to shoot using my left hand to aim the ball and my right hand to launch it. He'd hang out at the court with me for hours, running drills, playing H-O-R-S-E, just shooting around.

But telling jokes was how Robert and I really bonded, how we really connected. That was always my goal in our conversations—to see how fast, how big I could make him laugh. He'd have this big, wide-open mouth, laughing so hard he was gasping, barely able to breathe, tears rolling down his cheeks. Robert was the best audience a wannabe comic could imagine.

He'd tell his own jokes, too. Not actual good jokes, more like the kind of jokes you hear in a dentist's office. "Jo, you wanna hear a joke?" he'd say, and then it would end up being something about a priest, a rabbi, and a minister walking into a bar, and you'd have to pretend to laugh your ass off because he had the worst delivery ever.

But I didn't care. I'd fake-laugh for him forever, because he was my brother.

As cool as Robert was, though, I started to realize being cool had some downsides. Those older kids he hung out with had a lot of time on their hands. This was back in the 1970s before teenagers had smartphones and social media to keep them busy. What they had was drugs—lots and lots of drugs.

Soon after we got to Illinois, I was hanging with my brother in his amazing bedroom when he went in his closet and pulled out one of his many shoe boxes. It was on the left side of the top shelf, buried under a bunch of his shirts and another shoe box. Except this box didn't have shoes inside.

"What's that?" I asked him.

He gave me a look I'd never seen from my brother before. He wasn't laughing—he was dead serious.

"They're kind of like funny cigarettes," he said. "Don't ever tell Mom and Dad about these. And don't *ever* smoke these yourself, okay? You don't even *touch* these things."

"Okay."

"Promise me," he said. "*Promise!*"

"I promise."

I guess he knew what he was doing was wrong. He knew the devil had gotten to him, and the angel in his heart tried to protect

me. I'll always love my brother for that. But I so wish he had followed his own advice.

It all went down later that year.

I woke up in the middle of the night, groggy and confused.
It was pitch-black, but a horrible, terrifying sound was echoing
through our entire house. Then I realized what it was. It was Robert, screaming.

I ran to his bedroom, the walls glowing pink and blue and yellow from those velvet posters, and I saw my brother jump out of
his bed, his eyes wide and his fingers curled into claws.

"I'm a tiger!" he screamed. *"Stay back, I'm a tiger!"*

My mom and dad rushed in. My dad pushed me aside and
tackled Robert, pinning him down on his bed as my mom pleaded
with her son.

"What's wrong? What happened? What's wrong?"

"I'm a tiger!" he kept shouting. *"I'm a fucking tiger!"*

It took a team of cops to finally get him under control.

We found out later that Robert's funny cigarettes hadn't just
been weed. He'd moved on to harder stuff, hallucinogens like acid
and angel dust. That's what he'd smoked earlier in the night, and
it hadn't just sent him on a bad trip—the dust had helped trigger
a change in his brain chemistry. I'd never noticed anything wrong
with him before, never experienced him being violent or out of
control. Of course, I was just a little kid. Maybe I didn't want to
see the signs that my big brother wasn't right. Maybe none of us
did. I don't know. But that night, whatever string had kept my
brother's mind tied to reality just snapped.

Shortly after, he was diagnosed with clinical schizophrenia.

From there on out, my cool brother, the guy whom I'd idolized,
who'd laughed at my jokes, looked out for me and taught me how
to play basketball, turned into someone else.

I'd try to have conversations with him, and sometimes they'd start off normally. We'd be joking around one second, then suddenly he'd kind of drift off, get this look in his eyes and start mumbling under his breath, and before you knew it Robert was on another plane.

"I had to fight crime last night, did you know that, Jo?" he'd say, his eyes getting wide. "Yeah, you gotta promise not to tell anyone, but I'm actually a superhero. I work with Dad sometimes, yeah, because he's a famous spy, too."

He'd go on and on and on, repeating the same thing over and over again. It was like a switch was flipped. One second I'd be talking to my brother, the real Robert, and the next second he was gone, replaced by a fake Robert, this strange person I didn't even know.

"Yeah, Dad's really Robert Conrad, he's a famous actor. Really he's a famous spy, but when he's not, he's undercover as Robert Conrad on that show *Baa Baa Black Sheep*."

I had a trick for getting him back, though. Whenever he stopped making sense, when he started rambling about fighting crime and all the dark, mysterious, nonexistent forces out to get him, I could still tell him jokes. I could still get him to laugh. And in those brief moments, my brother, the real Robert, would be sitting beside me again.

But the rest of my family didn't have that skill. They couldn't rely on being funny to relate to Robert like I could. As Robert fell deeper and deeper into his mental illness, he became angrier, harder to control, and increasingly violent. He slowly began tearing us apart. And I began to learn that there were some problems even humor couldn't solve.

∽

"BE CAREFUL!" WILLIAM TOLD ME. He was one of my new friends in Tacoma.

"I *am* being careful!" I said, grabbing the contraband from him and totally not being careful.

"My dad doesn't know I took it, if he finds out I'll get busted so bad!"

"Dude, relax!"

I turned it over in my hands, staring at it in awe, my heart pounding like crazy. I wasn't even in high school yet. Kids like me weren't supposed to be messing around with this kind of stuff. It wasn't drugs. It wasn't porn or cash or even anything technically illegal.

It was a cassette tape. *Richard Pryor, Live in Concert.*

People had been telling me I was a natural comedian for a while now, ever since I was six years old. My aunt back in the Philippines, a few of my friends, some of my teachers—not always in a tone that made it sound like a compliment. But I'd never really understood what they meant.

A comedian? What's that?

Then we moved to Washington, and William had told me about this guy called Richard Pryor, about this tape his dad owned that he wasn't supposed to listen to, that he of course listened to, and how it was the funniest shit he'd ever heard in his life.

I put the tape in my boom box. And what poured out was unlike anything I'd ever experienced.

What spewed forth was a stream-of-consciousness riff that seemed somehow both completely spontaneous and meticulously constructed. Richard Pryor talked shit to his audience. He used the n-word, the f-word, and every four-letter word that existed, including a bunch I didn't know about at all. He jumped from pet horses to heart attacks to John Wayne to the death of his father.

He talked about issues that usually made people angry—racism, how white and Black people treated each other—except when *he* talked about it, everyone laughed and laughed and laughed.

My jaw dropped.

"You can say this stuff? Like, in public? In front of people?"

William shrugged.

"Yeah," he said. "I guess."

I thought for a second.

"And you can get paid money for it?"

"Oh, he totally makes a lot of money. I mean, listen to him—he owns mansions and shit!"

I finally figured out what a comedian really was.

I loved Richard Pryor so much I even started doing one of his bits for my friends, my family, pretty much anyone who would listen.

"You know Richard Pryor?" I'd say. "Have you heard this guy?"

Then I'd go into his riff about a guard dog he owned that was so friendly he'd guide burglars around to every room in the house, showing them exactly what to steal—except when the burglars wanted to leave the dog wouldn't let them, because he wanted to keep playing. By the time the cops showed up the burglars would be begging to be arrested because they were so tired of playing with his damn dog. I didn't just do the bit, I'd *perform* it—mimicking Richard Pryor, doing all his voices, even barking like his dog. It always killed. I loved seeing people respond to each beat in the joke; I'd be feeding off their energy, feeding off their laughter, trying to get an even bigger response every time I told it.

But that Pryor cassette was my gateway drug. I needed more. I needed to do more than just hear comedy; I needed to see it.

My family had our new TV, but with three kids to take care of my parents weren't spending any extra money on cable. Besides, this was still the early 1980s. Only fancy people had movie channels. We did have a VCR, but it was so old and ghetto the remote control wasn't even wireless. Seriously, there was a thick black *wire* going from the VCR to the remote, and we'd trip over it, get tangled up in it. I don't even know how that thing qualified as a remote control. More like a long, really inconvenient button—I think all it did was turn shit off and on. And of course we barely owned any videos, didn't even have a membership to a video rental store. But I was lucky. Another one of my friends was the first guy I knew who had his very own membership, which of course made him the richest person in the world.

Private jet? Who cares. Giant yacht? So what. Wait . . . did you say you can go to a place and get as many movies as you want and watch them at your house? Fucking **awesome***.*

On a Friday night, that little video shack was the place to be, man. It was like nothing we'd ever seen back then, like an amusement park with every movie you'd ever want. New releases, action and adventure, and back in the corner of that tiny little room with its mysterious swinging saloon door: the adult section. My buddies and I would go, dare each other to sneak a peek, and play all dumb whenever we got caught.

"Josep, get the fuck out of there!"

But the best section for me by far was standup comedy.

The first time I watched *Eddie Murphy: Delirious*, I saw Eddie on that stage in his gleaming red leather jacket and pants, with his black belt and shoes, and his gold chain around his neck with its huge gold pendant. I saw his hilarious expressions, his spot-on impressions, the way he looked directly at his audience and connected with them, enchanting them with his amazing laugh. And it was over. I knew.

I wasn't just gonna be funny. I was gonna be a comedian, just like Eddie.

గ

BY THE TIME MY FAMILY moved to Tacoma—six years after that horrible night in Illinois—my brother Robert's schizophrenia had become a massive strain on all of us. Especially my father.

When we arrived back in America, the military hadn't issued my dad a house yet, so we spent a few nights in a motel near base. It was only three days before we had to call the cops to break up a fight between my dad and my brother.

And by "fight," I don't mean they were yelling at each other or wrestling on the ground. I mean a full-on, straight-up fistfight.

My brother was only nineteen, and he was tiny, about five feet eight and 140 pounds. But man, you did *not* want to fight Robert. When he went off, he went *off*—losing his shit, no inhibitions, no fear. He didn't just throw punches, he'd kick you, he'd get you down and he'd *keep* kicking you, in the stomach, in the ribs, throwing his entire body into hurting you, this ball of wild aggression that was impossible to control.

When he went into one of his frenzies, no one near him was safe—not even my mom. I remember her coming to pick me up from school once back in the Philippines when I was little, and she had a black eye. That's not something you forget, you know? Your mom with a black eye. She said we couldn't go home because Robert was in a tough place, having one of his spells. So, we spent the afternoon just driving around, trying to wait it out.

Thankfully, though, my father did his best to take the worst of it for all of us.

My dad was a couple of inches taller than Robert, and he could handle himself in a fight, but he didn't want to hurt this boy he'd adopted, the son of the woman he loved. He did want to defend himself and his family, which meant he was always at a disadvantage. Robert had bruised him, he'd cut him, he'd broken my dad's ribs. It was a case of one guy with everything to lose facing off against another guy who didn't give a damn about anything, and my dad never had a chance.

So there we were—we'd only been in America for a few days after four years in the Philippines, hadn't even been told where we were going to live, and all we could do was watch as a team of cops tackled Robert to keep him from beating the shit out of our dad.

"Robert, Robert, please just put your arms behind your back!" we shouted.

"No, no! They'll never get me! They'll never fucking get me!"

Probably sounds pretty crazy to you, right?

But to us, it was more like, "Whatever, I guess it's Wednesday."

Back in the Philippines, the fights had become routine, happening at least every other week, sometimes more. Just like the endless talk of fighting crime or being an international spy, a switch would be flipped. No warning.

One second we'd all be at the dinner table having a peaceful conversation about finding Robert a trade school because he wasn't getting along with the kids at his high school, and the next second he and Dad were rolling around in the front yard, my dad trying to protect himself as my brother punched, kicked, and scratched as hard as he could.

Robert wasn't even my dad's biological son. My father had been raising him since he was seven years old. Hell, my dad was only twenty-four himself at the time, but it was a choice he made. The other guy, my mom's first husband and Robert and Rowena's biological father, was completely out of the picture. His name was never even mentioned in our house. So my own dad stood up and accepted the responsibility out of a sense of duty. If he was gonna marry my mom, he wanted to be a father to all her children, not just his own. Who cared if they weren't white like him? Who cared if his own conservative parents didn't approve? My dad did the right thing.

He'd raised this kid, cared for this kid, loved this kid, and now this kid was beating the crap out of him every other week, sometimes more.

What made it harder was that we all knew this wasn't the *real* Robert. It was the disease, this faulty wiring in his brain. Something that none of us, including Robert, could control. He was given medication, but he hated taking it because it made him feel like a zombie.

What were we supposed to do, cram the pills down his throat? Get mad at him? There was no point! We couldn't reason with him, we couldn't argue with him or try to use logic. He'd just spew gibberish at us, going into his usual nonsense about saving the world or how my dad really was the actor Robert Conrad living undercover because he was actually a secret agent. And that was if we were lucky.

If we weren't lucky, Robert would kick a hole in the wall, and we'd be stuck acting like it was completely normal to have a hole in your damn wall. My sister Rowena would argue a lot with him anyway, and what did it get? Nothing except more fights, more drama.

My mom would always make excuses for him, always forgive him, always give him another chance, no matter how violent he got, no matter how hard to control. She cried about him constantly. He was her firstborn son, and she probably experienced a lot of guilt. We didn't know much about Robert's illness back then, didn't really understand it on a technical level. So it was only natural to blame ourselves. Was it something we did wrong? Was there something we could've done differently? Something we could do differently now?

But there wasn't. All we could be was frustrated. Frustrated and helpless. We loved my brother—my real brother—but there was nothing we could do to bring him back.

Pretty soon the stress and the anger infected my whole family. When the military finally assigned us our own house in Tacoma it didn't really matter, because none of us wanted to be there.

When we were at home, it felt like the tiniest thing would set off a huge argument between anyone and everyone. My mom, my dad, my sisters, me. Whether it was who my sister was dating, who left the TV on, or who forgot to put the milk back in the fridge. It didn't matter what it was; any little spark would blow up into something huge.

You couldn't fight Robert; it didn't solve a thing, so it was almost like we were searching for reasons to fight each other, just to release tension.

Robert then began to disappear, for days at a time. Days, then weeks. He started dressing differently. Black zippered boots, jeans, and a rugged jacket. Street wear. We had no idea where he went, where he stayed, how he got food, or what drugs he might be doing. But he'd always come back, and my mom would always take him back. Home was a more stable environment, and he didn't do drugs around us, but inevitably the cycle of violence would start all over again.

Then, one day, my dad left, too—but he didn't come back.

We'd barely been in Washington a year. There wasn't any special buildup to it. We didn't have some big talk about where my father was going or why it was happening. It just kind of happened. He was there one second, gone the next. Even after he left, we pretended nothing had changed. Discussing that kind of thing isn't really big in Filipino culture, even today. Talking about our feelings, being open about our personal trauma, it's not something we do well. It's not part of our vocabulary. And back then, in 1982, divorce was still pretty rare in America, still a taboo subject.

So, I didn't know why my father was gone. I didn't know what I was supposed to do about it or how I was supposed to feel. I just knew one thing.

I didn't have a dad anymore.

✺

I BEGGED MY MOM FOR MONTHS, literally begged her.

"Mom, please, please, please, *please* can you get us HBO?"

"Josep, why would I pay money for TV when we get it for free? Ha? Ha, Josep? *Why?*"

I'd fall to the floor of our apartment—this little place she'd moved us to soon after my dad left—on my hands and knees, tears rolling down my cheeks.

"Oh my God, please! I have to have it!"

"No, you don't!"

"Please, I have no life! All I have is TV! I do nothing on the weekends! Nothing!"

"Fine, so go get a life. No HBO!"

"I'll die!" I sobbed, wriggling on the ground in agony. "I swear to God, I'll *die* without it!"

"You will not die, Josep! We are *not* getting HBO!"

But I didn't give up. I kept asking, I kept begging.

Thanks to the JCPenney raffle and my bloody fingers, I had

this massive color television right here in our living room, but there was no great comedy to watch on it. I couldn't rely on my friends with the occasional rented movie or secretly borrowed tape for my fix. That wasn't nearly enough. I needed my own steady stream of standup, laughter I could plug directly into my veins whenever I wanted it, which was pretty much all the time. I needed HBO.

Honestly? It wasn't only a matter of entertainment; it felt like a matter of survival.

My dad was gone, and my brother, Robert—not my real brother, my fake brother—seemed to be getting worse by the day, taking his anger out on the rest of us now that his punching bag had disappeared. Even my jokes weren't calming Robert down anymore. Every second I was home I was walking on eggshells. My whole family was.

Is Robert happy now? Is he acting normal? Okay—don't set him off, make sure you smile, tell him your jokes, keep him laughing, always laughing, never stop laughing—

Shit. Did he get the look in his eyes? He's whispering to himself again, doing that thing where he mutters and babbles and giggles and doesn't make any sense—shit—be careful, give him space, don't set him off, don't push him too hard—shit—shit—shit—

One wrong move and everything would shatter.

I knew now that comedy couldn't fix all the shit in my family. I knew that making people laugh wouldn't magically make my dad come back. Or make Robert stop abusing us. But maybe comedy could do something else. Maybe it could help me escape.

One day, as I pleaded and cried on the floor of our apartment for what was probably the millionth time, my mom finally looked at me and sighed.

"Stop, stop, Josep!" she said, switching to her kind, sweet, good-cop voice just like that. "Breathe, Josep, breathe! My God, it's just HBO, you're going to die!"

"I know!" I wailed. "That's what I've been telling you!"

"I know!" she said. "That's why I'm getting you HBO!"

And just like that, I had it—access to my very own standup heaven.

George Carlin, Robin Williams, Whoopi Goldberg, and of course Eddie and Richard. (It only took a few days and I was on first-name basis with all of them.) I'd watch all their specials on HBO and any other cable channel randomly airing comedy and just laugh and laugh and laugh.

Of course, back then there was no such thing as streaming or on-demand, which meant that I had to wait for the specials. Eight p.m., ten p.m., midnight, two in the morning. Whenever comedy was on, I was watching. I was scheduling my whole life around the TV guide, poring over the pages and scribbling down dates and names frantically in my notebook.

Louie Anderson on Tuesday—I gotta catch that! Letterman on Thursday? Can't miss it! Bill Maher on Friday? What a fucking week!

Everything else in my life was chaos, but my comedy viewing was planned down to the minute.

I'd grab the few old-ass VHS tapes we had lying around, the kind almost every family in America owned, even poor ones like us. *Jaws, Superman, Star Wars*—who needed the classics if I could have Carlin instead?

Put a little Scotch tape on the safety tab, switch the VCR's record setting to EP, and bam! I could cram six whole specials on a single *Indiana Jones*. Fucking golden.

Now, anytime of the day or night, I could pop in one of my tapes and lose myself for hours. Billy Crystal, Ellen DeGeneres, Robert Klein, Richard Jeni, you name them. I started out watching, but pretty soon I wasn't just watching—I was studying. Their timing, their mannerisms, the way they moved onstage. Soaking up every second, trying to understand what made them so fucking funny.

I'd watch them, I'd be engrossed, and I'd forget. For just a few minutes, I'd forget about my violent brother, my miserable family, and my father who'd left us all. While those tapes played, none of that shit even mattered.

I'd watch them, I'd study them, and more and more I'd dream about what I'd do when I was up there on the stage someday.

3

THIS CRAZY THING CALLED DIVORCE

Jo Koy's Chicken Adobo

Chicken adobo *is one of my favorite Filipino dishes. It's easy to make and it is delicious! I put my own spin to it and make it with chicken wings . . .*

SERVES 2–4

INGREDIENTS

2 tablespoons vegetable oil

2 pounds chicken wings

5 garlic cloves, minced

½ medium onion, medium diced

¼ cup soy sauce, plus more if needed

2 tablespoons brown sugar

3 tablespoons white vinegar, plus more if needed

4 dried bay leaves

2 eggs

4 cups uncooked jasmine rice

INSTRUCTIONS

1. Preheat the oven to 375°F.

2. In a large saucepan or wok, heat the vegetable oil over high heat. Add the chicken wings and fry until browned, about 10 minutes.

3. Add the garlic, onion, soy sauce, and brown sugar and stir well to coat the wings. Cover and cook for 10 minutes on medium heat.

4. Add the vinegar and bay leaves. Cover and cook for 5 minutes more on medium heat.

5. Transfer the contents of the saucepan to a large pan and bake uncovered for 25 minutes.

6. Meanwhile, cook the rice according to the package instructions. Hard-boil the eggs. Let cool, then peel and slice in half.

7. Serve the chicken wing *adobo* with the rice, drizzle sauce from the pan over the rice. Add soy sauce and/or vinegar as needed. Garnish with the slices of hard-boiled egg. Dig in and enjoy!

Picture it, right?

This tiny little brown woman with huge glasses walking down the streets of Tacoma, tapping random people on the shoulder, stopping them in the middle of their day, totally out of the blue, and asking them a single question:

"Exchuse me, exchuse me—are you Filipino?"

A terrified Mexican lady shakes her head, and walks away as fast as she can.

"Hello, hi, nice to meet you—are you Filipino?"

A baffled Korean man pulls his little kids close and sprints across the street.

"What about you? You look kind of dark—are you Filipino? Ha?"

A white lady who just happens to have a really good tan runs for the fucking hills.

That was my mom at the beginning of 1983, right after my dad left us. So if you were in Washington State right around then, and you were any kind of Latino or Asian or had slightly excessive pigmentation of the skin and you remember being publicly harassed by a strange Filipina lady, congratulations—you officially know what it's like to have a Filipina mother.

But please don't hold too much of a grudge, okay? Think about what it meant to be divorced in the early 1980s. These days it's no big deal. Happens all the time; if anything, it's almost weird to meet people whose parents *aren't* divorced. But back then, divorce was something few people did and even fewer talked about.

I'm sure there were support groups here and there for divorced single moms, and if you were rich and white, you could probably hire a decent lawyer to represent you. But my mom had none of that. She was a recent immigrant who had a bunch of kids, little money, and almost no support from the husband who left.

When her husband left, Josie Herbert was on her own. Here's a hundred bucks and have a great life.

At first when my father left he moved in with a friend just a few blocks away. But pretty soon he was gone altogether, off to Phoenix, Arizona, to become a flight attendant for America West Airlines, a job he's kept to this day (though America West is now merged with American Airlines).

We almost never heard from him, saw him even less. One time one of his flights brought him to Tacoma, so he gave us a call. When I got the phone, he asked me how school was. Okay, I said, thanks for asking.

"Well," he said, "I won't have time to see you on this trip, but I promise I'll try my hardest to see you next time I'm in town."

"Okay, cool," I said. "You know it's my birthday today, right?"

Guess what? He didn't know.

My father drove over that night and took me to Denny's for my birthday. Found time in his schedule for a Moons Over My Hammy with his son. And you know what's saddest of all? I was still excited to see my dad. *Oh, he's coming! He's coming and he's gonna take me to a restaurant, restaurants are so fancy, I can't wait!*

I got a country-fried steak. I didn't hear from him again for weeks.

And his parents—my grandparents? They actually lived in Seattle, just sixty miles away. They'd moved there even before we got to Tacoma—I have no idea why—and I think my dad may have even requested his transfer to Washington to be close to them. But I still never saw them myself. Even when my dad went to visit his parents, he usually went alone. We had no relationship. It was as if their grandson didn't exist.

I felt a lot of anger toward my dad. A lot. I felt rejected, betrayed. He left when I was a little kid, not even thirteen yet. Those are prime father-son years, when you form your tightest bond, create your strongest memories together. Going on trips, playing sports, talking about girls, figuring out life. I didn't get any of that.

I was so jealous of my friends and their dads. I especially missed all the sports. My buddy William's dad did all sorts of cool stuff with him. They watched basketball together, baseball. They played tennis together, golf, everything you could think of. I had no one at home to watch a game with, much less play something. What was I gonna do—ask my mom to toss around the football with me?

At that age, I didn't really know how to express any of this— the rage, the loss, just how unfair it all was. My mom did, though. She talked shit about my dad all the time.

Your dad is rotten. He's no good to you. Why do you even bother talking to him on the phone? He's a waste!

Over time I'm sure I started to internalize her words. And honestly, who could blame her? From her perspective, she was killing herself raising this family all by herself. My dad would promise financial support sometimes, but he hardly ever delivered. She had one official job at the bank, but it felt like she was there all the time, and she had a million side hustles going to make ends meet.

There was barely time for her to cook during the week, so a lot of time dinner was something cheap like frozen pizza or pasta—and the fridge was never very full. So, a phone call from my dad was nice and all, but it didn't help her pay the bills or buy us food. And it didn't help parent the children, either.

Plus, she wasn't just taking care of me, Robert, and Rowena now. She and my dad had started the adoption process for a second girl before we all left the Philippines.

Gemma was a year older than me. Her mom died when she was young and her dad was abusive, so she was being raised by her aunt, who happened to be good friends with my auntie Lynn, a lesbian who was so butch I basically had an uncle.

Auntie Lynn smoked Marlboro Reds, always tucked her pressed button-up shirt into her pressed khakis, and had a nice belt from Sears. She even wore the same kind of underwear as me—men's Fruit of the Looms, size 32, small enough that if I needed clean underwear I could just go in her drawer at her place and borrow hers.

No one in the family gave a shit that Auntie Lynn was gay. Filipinos are so busy worrying about being broke that they don't have time to worry about stuff like sexual orientation. But we did care about her as a member of our family.

So when she asked us back in the Philippines if we could raise Gemma, this little girl her friend was taking care of, my parents agreed. Auntie Lynn wanted Gemma to go to the United States, where she could get an education and have a better life. But the adoption took a long time to go through, so Gemma didn't arrive in America until 1983—right around when my dad walked out.

Great timing, right?

My mom was a thirty-seven-year-old immigrant. She'd barely

been back in America a year, she didn't know a soul except for her own family, and now she was caring for two sons, one of them violently schizophrenic, and two daughters, one of them adopted. Her husband had up and left. She was a long way from being that idealistic young hippie in go-go boots and a miniskirt who'd managed a band, fallen head over heels in love, and dreamed of moving to the land of opportunity.

I wasn't the only one who felt angry and betrayed. My mom had never run from hard work and responsibility, but this wasn't what she signed up for when she moved to America. She was committed to staying—the economic advantages to living in the States far outweighed anything in the Philippines—but life was hard. And she was lonely.

We needed a community fast. A place where we could feel at home, where we could feel supported, like we belonged. In short, we needed to find some Filipinos.

It wasn't easy. Going up to brown people on the streets wasn't really working, and there was no such thing as Facebook Groups. But eventually, we found a place where everyone was like us, where we could simply be ourselves—and in the words of the biggest pop star of all time, it was off the wall.

∽

"JOSEP, DO IT!"

"I'm tired, Mom!"

"I told everyone you would do it, and now you have to do it!"

"I don't know . . ."

"Come on, you're embarrassing me!"

Honestly, I wasn't tired at all, and I had no problem doing what my mom was asking me to do, but it was so much fun for *her* to finally have to beg *me* for something, I was gonna milk it for all it was worth.

"Fine, I will if you say 'please.'"

"Josep, I will not say 'please'!"

She wasn't trying to get me to do my chores or my homework. She wasn't asking me to wear some special outfit she had chosen for me. No, we were standing in a big hall right next to a Catholic church, in front of fifty people we hardly even knew, and my mom was trying to get me to moonwalk.

"But Mom," I said, "I always have to say 'please.' Why shouldn't you have to say 'please'?"

"Because I'm your mother!"

"Well, I'll have to think about it."

"*Josep!* Do 'Billy Jean'! Now!"

To be fair, this was a high-pressure situation. The people she wanted me to dance for weren't just any people—they were Filipinos, like us.

That's right. After asking around for months, my mom had finally heard through the grapevine about a group of Filipino immigrants who met up every couple of weeks on Sunday at a local Knights of Columbus.

The building itself was nothing special. Just this huge box with cinder-block walls and cracked concrete steps leading up to the front door. And above it sat a giant crest, with a sword and an axe and the letters "K of C" painted on it.

But inside? Inside we found a magical Filipino wonderland. There were tables and tables of all the most delicious home-cooked Filipino food you could eat. My favorites like chicken *adobo*, so tender and garlicky, beef *caldereta*, this thick stew made with veggies and liver spread, and shrimp *munggo* with its beans and tomatoes and onions—and *all* of them with extra *patis* fish sauce I spooned on top. My mom was so busy working during the week that usually we just had frozen, easy stuff for dinner. Even on the weekends she'd only have time to cook a couple of things. But here was every dish I could imagine, all in one place. Oh my God, it was heaven.

There were so many Filipinos in this building, I thought the Filipinos actually *owned* the Knights of Columbus. Like, was this some exclusive Filipino-only club? A secret brown society?

Later I found out that the K of C is kind of like a Catholic Moose lodge you can find connected to churches all over America, usually filled with old white dudes who want to hang out and do service projects. We just rented the space from them sometimes. And on the days we did, it was all Filipino, all the time.

Now those Filipinos needed to be entertained—and my family needed to make a good impression.

Of course, my mom knew exactly what she was doing when she ordered me to moonwalk. My first gift might've been making people laugh, but my second? Dancing like Michael Jackson.

Just a few weeks earlier I had started the seventh grade. In Washington, that meant the beginning of junior high. I was now attending Spanaway Junior High, a brand-new school with brand-new kids to win over. Again.

But at least this time I'd known someone going in. My sister Rowena was friends with an older kid who went there named Ed, and the first week I was there he agreed to let me perform with him and some buddies in the talent show that kicked off the new school year. He probably just felt sorry for me, but no one was feeling sorry for me after I rocked my dance number in front of a gym full of kids.

I broke that shit *down*, man. Everyone cheering and screaming, rushing the court and asking me where I learned how to dance like that. I even got my first girlfriend off that routine, Dina Del-Vecchio, who gave me my very first kiss.

So, I was good enough for the lips of Dina DelVecchio, but was I good enough for the Filipinos at the Knights of Columbus? My mother was going to make me prove it, apparently.

Don't forget—my people, we've got entertainment in our blood, running through our veins. People as poor as us, all we've *got* is entertainment. Singing, dancing, laughing—that's what sustains us in life, gets us through all the hard times. Given that, we've got high standards. We've seen every kind of act, every kind of bit you can imagine. If your shit ain't up to snuff, we're gonna let you know it.

The tables and folding chairs were pushed aside to give me room to dance in the center of the hall. All eyes on me as "Billy Jean" started up on the old K of C loudspeaker.

I was planning to copy one of the best break-dancers out there, Mr. Freeze from the Rock Steady Crew, who had this move with a real umbrella where he pantomimed as if the wind caught it and slowly pulled him backward into the moonwalk. But at the last second, I decided to put my own spin on it.

I struck an Egyptian pose, working my arms like King Tut, moving to the music. Then slowly started gliding backward on the balls of my feet. *Back, slide. Back, slide.*

Bro, it was like I was walking on water, like the whole floor just vanished, like it was just me, my feet, and my liquid moves.

I could feel the energy in the hall ignite, the Filipino crowd clapping their hands to the beat, whistling and cheering me on as I started popping and locking.

If everyone wanted Michael Jackson, I *gave* them Michael Jackson—maybe even better, that's how good I had him down. I'd mastered MJ for the same reason other Filipinos were experts at entertaining themselves—I was so poor it was all I had. Back at home, I didn't have an Atari, and with my dad gone I didn't have anyone to play sports with. But what I did have was a shitty piece of cardboard on the floor of our little apartment, right next to this old brick fireplace in the living room. I practiced on that thing every day—head spins, windmills, every breakdancing move you could imagine, just inches away from all the brick and mortar. I could've busted my head open on that thing so easily, but I didn't care. Just like comedy, dancing was my passion. It was the only escape from real life I had.

Back in the Knights of Columbus, my song finally came to an end and the crowd *exploded*.

At the very front stood my mother, smiling ear to ear. We were in. The K of C Filipinos loved us. We had found our people. I knew this was important, but I didn't really understand how much it meant to us, how much it meant to my mom, until she gave me a gift.

It was a white sparkly glove just like Michael Jackson's. She'd sewn it herself at home, sequin by sequin. It was tiny, just big enough for my adolescent hand, and I wore it every single time we went to the K of C.

People these days like to ask me why I talk about being Filipino so much onstage. After all, I'm a half-breed, just as white as I am Filipino. And I'm not ashamed of the Caucasian side of my identity. In a lot of ways, it's shaped me just as much as the Filipino side.

But when shit got real for my mom and our family, when we had nowhere to turn and desperately needed help, the Filipinos took us in, no questions asked. They never looked at me and said, "Hey, where's your dad's family? Why don't you go hang out with them and eat their food?" They accepted me—both of my halves—for exactly who I was. They accepted our whole family, my brother with his outbursts. My adopted sister. All of us.

I was home. I still have that glove to this day.

❧

THIS DIDN'T MEAN THAT ALL our problems were magically solved.

Just like all the other Filipino families, my mom brought a dish to share each time we went to the Knights of Columbus. Her offering was always *lumpia*, these incredible little egg rolls filled with pork. But she made enough so she had plenty left over, not for us to eat at home, but for her to sell on the side.

The price was fifteen bucks a bag for friends, coworkers, or total strangers—anyone willing to pay for some gourmet Filipino deliciousness. She'd carry that shit around in her goddamn purse, ready to whip them out at a moment's notice.

What, you hungry? You look hungry, here, take some lumpia*! Here!*

Lumpia would fly out of her purse and into the eager, unsuspecting hands of the hungry person. In a flash, they'd gobble them up.

Okay, that's $15. Pay up!

Back in the Philippines, with my dad's military pay and a strong dollar, we lived like kings. We had a nice house just off base with a maid and a gardener who washed our car for us. They even had their own "quarters." Imagine that—our house was so big that the maid and gardener lived with us. That's how rich we were back in the Philippines.

But in America, we were scrounging for nickels and dimes between the couch cushions to make ends meet. Yes, my mother had a job as a loan officer at a bank, but she also had four kids to feed, house, and clothe, not to mention all the money she was sending back to the Philippines to put basically every one of her second cousins' kids through school—which, by the way, is something pretty much all Filipino Americans do for their relatives back home. My mom was working day and night, hustling for every dollar she could find.

If we had twenty dollars for groceries, here's what we bought for our house: a stack of three-for-a-dollar Tostino's Pizzas, frozen burritos, a package of ground beef, some spaghetti, and ramen, so much ramen. That's all we ate. These cheap, fast, easy-to-make foods were always on heavy rotation along with any leftovers from the K of C she could store in those old Cool Whip and Country Crock containers.

When I got to go to McDonald's—that was rare, like gourmet, like "Mom must be in a really good mood today"—I didn't get to enjoy my favorite Quarter Pounder with Cheese (hold the onions, swimming in ketchup) like a normal kid; I had to load up on extra "supplies" as some sort of payment. We'd be leaving the restaurant, and my mom would stop me at the door, sending me back in to steal ketchups!

"For the house! For the house!" she'd say. "Go back in and get us some napkins, too."

"Why do we need napkins?"

"Because your birthday is coming up! Now go! Napkins!"

I'd go back inside, stuffing my pocket full of napkins. I'd look at my mom, so fucking mad. She didn't care.

Fill the other pocket! she'd mouth at me.

At my birthday, my mom would pass out slices of cake. Each one would have a napkin, and none of them matched. Popeye's, KFC, McDonald's, whatever we could get, whatever was free. No Transformers-themed birthday for me.

But hell, at least we had the cake.

For a while, I stopped eating lunch at school altogether. I didn't want to ask my mom for money to buy anything, because I knew we didn't have it, and she was so busy I don't know if she ever noticed I wasn't taking anything with me in the mornings.

Lunchtime would roll around, and I'd be too embarrassed to get a free lunch ticket. Didn't want my friends to know how poor we were.

If I got lucky, I'd search our sofa cushions and find forty cents, then buy myself a Grandma's Cookie out of the vending machine. That would be my lunch.

This was how I experienced my parents' divorce. My sister Rowena felt the effects differently.

Now, Rowena is a firecracker, and she can clash with anyone—including me.

The first time I ever stole something I was shopping at the base exchange with Rowena and my dad, right after we'd moved to Tacoma. I was browsing albums in the record store like the innocent child I was, when suddenly Rowena walked over, opened up her bag, and showed me all this jewelry she had swiped from a display.

"It's so easy!" she said. "Look how much I got!"

This shit wasn't even real. These were like gold-plated necklaces and bracelets, the kind of stuff that turns green after a day. But to me, it was a revelation.

A few minutes later, I walked out of the record store with a couple of goodies in my own bag—two album singles, "Buffalo Gals" by Malcolm McLaren and the World's Famous Supreme Team and "Human Nature" by Michael Jackson, which I'll never forget because MJ was wearing this sick white outfit with a yellow vest and bow tie on the cover.

A few minutes after that, I was sitting in the mall cop's office, arrested for shoplifting. My dad was there, furious, and Rowena was there, too—furiously mouthing the words "Don't fucking say anything!" over and over again.

She'd stuffed the jewelry in her bra. She got away with it home-free.

Me? I got my ass reamed out by my dad. Took the blame for the whole damn thing.

Not only did Rowena not have my back, but she didn't even thank me for taking the fall for us both. Worst of all, to this day she says I'm making *the whole thing up*. To this day!

But that's nothing compared to the way Rowena and my mom can push each other's buttons.

Their relationship is something special. Almost like they're twins. They both have strong wills and fiery, vibrant personalities. They live life big, and they live it on their own terms. And if they disagree with you about something—anything—they will never back down. Ever.

Being twins has its good side. When they're getting along, they're the best of friends, completely on the same wavelength. Talking, laughing, having fun in their own private world.

But it can also be bad. If I could count the number of times they've hated each other, made up, then become friends again— well, I'd actually be good at math. Something can happen, some argument or fight for a reason that seems completely petty, completely insignificant, and suddenly all that talking, laughing, and having fun just stops. When I say "stops," I mean it. They literally won't speak. No contact at all. Not for days—for years.

We're talking arguments over everything from who Rowena should date to where she should work to who left the empty jar of mayonnaise in the fridge. A few years back, before my career really took off, Rowena very kindly gave me her old truck so I could drive back and forth between Vegas and LA. I ended up spending almost all my time in LA, so I told my mom to go ahead and sell the truck for me. Rowena finds out, gets pissed at my mom for not consulting her about it, next thing I know she and my mom aren't talking for five years. Seriously. Even now, I still don't understand how that was my mom's fault.

One Christmas, I finally had it. I wanted my family celebrating the holidays together again, so I invited everyone out to dinner at California Pizza Kitchen—without telling my mom or Rowena that the other one would be there. They both showed up, sat on opposite sides of the table, wouldn't even *look* at each other at first. And by the end of the night, they were splitting a pepperoni, talking and laughing like they'd been best friends forever.

That's just how it is between them. That's their energy.

And way back then, after my dad walked out? That was the peak of our family's volatility.

Our home life was now miserable because of my brother's mental illness, and once my dad was gone, it was worse. My mother's life was spinning out of control, so her instinct was to hold on even tighter, to become stricter, more authoritarian, and Rowena didn't take to that so well.

My mom also wanted her children to start contributing financially to the family. Her attitude was, "Hey, if you can work, you can help." I was still in junior high when my dad left, and Gemma was just a little older than me, so we couldn't get real jobs, but Rowena was sixteen years old. Her first jobs were at fast-food joints to make a little extra money, and by the time she was eighteen she was working full-time at Wendy's as a shift manager.

She thought she was a fucking millionaire.

"Look at this shit!" she'd say, showing me her paycheck. "I'm rich!"

She was happy to give my mom some of what she earned—but she didn't want to give up *all* of it.

Rowena was a teenager, and she wanted to have a life, hang with her friends, go out to parties, spend her money on clothes and restaurants, just like any normal teenager would. As a result, she and my mom fought constantly.

"Where are you going?" my mom would shout. "You're just wasting your money! No more going out, save it instead!"

But Rowena wouldn't listen. She kept going out, and kept going out—and eventually my mom told Rowena to go out and stay out. They had their final showdown in our living room, Rowena coming in hot like she could call my mom's bluff.

"I'm sick of these fucking rules, Mom!" she shouted. "I'm old enough to take care of myself! Brian and I have been looking for a place, and when we find it, I'm out of here!"

My mom looked her right in the eye:

"Are you crazy? Get the fuck out of here *right now*!"

Rowena didn't even flinch.

"Fuck it," she said. "I'm out of here."

That was some gangster shit. She graduated from high school and moved in with her boyfriend, Brian, a tall, half-deaf Black dude who'd been a star triple jumper on the track team and who wore an "I ♥ NY" sweatshirt wherever he went.

Which was all fine and good for Rowena, but put yourself in my mom's shoes. She'd sacrificed everything to support us. *She* didn't go out to parties at night, *she* didn't have a life, because she was too busy taking care of us. And now my sister wanted to leave so she could go out and have fun whenever she wanted? Fine—see how easy it is out in the real world.

I still remember Rowena's last day at home. Loading her bags into the car out front and calling up to me as I watched from the window.

"I love you so much, Jo!"

I had tears in my eyes. This was my *sister*, after all. She could be tough to live with, sure, but we'd been through so much together. Our family moving from base to base, our brother turning violent, our father leaving us. I loved her. I admired her strength, her desire to be independent and go it alone. I turned to my mom.

"Mom, Rowena's gonna die!"

My mom looked at me as cool as you can imagine.

"Well then, let her die!"

She didn't mean it. At least . . . I don't think she did.

☙

"OH-OH-OHHHH! MERRY CHRISSMAS! OHHH-OHHHH-OHHHHH!"

We were at the Knights of Columbus for the annual Filipino community Christmas party. Robert wasn't there, of course, and once Rowena moved out she stopped coming, too. But my mom and Gemma and I still came all the time. And now I was standing in a long line of other Filipino kids, looking up at a dark brown, rail-thin old man wearing a red suit with a scraggly white beard dangling from his ears.

"Oh-Ohh!" he shouted. "Here is Shanta Clawss with his gifts for you! Oh-Ohhhh!"

This guy couldn't even say "ho-ho" right, and I was a full twelve years old—way too old to be sitting on some stranger's lap asking for presents. But you know what? I didn't even care. I loved holidays at the K of C—Easter with an egg hunt for all the kids, Thanksgiving with even more amazing Filipino food than usual, and Christmas with . . . this guy. So colorful, so bright, everyone laughing and having a good time and forgetting about the hard stuff of life.

"Oh-oh-ohhhh! Come here, littuh boy! Sit on the lap of the Shanta!"

My mom gave me a nudge. She wasn't just a member of the community anymore, she was one of the main organizers.

"Josep," she whispered loudly, "go sit on his lap! Go!"

For once, we didn't have to argue. I climbed up onto the Santa's lap. I wasn't a tiny kid anymore, and his legs were like toothpicks. His face was so thin I could see his pointy chin sticking out above his drooping fake beard. The thing had nothing to stick to!

"So, littuh boy," Shanta said, completely oblivious to the fact that I was almost a teenager. "What you wan for Chrissmas this year?"

I started to open my mouth, then I stopped.

As great as it was to be part of this community, so much was still missing from our lives. We were still broke, my brother was still abusive, and now my sister was gone, just like my dad.

He'd actually brought me a Christmas gift for once—from his parents, my white grandparents who I barely ever saw. I don't know why, but they had finally remembered me. Maybe they'd sensed that my relationship with my dad was deteriorating and they wanted to help. Maybe they saw something in a store that reminded them of the grandkid they barely knew. Maybe there was no reason at all. I really don't know. It was a Christmas miracle.

There was one problem, though. There was *only* a gift for me.

"What about the other kids?" my mom said to my dad. "If they can't give presents to the other kids, then Jo can't have his!"

It wasn't fair! My sisters and brother weren't even really *related* to my dad's parents. They were a hundred percent Filipino, not a half-breed like me. Besides, Robert and Rowena were older and barely ever around; why did they need presents at all? Gemma was adopted! I started crying. I wanted my present.

"No!" my mom said. "You can't open it, they'll be jealous! Throw it away!"

I threw my present away.

I was devastated. And though at the time I couldn't see it, I know what my mother was trying to show me. That my dad's parents, even though they were technically related to me, weren't my real family. My real family stuck together. My real family was brown, like me. My real family was the Filipino community at that K of C Christmas party. And she was right.

But you know what? Even that wasn't perfect.

The more involved we became, the more complicated it became with the Knights of Columbus crew. It wasn't just about holidays and good food and moonwalking to "Billie Jean"—it was also about drama. Gossip.

Tsismis, in Tagalog.

It didn't even matter what we were gossiping about as long as we were gossiping about something. Someone was always fighting, someone was always trash-talking, someone was always backstab-bing. Always.

Don't talk to that family anymore! Their daughter is doing drugs, and if you talk to them, you'll do drugs, too. Then I'll kick you out of the house and you can go live with them. Is that what you want?

No—sobbing—I don't want to live with another family!

Exactly! Because they all do drugs!

Of course, no one's daughter was really doing drugs, and eventually everyone would make up. There would be hugs and kisses—*it's good that we went through that, it was healthy!*—there would be peace for a couple weeks, and then it would start all over again with someone new and some other bullshit story.

With everything going on in my family—a brother who was institutionalized, a sister who'd left, a father who'd walked out—I can't believe we were never targets ourselves. Maybe we were. Maybe my mom managed to insulate me from it somehow. But if that was the case, she definitely didn't protect me from gossip about other families. If anything, she relished it.

I think partly the *tsismis* served as a weird form of entertainment, a distraction from all our own personal problems. I don't know, maybe that's not a white thing or a Filipino thing—maybe that's just a human thing. Maybe we're all just drawn to trouble. We like to keep our lives complicated to keep things interesting. Whatever it is, we couldn't help ourselves. No matter how much we tried, there was nothing in our life as a family that was truly sacred, nothing that was totally pure. Even when we found some form of happiness, we'd somehow find a way to fuck it up and add turmoil.

Back at the K of C, Filipino Shanta jostled me on his bony knee.

"So, tell me!" he said. "What you wan?"

There was so much to ask for, I didn't know where to begin.

4

"I WAS **RIGHT**. YOU SHOULD'VE **DIED**."

My best friend in high school was this Korean kid named William. All my good friends back then were Korean, I think because they all ate rice as much as I did.

Seriously—at school there weren't many other Filipinos, but I'd see these Korean kids eating rice all the time like I did at home. They came from immigrant families just like me, so I gravitated toward them. We'd relate over our shared brownness. Instant ethnic friends.

William was my best friend out of all the Koreans, and he had money. His mom owned a restaurant, and whatever William wanted, he got.

When we were in the ninth grade, William wanted a motorcycle. And boy did he get one.

It was a Yamaha YZ80 dirt bike, bright yellow with a black seat, and a top speed of 55 miles per hour. It didn't have headlights; in fact it wasn't even street legal—so naturally we rode it on the street at night constantly. And it drove my mom crazy.

"Josep, you ride that, and I swear to God you're going to die!"

"Mom, it's fine," I said. "I'm totally safe."

"What, do you want to die? Is that it? Ha?"

"No, Mom, I don't want to die."

"Or maybe you want to kill me from worrying. Yes, that's it—you want to kill *me*."

"No, Mom, I don't want to kill you."

"No, no, maybe it's better if I die anyway. I go to heaven, at least I don't have to worry anymore. Go ahead, keep riding the motorcycle."

"Fine. *Fine!* I won't ride the motorcycle anymore!"

I obviously kept riding the motorcycle.

I was in a dark place. The rain never fucking stopped. We were so poor I didn't eat lunch half the time. Rowena and my mom still fought a ton. And Robert would show up on our doorstep and wreak havoc whenever he felt like it.

One night, Rowena and Robert were both over and *they* decided to get into it. Robert being Robert, he started yammering on about how my dad was really the actor Robert Conrad, and he was actually a double agent for the US government. The kind of stuff he said all the time, and if you were smart, you just let him say it, crossed your fingers, and hoped he wouldn't turn violent.

But Rowena being Rowena, she couldn't let it go.

"Why do you always say stuff like that, Robert? Dad's *not* Robert Conrad! Shut the fuck up!"

Next thing you know, she was screaming, and he was dragging her down the stairs by the hair like it was nothing at all.

Imagine living with that kind of chaos all the time. Imagine having to experience that kind of trauma and then go to class the next morning with this big smile on your face like nothing was wrong. Like you hadn't just spent the night terrified of your brother, like you weren't just about to have a single cookie for lunch. That was my life in high school.

But what hurt most was not having a dad around.

I don't just mean someone who could provide for us financially. I mean I missed having a Man around the house, you know? "Man" with a capital "M." A father figure to guide me, provide me with a moral compass, or even just hang out and shoot the shit. I saw what it was like for William to have his own dad around to play sports with, watch games on TV. Nothing big, nothing monumental—just spending time, just being there. And I'd try to compare it to the memories I had of my own dad from when I was younger, and I'd realize I didn't even *have* any memories. There was just a blank where my father should've been, just a hole. I sensed that absence, I was aware of it constantly. A father figure, a strong masculine presence—it didn't exist in my life.

Instead, I had my mom.

And my mom did an *amazing* job raising my sisters and me, especially considering all the shit she had to deal with, and the fact that she was doing it all on her own. What she had to do just to keep us *alive* was nothing less than superhuman. I respect her hustle so much, and I'm incredibly grateful.

But let's be honest. She didn't exactly make things easy on us—or on herself, for that matter. Don't get me wrong, I didn't make things easy for her, either, I know that. I was strong-willed, I was rebellious, and I got into trouble all the time. But I was a kid; that's what kids do. To this day, my relationship with my mom is so complicated, so contradictory, I can't describe it in a way that makes sense—unless you're Filipino. Even my Korean friends don't get it!

But if you're Filipino, you get it, because Filipino moms all do what my mother does. The constant bickering that never really stops or starts, it just is. The ping-ponging from love to punishment, from indulgence to guilt, back and forth, back and forth, over and over. Putting you on a pedestal one day only to tear you down again the next.

Hell, Filipino moms even all *look* the same. Look at a photo of any Filipino dude's mom, and you'll see the exact same woman. Same short hair, same huge glasses, all the way down to the same Louis Vuitton purse. And if they don't have a Louis Vuitton purse, they all *want* a Louis Vuitton purse—because in our community, that is the ultimate status symbol for any mom.

Hey, Mom, what do you want for Christmas?

Son, as long as my family and my children are healthy and happy, I don't want anything else.

Well, Mom, we're all happy and healthy, so . . .

And maybe a Louis Vuitton purse . . . to carry all my pictures of you so I can remember just how happy and healthy you are.

Once they get it, that Holy Grail of Filipino maternal status, they will not let that baby go. They clutch it tight to the left side like a vise, guard it with their life. Always. They won't hold it anywhere else, even if you tell them to.

All Filipino moms are like that. All of them. God forbid my mom ever passed away, but if she did, all I had to do was walk into another Filipino's house. Bam—hello, new mom. I'd be fine.

In Filipino culture, sons are worshipped. In some ways you can do no wrong, even when you're being a total fuckup. On weekends, for example, William and I would go hang out in the 7-Eleven parking lot, offering random dudes a few bucks to buy us wine coolers. You know that old game, because you all played it.

Here's thirty dollars for a case of Bartles & Jaymes, you can keep the change. Exotic Berry, please!

I'd get fucking drunk, right there on the side of the road, then call my mom from a pay phone to come and pick me up—

collect!—and she wouldn't even care. She'd act like I wasn't blatantly slurring my words and acting like a moron in front of her.

If I made it so obvious that even she couldn't ignore it—if I was all, "Hey Mom, I'm drunk right now. D-R-U-N-K. Drunk"— even then she'd find ways to make excuses for my bullshit, and brush it off.

"Oh, it's the weekend, you're just tired, letting off some steam. It's okay, boys will be boys."

Now if I had been a girl, if I had been Gemma or Rowena? Totally different.

"What are you doing in this parking lot like some floozy? It's dangerous out there! Some stranger will take advantage of you; you'll get pregnant! You'll embarrass the family, and it'll be all your fault!"

Filipino moms are *strict* with their daughters, man. Trust me, Rowena isn't the only one who's been kicked out of the house for not following her mom's rules. Every Filipino girl who's reading this book right now, you know what I'm talking about. You know! Thank God neither of my sisters really minded that I had it so much better. It's so baked into our culture, they just accepted that I'd always get babied by my mom. They didn't necessarily encourage it, but they weren't gonna rock that boat, either.

But there's a flip side to all that adulation the Filipino sons get. That adulation comes with a side order of incredibly high expectations, so ridiculously high they're *impossible* to live up to.

Look at me. My grades in school were so bad. Horrendous. I can't believe I have a high school diploma. I honestly think I got a C-minus in gym.

As far as I was concerned, grades weren't important because I knew I was going to be a comedian. My education was the standup specials I watched, over and over again, analyzing every comic's timing, joke structure, and delivery. That was *my* school. But that dream was still private, a secret I kept to myself. And my mom had much bigger plans for me.

"It's fine that you drink at 7-Eleven on the weekends, Josep, because then you can study extra hard during the week and become a doctor or a lawyer."

"But Mom . . . you've seen my grades."

"It's okay, Josep! You'll go to a community college, take your electives, transfer them to a major college, and *that's* when you become a neurosurgeon."

She possessed an astonishing level of denial, it was almost delusional—and frankly, really confusing to manage while I was growing up.

But—and here's the big "but"—when you broke through that delusion, when you actually managed to disappoint her and fail to meet those colossal expectations, you'd better watch the fuck out. Because that's when that frail little lady, that tiny, smiling Filipino angel, would turn into a raging, powerful demon.

This aspect of her being was something she hid entirely from the outside world. William and all my other Korean friends, they loved my mom. Around them she was a social, fun-loving, happy-go-lucky woman. Around them she was the consummate "cool mom." She wouldn't let *anyone* see the she-devil she could turn into behind closed doors. Anyone.

Until she caught me riding that motorcycle again.

Actually, she didn't catch me. A cop did.

It was late at night. William and I were hanging out at his place, so I borrowed his Yamaha to get home. No headlights? No problem. I kicked off, blazing down the dark street, hugging the shoulder.

Suddenly I spotted headlights behind me, coming up quick like the jerk was gonna run me over. So, what did I do? I went even faster.

Bbbbbbbbvvvvvvvvvvvvvvvvvveeeeee!

That's when he threw the police lights on.

Fuck.

"Are you crazy?" he said after I pulled over. "I didn't even see you. I could've run you over!"

"I'm sorry, Officer," I said, preparing myself for the worst. Prison, electric chair, death by firing squad—whatever it was, I would take it like a man.

"Leave the bike on the side of the road and get in my car," he said. "I'm taking you home."

"Please God, no!" I wailed like a baby. "Please, Officer, take me to jail. I wanna go to jail!"

Not happening. He threw me in the backseat and all I could do was beg as we got closer and closer to our house.

"Please, sir, you don't understand . . . jail, juvie . . . you can even call my dad if you want, I never see him anyway."

He shook his head.

As we pulled up outside you could actually hear my mom yelling indoors. She had both of my sisters there, and of course it was all their fault that I was out so late. Clearly, I was missing. Of course I had been kidnapped.

"Where the fuck is Josep? How do you not know where he is? If we don't find your brother, I'll kill both of you!"

Now the cop could hear this too, okay? So he was getting a taste of what I had in store for me. My eyes welled with tears, and I gave him the saddest, most pathetic look I could manage in one last-ditch attempt at mercy.

"Please?" I whispered.

He hesitated—but only for an instant.

"Come on," he said. "Let's go."

He walked me up to the door and knocked. My mom, who just seconds before had been screaming at the top of her lungs, suddenly went silent.

"*Sssssh!*" my mom said behind the door. "*Be quiet. Stop crying.*"

The door slowly swung open, and there she was—the frail little Filipino angel the world knew and loved, smiling and as polite as can be.

"Good evening, Officer," she said meekly. "How can I help you?"

The cop cleared his throat, only slightly disconcerted. Back behind my mom I could see my sisters, also putting on their best, brightest, least emotionally traumatized faces.

"Good evening, ma'am," the officer said. "I'm sorry to report that I saw your son on Spanaway Drive doing about forty-five miles per hour on a motorcycle—"

WHACK!

He never got out another word. As soon as he said "motorcycle," Frail Little Filipino Angel smacked me, full upside the head, so hard it left my ears ringing and a giant red mark on my face. She put *so much* energy into maintaining that perfect, innocent façade for everyone else, but in that second, it didn't matter—the thought of me on that dirt bike, putting my life at risk and, more important, disobeying her direct order, shattered it instantly.

The cop's jaw dropped. My mom yanked me inside and slammed the door in his face. He didn't even bother knocking again. He probably figured that whatever illegal activity was going on inside was far worse than any discipline he could suggest.

That was the only time my mother ever smacked me—and honestly, other than a few broken capillaries in my cheek, it's not like it left much physical damage. We're talking about a four-foot-ten

Filipino lady, after all. But my mom didn't hurt you with physical punishment. That wasn't her thing. Her thing was psychological.

The relentless ridiculous expectations, the constant demands that I be someone other than myself, the implication that who I really was just wasn't good enough for her. And more than anything else, the words. Hours and hours of screaming, arguing, nagging.

No, the truly bad part wasn't the smack—it's what came after.

I told you never to ride that motorcycle! Do you see how you embarrass me in front of that policeman!? How you humiliate me? Do you know how much pain you cause me when you don't do what I say? No son has ever treated his mother so harshly, so cruelly! And you say you love me! I cannot believe my own flesh and blood would do such things!

Over and over and over again, all through the night.

It sounds funny when I do it in my act, but when you're in the middle of it, when you're living it, it's not funny at all. I'd feel mentally broken down. After an hour or two, I'd want to scream, "Please, just hit me! Punch me, kick me! Get it over with!"

That scene describes my life in the first few years of high school. None of the quiet strength you might receive from a father figure. But lots of volatility, lots of instability, plenty of screaming, and the constant feeling of being one short step away from falling over the edge.

That may have been the last time my mother smacked me. But it wasn't the last time I rode the motorcycle. Because as much as that slap hurt my face, I still needed to find ways to act out all the confusion and rage that I had inside of me.

es

MY MOTHER WORKED CONSTANTLY to keep us afloat. Gemma had gotten a job at Taco Bell to chip in. Rowena used to help out, but once she left she needed her Wendy's paycheck to cover her own living expenses—and my mom didn't really fault her for it, given that she'd been kicked out. So, I decided I needed to step up and contribute to my family's finances.

I got a job as a dishwasher at a Chinese restaurant.

As soon as the bell rang at the end of the school day, I hurried over to the restaurant, where I was slated to work until nine every night. I was so excited on that first day. I was gonna make *money*. I was gonna get a *paycheck*. I was gonna help my family like a *real man*.

Then I walked into the steaming-hot kitchen, I breathed in the thick, damp air that smelled like a toxic mix of dish soap and chow mein, I reached my hands into the scummy water full of dirty plates and woks, and I realized something truly profound:

I fucking hated washing dishes at a Chinese restaurant.

But I did it anyway. Night after night, dish after dish, pot after pot, as the skin on my fingers shriveled, slowly eaten away by the muck. The only thing that kept me going was the fried rice the owners let me eat for free. I lived for my half-hour lunch break, when I'd collapse in my chair and shovel that greasy goodness down my throat. God, it was delicious.

The problem was that I didn't just hate washing dishes at a Chinese restaurant; I was also horrible at washing dishes in a Chinese restaurant. I was so incredibly slow that pretty soon I didn't even have time for my precious fried rice breaks anymore. The restaurant couldn't operate without at least some clean dishes, so I had to keep going or the whole damn place would shut down.

"Just wash!" the owner would shout. "We bring food to you!"

I'd stand there with the high-powered spray nozzle in one hand and a dirty plate in the other as a waiter spooned rice into my mouth, one bite at a time. I was like a prisoner.

I could hear the chefs talking about me, and I know this because my name was the only thing these motherfuckers were saying that *wasn't* in Chinese. I don't know what the hell they were saying, but I could tell by their tone and their death stares that it wasn't good.

I was sweating and washing, sweating and washing. The whole six hours this was happening, the owner kept walking up to me at the sink, shaking his head and yelling.

"Look, wash pot *first*! Wash pot *first*! Why you wash plate? We have so many plate!"

I'll tell you why I kept washing the plates—because they were so damn easy compared to all the fucking pots! Those things were covered in burnt sauce and rice; it was so hard to scrape off. Of course, the pots and woks were exactly what the chefs needed to do their work; they didn't give a shit about my plates, but I didn't care—just hand me another plate please.

"No, no, no!" the owner would yell. "Here, like this!"

And he'd grab the spray nozzle out of my hand and blast that hot water—

Weeeehhooooooooooosh-weeeeeehoooooosssshhhhhh—

And I swear to God that guy knocked out ten pots in three minutes. I couldn't fucking believe it.

"Oh shit! Can you keep cleaning those pots? I'll do as many of those plates as you want, but if you could just keep going . . ."

And suddenly both the owner and the chefs were all swearing about me in Chinese.

"That's nice," I said. "But could you hurry with those pots? I'm backed up here, and I'd really like to eat some more fried rice."

I lasted two weeks as a dishwasher at a Chinese restaurant. But I didn't give up.

I got a gig at a sushi restaurant, and for some reason the owners there thought I'd make a good waiter, even though I was the one guy in the whole place who hated sushi.

Surprise, surprise, I was the worst waiter ever.

The head waiter who trained me was this woman with big horn-rimmed glasses, and she could memorize every single order she heard. Didn't have to write down a thing. I couldn't believe it.

"How the fuck are you doing that?"

They gave me one of the big long checklists to use, like every sushi restaurant has, but it took me too long to hunt down each individual item and mark it off the list, so instead I came up with the brilliant idea of using Post-it notes. Swear to God. So while all the other waiters were working so hard, memorizing all their shit, I was this Tasmanian devil of stationery, running around leaving Post-its all over the bar, all over the fridge, all over the floor. Of course, no one knew what tables the orders belonged to, including me. Brilliant idea, my ass.

Despite all this chaos I was causing, the head waiter in the horn-rims decided I was ready for the Wednesday lunch shift, the craziest shift of the week.

I got there, and the place was so busy and so loud it sounded like a whole football stadium was packed into this sushi restaurant. She gave me the smallest section in the place, but man, it was so hard. I was rushing everywhere, Post-it notes flying behind me, while I attempted to balance a million tiny hand grenades, these boiling, searing-hot bowls of miso soup.

"Be careful!" the head waiter shouted at me. "Don't pick up the bowls of soup from the top lid, Jo, always hold them from the sides. Otherwise the lid can come off and the steam can burn your hand!"

"Okay, okay, okay!" I say, barely keeping up.

Meanwhile, in my brain, I'm like "What the fuck did she just say?"

I got to a small table with a single customer sitting there, this big white guy in a tweed sports coat and a button-up shirt, like a pompous, self-important community college professor who was pissed he didn't get the gig at Harvard. I hand him his miso, and of course, I hold it by the lid on the top of the bowl.

As I'm pulling it off the tray, the lid opens, the steam hits my hand—

"OHHHHHHH!"

And guess what I did?

I threw that bowl of soup directly at tweed guy, not giving a shit about him whatsoever, just wanting to get that hot-ass soup as far away from me as possible, sucking my poor burned pinky finger.

"AAAAHHHHHHHH!"

Professor asshole screamed.

And the whole restaurant went silent.

Oh my God oh my God oh my God! Shit, shit, shit!

He started tearing at his shirt, pouring water on his hands. I just stood there, sucking my finger, the whole restaurant staring at these two burned idiots.

"Um, man," I said. "I'm so sorry. Here, um—"

I started wiping the seaweed off his shirt, patting him down with a napkin. I'm telling you, this guy was pissed. He was so mean.

"That won't do a thing! What is wrong with you? I can't believe you're a waiter!"

It was a fair statement.

Once he got his shirt off, it was clear that his burns weren't so bad. But the restaurant did have to get his whole outfit dry-cleaned. Of course, they took the cost of the dry cleaning out of my tips.

I lasted three weeks at that place, just long enough to actually try sushi and find out I loved it before they fired me.

I didn't give up on the whole job thing, though. I found another one at McDonald's, but I never showed up on time. Then I found another one at Burger King, but I couldn't keep up with the burger conveyor belt. Then another one delivering papers where I gave every house on the block a paper whether they had a subscription or not. Then another one stocking shoes where I had to wear a shirt and tie even though I was always stuck in the back.

Every job I had, they ended up hating me. Never lasted longer than three months. No idea why.

⁓

IT WAS A SATURDAY AFTERNOON, and my dad was gonna actually spend time with me for once.

I was at William's house, where my dad was supposed to pick me up to take me to lunch with my sister Rowena. It was beautiful out. William's Yamaha was calling to me, and you know what? I had spent 99 percent of my life wondering where the hell my dad went. I wanted him to see how it felt for once.

Fuck it, I thought.

I grabbed William's dirt bike, and William's brother grabbed his, and we took off to ride the trails. Motorcycles were technically banned from the trails, but no one really followed those rules, and I *definitely* didn't.

I was blazing on that bike, crisscrossing the park, seeing just how fast I could push it. I wasn't wearing a helmet, I wasn't even wearing pants—just a T-shirt, an old pair of shorts, and some tennis shoes. I could practically hear my mom yelling at me in my head.

Slow down, Josep! You're going too fast! What are you, crazy? You'll die!

I grinned, laughing to myself, and then . . . collided head-on with another motorcycle.

I was taking a corner at full speed, and the guy came out of nowhere. He smashed directly into my right leg. I flew off the bike and through the air and landed five feet away. My leg snapped like a twig.

As soon as I hit the dirt, my broken femur tore through the skin above my knee. I could see about an inch and a half of jagged bone, along with torn muscle fibers jutting out of my skin. Bone fragments were scattered all around me in the dust, and my knee was twisted in a sickening, bizarre way.

Screams filled the air. Who was making all that noise? At first I thought it was me, screaming in pain. But I was silent. In shock. It was everyone around me screaming in horror.

I tried to stand up.

"No, no, no! Don't try to stand, do not try to stand!"

I looked up and saw a substitute teacher I had a few weeks back. I had been such a jerk to her, fooling around, never paying attention, and here she was, trying to help me. Man, I should really be nicer to my substitute teachers.

I tried to stand again.

"Dude, do *not* stand! Your leg looks like a fucking shish kabob! It's meat on a stick! DO NOT FUCKING STAND UP!"

This was William's brother. I decided not to stand.

Someone called an ambulance. It took over thirty minutes to arrive, and I lost a lot of blood during the wait. I could feel myself getting woozy, and the pain was excruciating. When the paramedics finally showed up I asked them if they'd stopped for coffee along the way. Always the wise-ass.

"Hold still," the EMT said. "We're gonna try to lift you onto the stretcher, okay?"

I could feel my body being raised into the air, but it was almost as if we had forgotten my leg on the ground. It was so heavy, so dead.

I heard more screaming, but this time it was me.

They loaded me into the ambulance and turned on the siren. All of a sudden, I felt incredibly tired.

"Can you please just let me sleep?" I moaned to the EMT.

"I can't let you go to sleep, buddy," he said, waving smelling salts under my nose.

"Please, I don't want to be here," I said. "Just let me sleep."

"I can't, buddy. Your body's in shock."

We finally got to the hospital, and they wheeled me through the emergency room doors. My dad and Rowena got there a little while later. William's brother had called my sister. Tears were streaming down Rowena's face.

"Jo, are you okay?" she cried. "Are you okay?"

I nodded weakly. Even with all my pain and all my misery, one thing kept flashing through my brain as they took me into surgery.

"Please," I whispered. "Don't tell Mom."

༄

ALL RIGHT, SO THE TRUTH is I wasn't exactly a model son in high school. I was fucking up all the time.

I couldn't hold down a job, so I got some side hustles going. But unlike the jobs, my hustles weren't about helping my family—they were about helping myself. I was tired of getting by on vending-machine cookies for lunch. My friends owned their own motor-cycles, for fuck's sake. Me? I was stuck taking the bus.

Most of my hustles were harmless enough, the normal shit a lot of teenagers do, calling back to the very first time I swiped those albums with my sister Rowena. I started stealing candy from the 7-Eleven and sold it to other kids for pocket change. I shoplifted clothes I couldn't afford from Nordstrom's. I had an Izod jacket, and you could open the Velcro by the neckline and pull out the stuffing—leaving just enough space to hide a few shirts. I'd walk into the fitting room with two Polo rugby shirts and walk out with one, the other safely tucked away into my coat. If my mom ever asked, I just told her I'd borrowed them from William.

This way, when we got our pictures taken for our class ID, I wasn't dressed like some sad immigrant kid whose family could barely make ends meet. I was smiling away in my authentic $115 Ralph Lauren Polo rugby. None of that off-brand, Air Force base exchange bullshit for me.

But once I got a taste, I got hungry. My stealing went beyond little things I could justify as innocent attempts to level the play-ing field with my friends. It got dirty.

I had started hanging out in the library during lunch, because I didn't have any food to take to the cafeteria anyway, and I got to be friends with the librarian. I'd hang out with her at her desk. She thought I was funny, and she trusted me. I mean, why wouldn't she trust the poor kid who got laughs for attention?

One day she left me alone at her desk while she went to do some other work. For fun I took a paper clip and started messing with the desk's lock, pretending I was MacGyver. And that shit opened right up. Guess what I found inside?

A thick stack of public transit passes.

Those things were valuable, man. I knew because I took the public bus all the time. These were the kinds of passes that were good for a whole day, so you could use them to get all over the city, to the mall, to the movies, wherever. This was the school's private stock, so I convinced myself I wasn't really stealing from my friend the librarian, I was stealing from the faceless public school.

I grabbed them all, locked the desk behind me, and bolted. It took me about twenty seconds to sell two of them for five dollars each, and I used the money to buy myself a nice lunch. An apple, a brownie, and my very own slice of pizza, baby. I was living like a king!

But my victory glow faded pretty fast.

Later that day, the librarian came to one of my classes. She had a security guard with her, and he pointed right at me. I still had a bunch of the transit passes in my pocket and nowhere to hide them. I was busted. So, I just crumpled them up. Brilliant strategy, right?

They'll never be able to tell what these are if I crinkle them up! Mwahaha!

They took me to the office and made me empty my pockets. Somehow my diabolical ticket-crumpling failed to throw them off the scent, so I did the next best thing. I lied my ass off.

"Those are all mine! I bought them myself! What's wrong with that?"

"Right," the security guard said. "So, you just happen to be carrying around a big stack of transit passes on the same day that they go missing from the library."

"Totally."

Shit, I was a criminal fucking *mastermind*. My friend the librarian sighed.

"Jo, you were the only one sitting at my desk today."

"So?" I shrugged. "Maybe someone else sat there when you weren't looking. Maybe someone took them yesterday. All I know is I didn't take them."

Yes! Beat that logic!

The guard tossed a notebook onto the table in front of me.

"All our passes are numbered, and we keep a record of every single one. All those tickets in your pocket have our numbers on them. You stole them."

Shit.

"Uh. No, I didn't?"

Hard to believe, but my word just wasn't good enough for them. They called my mom, who had to leave work to come to the school and take me home.

"I have nothing," she said in the car. "I'm so ashamed. I can't even walk into that school anymore. This is the worst thing you've ever done to me. You're such an embarrassment, such a disappointment."

After that, my mother didn't even hit me with her usual endless barrage of words. There was no more shouting, no more screaming. Instead, she just cried the entire ride home.

I think this might've been worse.

❧

I HAD TO HAVE SIX surgeries on my leg after the motorcycle crash. I had fractured my fibula and tibia, and I had a compound fracture in my femur.

I was at the Fort Lewis Medical Center, because that was allowed by my father's insurance, and I was under my dad's plan until I was eighteen. After the doctors there cleaned all the debris out of my wound, my temperature spiked to 101 degrees. The doctors thought my leg was infected, and they'd have to amputate.

Right as they were preparing to cut my leg off, my temperature *suddenly* went down. It was like something straight out of the Bible, and the doctors saved it. They said I had a miracle leg.

Oh thank you, Jesus. I like my leg; keeping it attached to my body is a very good thing.

If my break had happened just an inch to the left, it would've severed a major artery and I would've bled out on the ground in the park before the ambulance ever arrived. An inch in the other direction, and I would've needed a full-body cast.

Instead, the doctors were able to set the breaks with giant metal pins, which was better than the alternative but wasn't exactly a picnic. The holes from where the pins were inserted kept filling with pus, so they'd have to be cleaned with cotton swabs and hydrogen peroxide every four hours. The burn was awful. A weight was attached to my shin to pull my leg straight, and I had to lie in traction in my hospital bed for five whole fucking months.

Oh, and guess what? My mom found out.

But if you're expecting my miracle leg to miraculously bring us together, you're in for a rude awakening. My mom still had to work all the time, she still had bills to pay and kids to support. And there I was, her favored son lying literally broken with pins coming out of his leg like some kind of Filipino Frankenstein. And all because I disobeyed a direct order from her.

In her eyes, this situation must've been just as infuriating as it was devastating. It did nothing to ease the tension between us. And my dad? He was business as usual, barely a presence. The person I did grow closer to was my sister Rowena.

I never saw it coming. When Rowena had lived at home we'd never gotten along. She hated being there. Whenever she was home, we argued. We argued about how she never backed down from my unstable brother. We argued about how mad she made my mom. We argued about how to defrost pork chops for dinner. We argued about the best way to iron my shirts. We loved each other deep down, but if there was something to argue about, we figured out a way to argue about it. Once she moved out, I almost never saw her.

All that changed once I was stuck in the hospital.

My sister visited me almost every other day, and her live-in boyfriend, Brian, tagged along, too. She brought me fast food all the time, which was pretty much critical to my recovery.

She even got me my own Walkman, which I desperately needed for my sanity during rehab. Think about it—I was looking at weeks and weeks of struggling to move my scarred, pin-punctured leg without any music except the sound of my own screams. But thanks to my sister's Walkman, I had my own personal recovery soundtrack, working out and dancing on one leg to Janet Jackson's "Nasty" and "Who's Johnny" by El DeBarge.

Shit, if El DeBarge can't inspire you back to health, you might at well pack it in.

But what I wanted, what I needed, what I *craved* more than anything wasn't a Whopper or even a Walkman—it was Brian's sweatshirt.

Like I said earlier, Brian was a six-foot-four Black dude who Rowena had been dating since high school. He was a star triple jumper on the track team, he was deaf in one ear, and he always wore this "I ♥ NY" sweatshirt. *Always*, like everywhere he went. That might seem a little weird to you, but remember—this was 1985. You couldn't just go on Amazon and have one of these things shipped to you in a fucking day.

If you wanted an authentic "I ♥ NY" sweatshirt, you had to travel all the way to New York City itself. I'm talking Times Square, baby—musicals and newsstands and porno theaters and hookers—and you had to buy one and bring it all the way back to Tacoma with you. Well, that's exactly what Brian had done, maybe on a trip with his family, I don't even know, and that's exactly why I wanted that thing for myself. That sweatshirt was cool, it was cosmopolitan, it was fashion, period.

And Brian would not give it up.

Before the accident, I'd beg him for it whenever I saw him, literally *beg* him, and he'd always shoot me down. He had this cloudy, deep voice, the kind that half-deaf people sometimes have, which somehow made his constant ridiculous denials even more infuriating.

"Brian, please, please, *please*, can I have your sweatshirt?"

"No, Jo. This is my famous sweatshirt, I wear it all the time, you know that!"

"Please, Brian, just to school for a day! One day!"

"No, I got this sweatshirt in New York! What if you lose it? I don't know when I'll be back in New York again! Maybe never!"

"But you're like seven feet tall and it's only a medium! It'll look so much better on me! It'll actually fit me!"

"No, I don't let anyone wear my famous sweatshirt! That's why it's famous! Now stop asking me!"

Eventually, I did. And then I broke my leg.

I'd been in the hospital for months. I missed so much school all the teachers just passed me. I got to skip summer school. It's probably half the reason I got my diploma. I was in that hospital so long even Janet Jackson and El DeBarge started getting tedious.

My birthday was around the corner. I was gonna turn fifteen trapped in the hospital with a bunch of fucking pins in my leg. I couldn't take it anymore. I never blamed the rest of my family for not visiting much. My mom couldn't exactly quit her job to spend time with me. My sister Gemma was still in high school and working nights. My dad was my dad. But lying there all day every day by myself was torture. I'd sleep just to sleep. Not because I was really tired, but just because I had to fill the loneliness with something. I was going to snap.

Rowena and Brian came on my big day. I knew they would—they were the only two who always made time for me. They were the reason to stay awake. Brian was wearing his sweatshirt. He looked me in the eye.

"Is there anything you want for your birthday, Jo?"

I had been waiting for this moment. I made my voice sound as meek and pathetic as possible.

"Can I have the sweatshirt?"

There was a long pause. I could feel the sweat beading up on my forehead, the pus collecting in my wounds. He sighed.

"Okay, I'll give you my sweatshirt."

I can't remember for certain, but I'm pretty sure all the nurses started cheering. My sister was appalled.

"You're gonna give it to him? Really?"

He took it off right there, and I never took it off as long as I was in the bed.

But you know what? That wasn't even the best part of my birthday. My mom came, too, and she brought me a cake.

My mom wasn't evil, she wasn't a bad person. She was just stubborn as hell. There was no way in her mind she could ever be wrong about anything. It just wasn't possible. She was right, she was *always* right, and that was reality. As frustrating as that was for me, that same stubbornness, that same iron will, is probably also what has helped her to survive as a single immigrant mom in America. To this day, I've never heard her apologize for anything. Not once.

But on that day, I think we both realized that something in

our dynamic had to change. I needed a father figure in my life, a strong, straightforward presence who could give me guidance. And she needed a partner. She was worn down trying to juggle all of this alone. She was lonely. She was exhausted. She was scared.

We all sang happy birthday and blew out the candles on my cake.

"Happy birthday, my son," she said as she sat next to me, rubbing my head.

"Thanks, Mom."

She leaned over, close to my ear.

"I was right," she whispered. "You should've died."

I never rode a motorcycle again.

5

FRED AND
TITTY BABY

There was one thing standing in the way of my mom meeting someone new after my dad left. One thing with two very powerful fists.

My brother, Robert.

Not my real brother, of course. My real brother would never dream of threatening my mom; he loved her with all his heart. But my fake brother, the schizophrenic one who took over Robert's body and mind, he was convinced that my dad was coming back. And he did not want my mom to see anyone else.

He didn't directly forbid her. He'd never say, "Mom, you cannot date people!" That wasn't fake Robert's way. Through a combination of sheer presence, physical power, and garbled statements, fake Robert would make his preferences known. He could be in the middle of one of his episodes, raving about how my dad was a spy, and it would come out of nowhere.

"Mom and Dad are getting back together! They're getting back together! Stay away from my mom! Stay away!"

Then the words would be gone, and he'd be on to something else. But the message was received. He didn't want my mom dating anyone, and we knew it.

Robert was extremely clever in his own twisted way. By this

point he was spending a lot of his time on the streets, but he knew how to manipulate the system to get what he needed. If life on the street got too tough, if the nights were too cold or his stomach was too empty, he'd attack someone, start a fight, and get himself arrested or institutionalized.

And bingo, just like that he had a warm bed and food to eat. He'd stay in the jail or institution for a while, start taking the meds they gave him, say all the right things to all the right doctors, then they'd release him—and he'd go right back to doing whatever he wanted to do.

I know it sounds kind of casual the way I talk about my own brother living on the streets or getting locked away in an institution. Your average, everyday person probably doesn't simply toss out "Yeah, so my bro was arrested the other day, probably won't see him for five or six months" like it's nothing. But in a weird way that's the most devastating part of a situation like ours—just how "normal" it becomes.

Oh, Robert's in an institution again? Did Mom admit him this time or was it the cops?

The cops.

Well, at least we know he's getting fed.

Yeah.

And at least he's not beating us up.

Yeah.

Where's the TV remote control?

But Robert knew how to manipulate his family as well. If he didn't feel like pulling his institution hustle, he'd show up on our doorstep. There were many cold, rainy nights when we'd hear that knock on our door. As soon as I heard it, my stomach would drop. I could feel the anxiety rattle my body, because I knew exactly what would come next.

He'd stand there, soaking wet, shivering and pathetic with tears in his eyes, saying he just wanted something to eat, just wanted to get warm, and we'd let him in. We'd always let him in.

Then, within minutes, he'd explode. Screaming his nonsense about our dad being a secret agent, and punching, kicking, scratching everyone in sight. And without any man around, without anyone to protect us, all we could do was take the abuse or call the ten cops required to drag him away. It was a merry-go-round of horror, and there was no way to jump off.

That was the other reason my brother never wanted my mom to date—maybe even the *real* reason, buried somewhere under all the other crazy rationalizations he came up with. He didn't want a rival. He didn't want competition. He wanted to know that whenever shit on the streets went bad, he could always come home and unleash without fear of being escorted right out the door by someone strong enough to handle him.

But during my junior year of high school, for a short time, it seemed like Mom finally found someone who could help.

Through a mutual friend she was introduced to a man she started dating. Robert was doing one of his longer stints in an institution at the time, so my mom was able to keep her new relationship on the down low. Her boyfriend was older, also divorced, with kids of his own he saw on weekends. His gray hair was done up in this slicked-back, fifties-style pompadour, and he had a thick mustache. My mom liked him well enough, I guess, but mostly she was looking for stability. Someone to help take care of her family, lend a hand (or fist, as needed) with Robert, and share her life with. I'm sure finding love would've been nice, but at this point in her life the main priority was simply not being alone anymore.

And so, shortly after they started dating, we ditched our apartment and moved into his house.

Here's a fucking shock for you: this was *not* a great idea.

I'm sure her boyfriend had only good intentions; the guy was helping our family out, after all. The problem was he never let us forget it. I got this cool room all to myself, the whole basement with its own entrance from the back of the house, but it never felt like *home*, you know? We were on his turf, we were living on his dime, and he made damn sure we knew just how lucky we were by reminding us of this fact, constantly. Needless to say, I fucking hated living there.

After living there for a few months, my mom and her boyfriend's relationship took a turn as well. There weren't big blow-ups, just the kind of disagreements you'd expect when two people who barely know each other decide to live together. Except there was one added layer—my mom ain't gonna put up with shit from *no* man. Compromise is not her thing.

I was sound asleep in the middle of the night when suddenly I felt someone shaking me awake.

"Josep!" my mom said. "Get your stuff and throw it in the car! Hurry!"

Now, maybe you'd think I'd be slightly traumatized by a dead-of-the-night evacuation order coming from my panicked mother. But bro, I couldn't wait to get the fuck out of that house.

"Hell yeah! Let's go!"

My mom had already rented us a new place. Even started furnishing it with the stuff we'd kept in storage. She was just waiting for the right moment for us to fly the coop. Maybe that moment came when her now-ex was out of the house. Maybe he was asleep. Maybe my mom just enjoyed the added drama of a late-night getaway. I don't know—I've honestly blocked it out of my memory.

But what I do remember is our new apartment. A tiny one-bedroom space that had to fit me, my sister Gemma, and my mom, not to mention all our earthly belongings. My mom and Gemma got the room, where they slept on all of our mattresses stacked one on top of another, surrounded by cardboard boxes full of our crap. I got the couch in the living room.

Our first night there, I lay on our lumpy, shitty sofa staring at the ceiling. I was thrilled we weren't living in the house of a man who was practically a stranger, but besides that? We were back on our own, back to living in constant fear of my schizophrenic brother, back to hanging on by a thread.

The American dream was supposed to be about new opportunity, about building a better life for you and your family. That's why my mom had dreamed of coming here from the Philippines when she was young. But no matter how hard she worked, that better life wasn't happening. If anything, life was getting worse.

I had no idea that night, lying on that couch, tired, uncomfortable, and sad, that I was months away from meeting the guy who'd turn it all around. Who'd love my mom for the rest of her life, who'd be the dad I so desperately needed, and who came up with a nickname for me that was so fucking wrong it was one thousand percent right.

He called me the Titty Baby.

ↄჟ

"MOOO-OM!" I WHINED. "I can't eat this stuff, it's disgusting! Can't you just, like, make me some chicken or something?"

"Josep, I spent all afternoon cooking that," my mom called from the kitchen. "Just eat!"

"Please, Mom? I seriously will gag if I take a bite. Pretty please? It'll only take you ten minutes! Pleeeeease?"

I could hear her sigh from the other room.

"Okay, fine, Josep. What, you want chicken? Ha?"

"Yes, please! Just chicken, that's all. Thank you so much!"

I considered for a moment.

"Oh, and could you please make sure it's boneless?"

She sighed again, louder than before, but I knew she'd make me what I wanted. She always did.

Though to be fair, the food I was staring at in front of me was legitimately, *objectively* gross. Filipinos got this dish called *dinoguan*. You take a pig's intestine, clean it out, chop it up, and boil it. And the broth the pig intestine is boiled in? The pig's own blood, of course. The dish comes out of the pot pitch-black, and you know what? If you taste it without knowing what it is, it is amazing.

But the second you realize what you're actually eating, you can't spit it out fast enough. This dish is Filipino to the core. Like, some Filipino foods have crossed over into the mainstream, right? You can find recipes for chicken *adobo* on Martha Stewart's website—*Martha Fucking Stewart*! But I don't care how open-minded she gets, Martha ain't gonna be posting about boiling pig intestines in its own blood. You'll only find *dinuguan* in the most authentic, legit Filipino restaurants out there. I mean, I love Filipino food—absolutely *love* it—and even I can't eat this shit.

Yet the dude sitting across the table from me, a gigantic, six-foot-three, 240-pound white-as-white-can-be hillbilly from the mountains of West Virginia, was just shoveling *dinoguan* into his face, licking his damn plate faster than our Chihuahua, Sissy.

The only moment he paused was to look at me in contempt.

"Shit, you gotta have a special goddamn meal?" he said in his thick country drawl. "You a titty baby, that's what you are. Still attached to your mama's titty. Just a goddamn titty baby."

I was speechless. I was insulted. I was ashamed. I fucking loved this guy.

"Fred," I said, "do you even know what you're eating right now?"

"I don't give a fuck what it is, Titty Baby, it taste good. You think my stomach cares what it's eating? My stomach is happy cuz it's full."

He then took a slice of Wonder Bread and started mopping up the sauce. And I was perfectly happy waiting for my specially prepared, boneless chicken. I loved my mom's new boyfriend—so much that I didn't want to ruin his dinner by telling him he was eating pig guts.

ↁ

IT WAS THE SUMMER AFTER my junior year, only a few months since we'd left my mom's boyfriend from hell. My mom met Fred the same way she met Satan-dude—set up by a friend, no Tinder or Match.com back in those days. And just like the last boyfriend, Fred was recently separated with kids of his own who he didn't live with. But as soon as I met Fred, I could tell he'd be different.

For starters, Fred was ex-military and had fought in Vietnam, like my dad, except he'd been Army, not Air Force. He'd had a long career, retired after twenty-three years. He was far from rich, but he had a pension and good benefits, exactly the kind of financial stability my mom was looking for.

But it really wasn't about the material things.

Fred exuded the kind of simple, honest strength that had been missing in our lives for so long. He had a square, chiseled face, big thick eyebrows, and when he frowned, he'd get this long, vertical crease like a butt crack between his eyes. He never said more than he needed to say, never bickered or made things complicated. He meant what he said and said what he meant, and it was like a breath of West Virginia country air.

His favorite nicknames for me were "Titty Baby" and "Bubba"—he called almost everyone "Bubba," but "Titty Baby" he saved especially for me—and he had no problem calling me this or telling me when I was full of shit, and even that was refreshing. I mean, my mom told me I was full of shit all the time, but somehow it always turned into drama coming from her, always exploded into this long, stupid, pointless fight. But when Fred told me I was being a pussy for ordering my mom around—"pussy" was another Fred favorite—there was nothing to fight about, because he was right.

I *was* being a pussy, I *was* being a titty baby. And it felt good to get a strong dose of straightforward, dad-style discipline. He was tough, he was stern, but he was just what I needed. With Fred, I felt grounded, protected.

Fred also happened to be the most indirect racist you'd ever meet. One of his favorite jokes—which I totally stole for my own act years later—was to tell me he was with my mom because he loved Chinese food.

"But Fred," I'd say, "we're *Filipino*."

"So?" He'd shrug, grinning. "Rice is rice."

Now, after everything we'd been through with my dad, you might've thought my mom would try to stay away from white dudes, look for someone from her own community. But first of all, Filipino guys weren't exactly falling off trees in Tacoma. And beyond that, in a weird way there was actually something comforting about how blatantly politically incorrect Fred was. After all, my mom never hated my dad because he was white, she hated him because she felt like he left her, because she felt betrayed. But a man like Fred would never betray us. If he wanted to say something he felt, he'd say it right to our face, even if it was offensive as fuck.

And, as much as we loved our big Filipino family at the Knights of Columbus, they were practically drowning in *tsismis*—gossip and drama and backbiting. Fred was the most unfiltered, authentic, what-you-see-is-what-you-get dude we'd ever met, no matter what color he was. And he was fucking hilarious.

Best of all by far, Fred liked sports.

That might not sound like a big deal to you, but it's hard to explain how important it was to me. I loved watching standup specials, of course—comedy was my passion, my dream. But it was something I enjoyed alone. Sports were different. Sports were about bonding, about watching games and talking shit with someone else. What was the point of watching Nate McMillan hit a huge shot for the Sonics if there was no one there you could high-five?

I'd had that kind of bond with Robert—the real Robert—years ago, before the schizophrenia took hold. Robert taught me everything I knew about basketball, how to shoot, how to dribble, and we had always watched games together on television.

That had been missing from my life until I met Fred. Fred was a Lakers fan, I was a Sonics fan. Fred was a Redskins fan, I was a Seahawks fan. Fred was a Dodgers fan, I was a Mariners fan. Together we'd spend hours watching games, sometimes talking, sometimes silent, just sharing in the experience.

It took me far away from the darkness in the rest of my life. Watching sports with Fred, I stopped thinking about being poor, about my violent brother, or the dad who wasn't around. For a short while, I could relax. I could simply be. But the hours hanging out with Fred were more than just an escape. They filled a void I'd felt for years without my father. Provided a sense of stability. Here was a man I could finally trust. Here was a man who wasn't going anywhere.

So even though my mom and Fred had only been together a couple of months, and even though we'd just gone through that horrible experience with her last boyfriend, I honestly didn't bat an eye when she told me Fred was moving in with us.

My mom, Gemma, and I had just moved into a new, much bigger apartment after the disaster of a one-bedroom. It felt like a palace compared to where we'd just been. The complex had a tanning bed and an indoor *and* an outdoor basketball court. The outdoor court was right behind our unit, so it felt like I could shoot hoops in my own backyard, like we lived in the suburbs or something. There was also the minor detail of having my own room with an actual bed to sleep on, which took things up a notch for sure.

The place was big, bright, with plenty of room for Fred. He just had one last test to pass, and it was the hardest one of all—he had to face Robert.

⁙

BAM BAM BAM!

It was the crack of dawn, and we were all asleep.

BAM BAM BAM BAM!

In my groggy haze I couldn't understand what I was hearing. Were we getting bombed? Were we at war? What the fuck was going on? Then I heard the screaming.

"Let me in! I want to come into my house!"

Oh, I thought. Robert.

BAM BAM BAM BAM!

He was trying to break down our front door. Thank God it was made of metal. I rushed out to the living room. My mom and Fred were already there. Fred was in his underwear. He'd only been living with us for a few days. *Welcome to our life. I wonder how much longer you'll last.*

My mom cautiously approached the door.

"Robert!" she called out. "Robert, go away! We don't want to fight!"

BAM BAM BAM BAM!

Fuck, he wasn't just punching the door—he was kicking it!

My mom looked at me and Fred, her eyes wide. She never wanted any physical conflict with her son; she wanted to avoid fighting at any cost.

"It's okay," she said. "The door is big, just wait. He'll leave."

BAM!

Robert did not leave.

Just like that, he broke in. He was wearing his favorite boots, stylish leather zip-ups with sharp little heels, and he used those things to kung-fu kick our big metal door wide open like a little Filipino Chuck Norris. He darted inside straight at me and pushed me against the wall.

WHAM!

But the *wham* I heard wasn't me against the wall—it was Robert, who had just been full-on body-slammed by Fred. Robert—pancaked and pinned to the ground by Fred—was now completely unable to move.

Holy shit! This was a new development.

"Get off me!" Robert yelled. "Get off!"

"I ain't moving, Bubba," Fred said. "You can try to move me but I'm 240 pounds. I need you to get out of this house."

Fred was speaking so calmly, so coolly, it was surreal. I mean, the guy was wearing nothing but his underwear, and he'd just done what it usually took a gang of cops to do!

"Get off me!" Robert yelled wildly.

"I'll let you up if you calm down," Fred said. "Then you gotta leave."

"Okay," Robert said, breathing raggedly. "Okay, I'm calm."

"You sure?" Fred said.

"Yeah, I'm sure. I'm calm."

"All right then."

Fred stood up and Robert took a swing at him. Fred blocked the punch like it was nothing, grabbed Robert, threw him against the sofa, and body-slammed him again. Didn't break a sweat.

"Look, Bubba, I can do this all day."

"Get the fuck off!"

Robert tried to throw another punch, so Fred punched him right in the face.

"You gonna calm down and leave quietly, Bubba?"

It was right around the time Fred punched Robert in the face that I decided Fred was my hero.

I know, it's fucking weird, right? I loved my brother, but here I was practically cheering on the man beating the shit out of him. It had been years since I'd figured out that real Robert, the Robert I knew and loved, was gone for good. I hadn't understood at all what was going on at the beginning—his first episode took place when I was only five. I actually thought he was doing it on purpose, that he was faking being sick and intentionally acting cruel and irrational. He'd get so violent so suddenly, I couldn't understand why the brother I loved simply couldn't control himself. I was angry, and I needed someone to blame—so I blamed him.

But honestly, even once I was old enough to understand that it wasn't his fault, it was still hard to feel real sympathy. I wanted to, I did. But the abuse we experienced was so intense—physical, psychological, the black eyes, the calls to the cops, never knowing what would set him off or why—I just couldn't. I'd actually have dreams about finding someone strong enough to beat him up. Seriously! He'd break a hole in our wall, we'd call the cops, and I'd sit there thinking, "I wish someone would come and beat the hell out of him."

I had accepted that no matter how much I wanted real Robert back, fake Robert was here to stay. Fake Robert had taken over my brother. That's just the way it was.

So maybe a little part of me felt guilty for feeling happy that Fred was beating up fake Robert. But mostly it felt like he was getting exactly what he deserved. Someone was finally standing up to him. The hero of my dreams had finally arrived. And I loved it.

"All right, Bubba," Fred said. "Now I'm gonna stand up nice and slow, and I'm gonna walk you to the door. And then you're gonna leave."

You know what? That's exactly what happened. Fred walked fake Robert to the door, and he left. We didn't even have to call the police. Robert never brought his violence to our doorstep again.

I hadn't just found my hero. I had found my dad.

ↄ

DESPITE THIS RUSH OF WARM feeling toward the guy, I'll admit it that it felt a little strange when my mom told me she was moving to Las Vegas and leaving me in Tacoma with Fred.

You read that right. Just a couple weeks after Fred moved in and kicked Robert's ass, my mother decided to move to Vegas so she could take care of her own mom, who'd been diagnosed with breast cancer.

My grandma, who we called Lola Tinay ("lola" means "grandma" in Tagalog), had moved to the States more than ten years earlier after marrying an American businessman back in the Philippines. First she lived in Los Angeles, then Provo, Utah, and she finally ended up in Las Vegas. She and my mom were close, they talked a few times a week, but we barely saw her.

You gotta remember that this was back in the 1980s, when flying was still a big deal. You'd get on a plane and you'd get your fancy little hot tray of food and the stewardess was always super nice to you and you actually had legroom. Flying was special, an event. It was also way too expensive for people like us. Shit, I couldn't even afford lunch *not* served to me on a plane. There was no way we were flying anywhere, no matter how much my mom wanted to see my grandma.

That all changed when Lola Tinay got cancer. A bunch of my other aunts had also moved to Las Vegas so it felt like we were the only members of the clan who *weren't* living there. Sure enough, once Mom landed in sin city, she decided to move our whole family to Nevada to join them and help out with my grandma's chemo.

There was just one catch. I still had a year of high school left, so Gemma and I would have to stay in Tacoma with Fred long enough for me to finish my senior year. Once I graduated—*if* I graduated, because it was never a guarantee—we'd meet up with my mom in Vegas.

"Mom," I said as she packed her bags, "you know we just met Fred, right?"

"Relax, Josep! You'll be fine!"

This from the lady who was so overprotective she nearly had a heart attack if I even mentioned the word "motorcycle."

My mom was gone the next day. My other sister, Rowena,

moved to Vegas, too, while Robert was reinstitutionalized. So it was Gemma, Fred, and me. All alone.

But you know what? As strange as it was, I was so happy. Not because my mom was leaving—I mean, I loved my mom, even though she drove me crazy. No, I was happy because I was finally gonna get to spend time with a father figure. A real dad. Maybe not my biological dad, sure, but someone who felt like one in all the ways that mattered. Gemma was living with us too, of course, and she loved Fred—he represented stability to all of us—but she was going to high school during the day and worked as a manager at Taco Bell on the nights and weekends, so she was hardly around. That meant I got Fred all to myself.

Soon after my mom left town, he took me to the mall to do some shopping. He'd just gotten a new credit card, and we decided to celebrate.

"I don't know how much money is on there, Bubba," he told me. "But let's go get some stuff."

Going shopping probably doesn't sound like much to you. Hell, I'd been to the mall before. I'd stolen some of my favorite Polo shirts from the mall. But to have my *dad* take me to the mall? To buy me things? Suddenly places I'd been to a million times before seemed brand-fucking-new.

*Whoa? A **Foot Locker**? Are you kidding me? This place is incredible!*

Fred bought me some shorts and shoes and a corduroy Lakers hat. I wore the shit out of that hat from that day on, and I didn't even *like* the Lakers. I was a Sonics fan.

And every night it was me and Fred in front of the TV, mostly watching sports. Football, basketball, baseball. We even caught the famous Dodgers game in 1988, game one of the World Series, where an injured Kirk Gibson hit a two-run walk-off homer in the bottom of the ninth to win the game for LA. Fucking Fred called that thing as soon as Gibson walked up to the plate.

"They gonna win this right here, Bubba. Watch this, they gonna hit it out."

"Whatever, Fred. No, they aren't."

"Put your money where your mouth is, Titty Baby. I ain't got no time to bullshit."

Kirk Gibson lost me a hundred dollars right there and then, but Fred never made me pay him back, which is exactly what a good dad does, especially when his son is as broke as I was.

As the weeks went by, and Fred and I had more time together, I began to see there were parts of Fred he'd been holding back. He wasn't just the strong, straight-talking man I loved watching sports with. There were demons—raw, conflicted emotion—lying just underneath.

And Fred drank. A lot.

We'd sit down after I got back from school to talk sports or watch a game, and next thing you know he'd be downing shots of Jack Daniel's and working on his second pack of cigarettes that day. I hadn't noticed him drinking much during the couple of months my mom had been in town. But it honestly didn't bug me at all. There are good drunks, and there are bad drunks, and Fred was a really, *really* good drunk. Funny, engaged—and revealing.

In most of my relationships—with family, friends, whatever—I spend a lot of my time making people laugh. And yeah, I make Fred laugh. But mainly I just love to listen and learn.

He and I took to watching the Vietnam movies that were so popular back then—*Platoon, Full Metal Jacket, Hamburger Hill*—

and bits of Fred's past started to come to light. I began to understand what had turned him into the kind of man who could and would, save my family.

℘

FRED HAD JOINED THE ARMY back in 1964. He was only seventeen, hadn't even graduated from high school yet, and he lied about his age so he could enlist.

That's right. During the Vietnam War, rich kids and hippies were lying about shit like bone spurs or going to Canada to stay *out* of the war, while Fred was lying his ass off just to get *to* the war.

"Why the fuck did you do that, Fred?" I asked him one night.

"Bubba, I was tired of digging holes in the snow on a mountain to take a shit," he said. "You never felt the cold if you ain't felt the West Virginia cold."

When I say Fred was West Virginia, I mean Fred was *pure* West Virginia. He came from generations of coal miners, the men who knew that if that canary died, you got the fuck out or you were dead, too. And that's what happened to a lot of Fred's family— they lived in those mines, and they died there, too.

Well, when winter hit, the mining didn't stop. Fred and the other miners would be deep in the mountains, surrounded by feet of snow, far from the nearest outhouse. If they had to shit, they had to shit, and there was nothing to do but dig a hole in the snow and take a dump right there in the freezing cold.

"Bubba," he said, downing his drink, "I wanted to fight a war in the sun."

So that's what he did. He got the hell out of mining and got into the Army. He went to Vietnam, and he'd barely set his boots on the ground before he got hit by shrapnel. Earned himself a Purple Heart and a Bronze Star—and the chance to go back home. But Fred had no intention of going home.

"That's just what I told 'em, Bubba. I said, 'General, send me back in. I don't wanna shit in the snow.'"

They sent him back out and he got shot by a sniper in his right shoulder. It ripped his collarbone to shreds and left tiny scraps of metal permanently embedded in his body. He got another Purple Heart, another Bronze Star, and a Combat Infantryman Badge, an extremely prestigious award that infantry can only receive during active ground combat.

This time, Fred went home, but he didn't go back to the coal mines. He stayed in the service until his retirement in 1988.

In our living room, twenty years and thousands of miles removed from the war that left him permanently injured, Fred and I would watch the battle scenes in these movies—mines exploding, bullets whizzing by, men dying left and right—and he'd show almost no emotion at all. Just sit there, glassy eyed, drinking his Jack, quietly taking it all in.

He was so calm, with the same demeanor of eerie cool he showed when he kicked my violent brother out of our apartment. It was unnerving. I had to know how he could watch all of those battle scenes, battle scenes he had lived through, and not even react.

Finally, as we stared at the television watching a pitch-black night battle flash on the screen, I decided to ask him a question.

"Fred, see all those bright white streaks flying through the air? What are those? Like some kind of bullet or something?"

"Those are tracer bullets, Bubba," he said. "They fire every third round so you can see what direction you're shooting in."

He went quiet, but after a few moments spoke up again.

"You know, Bubba, a lot of the way the movies show this shit, it didn't go down like that."

"What do you mean?" I said.

He shook his head and sighed.

"We got caught in an ambush once. I jumped in a ditch. I wasn't running out trying to be a hero or nothing. I looked up in the air, saw which way the tracer bullets were going, stuck my arm up with my gun and started shooting, just let it go. I didn't want to pop my head up, Bubba."

"Goddamn, Fred."

"All I wanted was dry socks," he said. "It was so fucking wet over there your feet would get all fucked up. That's all I wanted. Dry socks and weed."

I guess shitting in the snow really was horrible—if it was better to spend your life running from bullets with wet feet than coal mining in West Virginia, it had to be hell.

Fred finished up his Jack and fell asleep on the couch, out cold. That's how most nights were. We'd watch TV together. Fred would drink, talk, and make me laugh. I'd listen and learn. Then he'd pass out. The next morning he'd be up at six sharp no matter what, that military training still going strong.

It finally hit me. Fred needed our family to save him, just as much as we needed him to save us.

∽

I WAS A HORRIBLE FUCKING DRIVER.

I know, I know—insert Asian joke right here. But seriously, to this day I'll go to apply for auto insurance, and the agent will look up and say, "Oh wait, you look familiar. I know you from somewhere. You're Jo Koy, right? Uh, yeah . . . We're not supposed to insure you."

This was a huge problem at the end of my senior year of high school. I needed to go to prom.

I'd already failed my driver's test because I ran a stop sign—well, I didn't *really* run a stop sign, the stupid instructor just claimed I did and wouldn't change my grade to pass even when I told him he was wrong and I totally, absolutely came to a full stop. (Okay, fine, I ran the fucking stop sign.) But I needed to figure out a way to drive my date to prom. Not because I was particularly into my date, or even because I was planning to make out with her in the backseat after the dance, but because this was my senior prom and *everyone* was driving.

I sat with Fred on our apartment's porch one afternoon and made my case.

"You promise you won't get in an accident, Bubba?"

"I promise."

He looked me up and down.

"All right, I'm gonna let you drive the car, but don't do nothing stupid, okay?"

"Oh man! Thank you, thank you, thank you! I promise I won't do anything stupid! I swear!"

He gave me the keys to his Chevy Astro minivan with its ugly beige trim, and by the following night I'd ripped the whole side of the car open.

It wasn't even a cool, high-speed, high-impact crash. It wasn't some near-death experience I could brag about to friends. I was leaving this lame hotel party after the dance, driving very slowly, maybe four miles an hour, and I hit a fire hydrant. Just barely snagged it and watched in slow motion as it opened up the van's guts like a sardine can.

Fred knew as soon as I walked in the door. It's like he could smell it on me.

It was Fred at his best. There was no judgment, no anger, no fighting. He assessed the situation, spoke his mind, and acted. By which I mean he got his insurance to pay to fix the car.

"Fuck, Fred. I owe you so much."

He smiled.

"It ain't just for you, Titty Baby."

He was right. We needed that Astro for more than just my prom. And he wasn't saving my ass just to be nice to me. I was done with high school. It was time for Fred, Gemma, and me to pack up all our stuff and move to Vegas, where my mom was patiently waiting for us to create a real family—and where I'd finally make my standup dream a reality.

Once I got up the courage to actually tell someone about it.

6

LOOKING FOR GOLD

Pancit

INGREDIENTS

1 pound uncooked rice noodles
¼ cup vegetable oil
1 cup shredded chicken
4 garlic cloves, peeled and minced
½ onion, medium diced
2 carrots, thinly sliced
4 celery stalks, thinly sliced

½ half head green cabbage, medium diced
¼ cup soy sauce
1 teaspoon ground black pepper
4 scallions, thinly sliced, for garnish
2 lemon wedges, for serving

INSTRUCTIONS

1. Take the noodles out of the package, place in hot (not boiling) water until softened, about 5 to 10 minutes. Drain in colander, set aside.

2. In a large saucepan or wok, heat the vegetable oil over medium heat. Add the meat and cook until browned, about 7 minutes. Add the garlic, onion, carrots, celery, and cabbage and cook, stirring often, until softened, about 5 minutes.

3. Add the softened noodles, soy sauce, and pepper. Stir to combine, remove from the heat, and serve.

4. Garnish with the scallions and serve with the lemon wedges alongside.

Fred, Gemma, and I left Tacoma the week I graduated from high school.

It was the summer of 1989, but driving southeast across the desert, it felt like we were back in 1889. Barren and empty, nothing around as far as the eye could see except sand and brush and the occasional roadkill. We were pioneers traveling through a Wild West wasteland, hunting for new green land to settle down, prospectors looking for gold.

But instead of a covered wagon, we had Fred's Chevy Astro with its ugly beige trim, reborn after my prom night catastrophe and loaded full of everything we owned on earth. Fred behind the wheel, me in the passenger seat, forbidden from driving ever again, and my sister Gemma, who somehow carved out a nook for herself in the back with all our boxes, holed up for a thousand miles in her own little cardboard nest.

And instead of lush green land, we found Las Vegas.

These days when you think of Vegas, you picture glitz and glamour, a city as much about high-end hotels and top-tier attractions as it is about gambling. You think of the fountain show at Bellagio, the gondolas at the Venetian, the Eiffel Tower at Paris. What happens in Vegas stays in Vegas, right?

But back in 1989, you didn't care about staying in Vegas—you were lucky if you got the hell out. None of the cool shit that people love about Las Vegas now was around back then. The big Vegas building boom didn't start until the early 1990s, and the south side of the Strip literally didn't exist. The most expensive hotel in town was the old-ass, crumbling Stardust, the Bellagio was still called the Dunes, and then it was just vacant lots. Man, we should've bought property—we'd be billionaires now! Too bad we were dead broke.

The truth is we could barely even afford the shitty little apartment we moved into. It was right behind the MGM Grand, not the amazing hotel that stands today, but the original built in 1973, a big ugly tower that's now Bally's. When it was first built it was the largest hotel in the world, with over two thousand rooms. I guess it passed for fancy back in 1989, but the area where we lived was anything *but* fancy.

Our neighborhood was strip clubs and bars and hookers and tramps and drug dealers and junkies and, oh yeah, our apartment. Honestly, the apartment felt more like a spot in a weekly rental motel, or a step above some kind of seedy flophouse. It was a big box of fourplexes, two units on top, two on the bottom, with the two on top sharing a balcony and the bottom two sharing a porch.

Luckily, we wound up in the only fourplex in that whole disaster zone that had cool tenants, and we would all look out for each other. Right next to us was an Ethiopian family, and they were really good people. We'd all hang out in our shared area out front. Fred would lean against the metal rail and have a smoke with our neighbor, or if I got locked out of our place, I would go next door and crash on their couch for a while. It was like a big crazy sitcom of characters—*one family of Filipinos, one family of Ethiopians, and*

one indirectly racist ex-Army vet move into a dump in 1980s Vegas,
hilarity ensues!

Then twenty feet away in the next fourplex over lived a guy who
spent day and night jacked up on cocaine. Real TGIF on ABC
material.

I hadn't felt this excited in my entire life. I was finally done
with all the Washington rain and gloom. The sky was blue, and it
was hot and sunny all the time. I could go outside and play basketball whenever the hell I wanted. Even though we lived in a crappy
neighborhood, we felt more secure than we ever had in Tacoma.
My mom's entire family was nearby. She'd finally found a man in
Fred who was both strong and stable. Robert was being taken care
of in an institution a thousand miles away, so we didn't have to
worry about him ever showing up at our door. Rowena was still
living on her own, but she'd started putting her own talent to use,
the talent of her amazing voice, and was booking gigs as a lounge
singer around town. It was a fresh start. We were a few steps closer
to that American dream.

And most important of all for me, now that I was done with
high school, I could finally focus on becoming a standup comedian.

There was just one problem. I had no fucking clue how to do it.

❧

"HELLO?"

"Um, hi," I said into the phone, doing my best to keep my voice
from shaking. "Is this, uh, Steve?"

"Yeah," the voice said, "this is Steve."

"Steve Schirripa?"

"Yeah," he said impatiently. "Steve Schirripa. Why?"

"And you, uh, book comedy at the Riviera, right?"

"Yeah, I book at the Riviera. Why? Who is this?"

Fuck, he wanted a name! My mind raced.

"Um, I'm Herbert Glenn."

"Herbert Glenn."

"Yes," I said, clearing my throat. "I'm a local, uh, Vegas come-dian, and I wondered if you, uh, needed a comedian. For your show. At the Riviera."

Long pause.

"Who the hell gave you my number?"

Shit! I hadn't expected that question. What should I say? There's no way I could tell him the truth—that I harassed the guy at the front desk until he finally broke down and just gave it to me. Maybe I should tell him I got it from another comic? But what if he asked for that comic's name? I didn't know any comics' names, because I didn't know any comics! Then he'd totally know I was full of shit, if he didn't already think I was full of shit, because I was so obviously, blatantly full of shit.

Click.

"Hello?" I said. "Hello? Steve?"

Oh well. Not too bad for a first try.

Back in high school, I had dreamed of being a standup all the time. I never told anybody about it, because I was too embar-rassed, but it's pretty much all I did. In the morning when I took a shower, I'd take our handheld showerhead and pretend it was a mic, telling jokes into it after an imaginary announcer introduced me to the roaring crowd.

Ladies and gentlemen! Live, from his bathroom and totally na-ked! Joseph Glenn Herbert!

None of the shit I said to the shower wall was very funny, but that didn't stop me from practicing my autograph on every page of our thick-ass phone book. I mean, having a great autograph was important, right? I didn't want to let down all my fans begging for my signature after my shows. Had to get that capital "J" just right—just cool enough without seeming like I was trying too hard. And of course, speed was important if I wanted to get through all my requests—hundreds of them, maybe even thousands.

"Why do you keep signing your phone book?" my best friend, William, asked when he caught me one day. "You think you're gonna be famous or something?"

My face turned red.

"I don't know," I said with a shrug. "I just like doing it."

"Dude, you're filling up the whole thing. You can't find any phone numbers!"

But there was one thing I never considered in all those hours and hours of daydreams, and that was how the hell I was actually going to book a show.

These days, in any big city like Los Angeles or New York or even Vegas, you can find an open mic almost anywhere. Walk down the street in LA and in ten minutes you'll find dudes holding comedy shows in their goddamn living rooms using floor lamps as spotlights and cheap karaoke systems as their speakers. Now, I'm not saying that doing those shows will make you famous, but still—it's a start, a way to meet other comics and become part of the community.

Back in 1989 there was none of that, especially in Vegas. All the comedy specials on HBO—and a couple of years later on Comedy Central—were great for people like me who loved to watch at home but horrible for live comedy. Who wants to go to a smoky club if you can watch the biggest comics in the business in your fucking living room? The open mic scene was dead on the Vegas

Strip, and I was just a kid so I didn't know a thing about how booking real, paid comedy gigs worked.

So I did the only thing I could do. I found a phone book that wasn't completely destroyed by my autograph and I started making calls.

There was Steve Schirripa, who became famous years later as Bobby Baccalieri, Tony's brother-in-law on *The Sopranos*, the booker at the Riviera. I tried hitting him up a few times, but he was one of dozens. I'd find the numbers for comedy clubs all over the country and cold-call them, asking if they needed someone to open for any of their acts.

I came up with a fake name each time I called, usually a random variation of my real name. "Glenn Joseph," "Herbert Joseph," "Joseph Glenn"—this was the one advantage to having three first names for a name. If none of these bookers knew who I was, what did I care if they laughed and hung up the phone? Besides, what was I actually gonna do if someone said yes—drive across the country to some random club in Boston or Chicago? I didn't even have my license. I was still forbidden to drive. I didn't even have any material beyond the garbage I spewed every morning in the shower.

I called clubs constantly, but nothing ever came of it. No one returned my calls. None of the bookers would take the time to talk to me. None of what I was doing was real.

But here's the honest truth. I liked it that way. Because deep down I was scared.

Yeah, I'd always been the funny guy in class or at parties or hanging out with my friends. But to get up onstage in front of a crowd? To tell jokes for a living? That was a whole new level of funny, something I'd never tried before. Stand-up had been my dream for as long as I could remember, but that only added to the pressure I put on myself. What if after all those daydreams about making it big, all those signatures in the phone book—what if I got up onstage and just sucked? What if I was a failure?

Ever since I was a little kid who was confused about his identity, insecure about his half-breed background, I had one thing to fall back on—I was funny. That was my identity. If I couldn't hack it as a comedian, if I couldn't look myself in the mirror each day and know I was the funniest guy out there—who would I be? I'd be no one.

I'd been afraid to tell anyone about my comedy dreams for a reason. If I hid them from people, I could enjoy the fantasy without worrying about the reality. Now was the time to finally face the reality, and the prospect was terrifying.

And the pressure I felt was more than internal. How was I supposed to take my dreams seriously when no one else did? Back in Tacoma no one I knew even considered entertainment to be a real job. These days anyone can hop on YouTube and become a minor celebrity for doing all kinds of things. Not back then. TV shows, movies, music, this was all mystical, magical stuff that happened someplace far away, made by glamorous people who lived lives we couldn't begin to comprehend. The idea that someone like me—a guy who almost flunked gym and paid strangers to buy him wine coolers at 7-Eleven on the weekends—could be famous was laughable, and not for the right reasons.

And that was just among the white people. The Filipinos? Fucking forget about it, man.

As far as my mom was considered, I was still destined for medical school. She'd wanted my sisters to go to college, but they'd decided to work instead—Rowena was singing on the side, but both she and Gemma had steady, good-paying jobs. Not exactly a college education, but the next-best thing. My brother, Robert, obviously wasn't going back to school. That made me our family's last great hope for that college cap and gown. So, no, I definitely did not tell Mom about my comedy dreams.

Filipino people are really talented, *so* talented. As I explained—when you're as broke as we are, you have to rely on yourself for entertainment, for singing, for dancing, for telling jokes, and this really is embedded in our culture. But for the exact same reason—because back on the island we're so used to having absolutely nothing—we also have a strong practical streak.

You're allowed to be talented until the end of high school. Then after that, it's "get a real fucking job." And if you're a first-generation American immigrant, the pressure is even worse, because as far as your mom is concerned the *only way* she's been successful is if you graduate from college and get a good white-collar job—because that's the American dream, and your success is her shot at that dream.

So, and I know I've said some form of this many times before . . . if you're a Filipino woman in America and you're reading this book right now, there's a really good chance you're a nurse.

Seriously, a Filipino family reunion is a great place to get injured, because as soon as you sprain that ankle you'll be surrounded by dozens of women shouting, "Put a cold compress on the head and elebate the peet! Elebate the peet!"

And to all you Filipino nurses out there, I'm not shitting on you for what you do. It's a great job, great benefits, great money. I'm just saying it probably wasn't your dream. That was your Filipino *mom's* dream. She wanted you to be a nurse because she knew it was practical, responsible, safe.

I know, I get it, because my mom was the exact same way. She'd had her own dreams back when she was young, remember? You think managing a rock band included a steady paycheck and good benefits? Hell no! She did that because she loved it. And she'd had to give it all up the minute she got to the States. It was time to be practical. She had mouths to feed.

As soon as she got to Vegas, she'd gotten yet another job as a loan officer at a bank, and when I moved there she started bugging me about going to college.

"Take a few classes, get your grades up, then you go to med school, no problem!"

So, yeah, I was scared. Scared of failure. Scared of not living up to my mom's high expectations. Scared of finally taking my shot.

Somewhere deep down I knew that all my cold calls wouldn't amount to anything. I was making just enough effort to tell myself I was trying, without really putting myself on the line. I wasn't risking anything at all.

I got through to Steve Schirripa again, and he gave me a little piece of advice.

"Look, kid," he said with a sigh. "You wanna try to make it in Vegas? Go to LA, do some open mics first, get something I can see on tape, okay?"

I hung up the phone.

Steve was the only booker who ever said more to me than "no." I don't know why he took my calls. Maybe I managed to wear him down. Maybe he's just a nice guy. Whatever the reason, his words gave me a brief moment of hope—and it vanished almost immediately.

Me? Go to LA? Yeah, right. I couldn't even handle Vegas.

And it was true. Yeah, it was warm and sunny in Nevada, but we lived in a dump, my comedy dream wasn't going anywhere, and I didn't even have any friends. At least back in Tacoma I had friends who knew me and liked me. At least back in Tacoma I didn't have to call someone a thousand times just to have a five-word conversation that ended in "no."

That's right. As crazy as it sounds given all my history there, moving back to Washington actually started to seem like a good idea. All my buds were still in town, and William had a cool place of his own. I could crash with him, get a job—somehow figure out how to not lose it—and spend the rest of my time hanging out and partying. It was the perfect plan!

It lasted maybe three months. Being on my own was *hard*, man. I was eighteen years old. I'd never had to pay bills before. I'd never had to cook for myself. I didn't even do my own laundry! In a weird way, I ran into the same problem I had with my comedy "career." I loved the dream of independence. But I was *not* prepared for the reality.

Fred had been right. I was still nothing but a titty baby.

I called up my mom on the verge of tears and went back to Vegas the next day. She hadn't even touched my old room.

"I knew you'd come back!" she said triumphantly.

And for the first time in my life, I actually started to buckle down.

I got a job at the mall selling shoes at Champs, and guess what? I managed to keep it. I'd learned from my past mistakes. I showed up on time and did my work with a smile. And, okay, it probably didn't hurt that I was dating my incredibly hot coworker. But what mattered most was I got my paycheck every two weeks, and I used some of the money I made to buy food and help my family pay the bills.

I took my driver's test, made sure to come to a full stop at the stop sign, and finally got my license. My mom then bought me a car, a Volkswagen Rabbit, and I used it to get to work and take

Lola Tinay to her chemo sessions—that is, until I crashed it a few weeks later when I collided head-on with another car that ran a red light in an intersection. For once it wasn't my fault, so insurance gave me a loaner to drive, and I was back on the road, going to Champs, helping my grandma, being a good son.

Soon after, I enrolled in courses at the University of Nevada, Las Vegas.

∽

TOTALLY COINCIDENTALLY, MOVING TO VEGAS also put me a lot closer to my biological dad—geographically anyway. He was just a few hours' drive away in Phoenix, even closer considering his job as an airline attendant meant that he could fly whenever he wanted. Phoenix to Vegas is a sixty-minute flight, if that.

But I didn't think this new proximity would change our dynamic. The guy had hardly been around the last six years of my life; what difference would a few hundred miles make? Besides, I had Fred now, someone who watched sports with me, someone who'd protected me from my brother's schizophrenic episodes, someone who was around. My dad had been able to fly to Tacoma whenever he wanted. I still almost never saw him. So I had no great hopes that we were going to instantly become best friends.

So, when my biological father suddenly decided to take me on a trip to the Grand Canyon, I tried as *hard* as I could to lower my expectations.

I mean, come on. My dad the flake was supposed to pick me up, take me to the airport, use a buddy pass he had earned to fly me from Vegas to Arizona, and then spend *time* with me in the Grand Canyon? There were so many ways he could screw it up! There was no *way* this trip was gonna happen! Get a fucking grip!

But I couldn't help myself.

When my dad pulled up outside our place that morning, I was beyond excited.

"Hey, Jo, how you doing?" he said as I practically jumped into his car.

"Awesome!" I said. "I can't wait to get there!"

"Absolutely," he said, hesitating a little. "Hey, did your mom give you any money?"

"Money?" I said, my voice dropping.

"Yeah," he said. "Not much. Just enough to cover food and stuff on the trip. You know . . . ?"

My mom had not given me any money. My mother had assumed that since this was my dad's trip, since he had invited me, he'd take care of the logistics and pay to feed his only son. Nope. Apparently not. My dad was totally fine waiting while I went back and asked my mom for cash.

I ran back upstairs. My mom looked up when I opened the door.

"What's wrong, Josep? Did you forget something?"

"Um," I said sheepishly, "Dad wants you to give me some money."

Swear to God, smoke started coming out of her ears.

"What. Did. You. Say?"

"Uh, well, Dad said—"

"This son of a bitch hardly ever paid me child support, he hasn't bought you clothes or food or a car, he hasn't done anything, and now he wants **money***?"*

"Just for, like, food," I said, my voice cracking.

There is nothing more terrifying than a Filipino mom who's gone into full self-righteous demonic fury mode. For all you non-

Filipinos out there, if you're ever close to one who's about to go off, straight up—fucking *run*.

"Stay here," she commanded.

She stormed out. And you know what? Even though I knew my dad totally asked for what he was about to experience, I kind of felt sorry for the guy.

I couldn't actually make out what my mom screamed at my dad over the next few minutes, it sounded like a series of high-pitched, muffled shrieking noises, but it didn't really matter. She could've been speaking in Tagalog or French, and the anger would've been just as powerful. It was like *Exorcist* level, beyond human language.

When she came back inside, her rage had just started to burn itself out.

"You're staying here. If he's too cheap to pay for his son's food, he doesn't deserve to be a part of your life. I'll take care of you. You can rely on me for everything."

A couple of minutes later I heard a knock at the door. It was my father.

"Can I talk to Jo?" he asked my mom.

My mom glared at him, considering.

"You can talk to him," she finally said. "But he's not going with you."

My dad nodded. I got up and went with him to his car.

My parents had split up when I was in the sixth grade. I wasn't a child anymore. I had graduated from high school. But in all the years since their divorce, we'd never really talked about it. About why it happened or how either of us felt. Not once.

So, in this weird way, my relationship with my dad, if we even had one, was frozen in the past. It'd never moved forward, never come back to life after that moment when he walked out on us.

Until now.

"I'm so sorry, Jo," he said to me as we sat in the car. "I promise this'll never happen again."

I looked up and I saw tears in his eyes. I'd never seen my dad cry before.

"I'm sorry about today, and I'm sorry about everything. I know I haven't been there for you, I know I haven't been around. I have no one to blame but myself. It's all my fault. I can't take it back, but I promise I'll change. I promise."

I realized I was crying, too.

I'd never experienced that kind of emotion from my dad. Yeah, he'd tell me he loved me. He'd hug me good-bye—the few times he was around. But he'd never talked about the past. He'd never expressed any sorrow or regret for how he acted. He just kept messing up, over and over again, and he never said sorry, never shed a tear. And because of that, I thought he didn't really care. I believed he didn't really want me.

I didn't need an explanation from my dad—then or now. I've never wanted him to tell me exactly why he left us. I do my best to put myself in his shoes, to see things from his perspective, to appreciate the stress he must've been under as a young man with a violent schizophrenic son and a family to support, and I let it lie. He hasn't given me a reason to this day, and that's good enough for me.

But hearing that he was sorry, seeing him break down like that, feeling his sincerity and his pain—*that* was real. That meant everything. I knew that whatever had happened in the past, he wanted me now. He loved me now. He'd be there for me for the rest of my life. And that's all that mattered.

It was the worst day and the best day of my life. It was the day my dad let me down for the last time, and the day he finally became my dad. My mom woke him up. Whatever she said, however she said it, it worked, and I'll always be grateful.

A few months later, my dad took me on that trip to the Grand Canyon. He paid for everything.

∽

SHOCKER.

I fucking hated college.

Honestly, I don't even know why they let me in the door. The math class they made me take was the closest thing to remedial they offered. It wasn't even Math 101, more like Math -1.

I started taking classes because it's what my mom wanted, but pretty soon the only reason I was showing up was to show off my new Air Jordans from my job at Champs. All that shit people talked about how all you had to do was "apply yourself" and you could be book-smart, that's all it was—shit. My brain wasn't wired for school, and it really didn't matter how hard I tried or how much my mom wanted me to succeed.

Finally I decided to take a class *I* wanted to take. I was gonna take a class on standup comedy.

Unfortunately, there are no classes on standup comedy. So, I found the next-best thing, or what seemed like the next-best thing: music theater.

Hard as it might be to believe, there was a method to my madness. I was still struggling with all my self-doubt about making my comedy dream a reality. Sure, part of the problem was simple logistics—I still hadn't figured out how to break into standup as a kid with no experience in Vegas. But a bigger issue was my self-confidence. I simply didn't have any experience getting up onstage and performing solo for an audience in a formal setting. Maybe the Musical Theater class could give me a low-pressure environment to get up in front of a crowd and get my feet wet. After all, I might be bad at school, but even *I* couldn't flunk Musical Theater. Right?

There was just one problem. Except for some karaoke back in Washington, I'd done very little singing.

Soon I found myself in an auditorium full of students whose only dream in life was to sing the fucking *Pirates of Penzance* in front of five hundred people, and the most I'd ever done was lip-sync "Billie Jean" at the local Filipino community center. UNLV is a pretty cool, diverse school, so even in this crowd I didn't really stand out physically, though I did always have the hottest sneakers. But there was no question I was out of my element.

All semester—or at least the times I bothered showing up for class—I struggled. As a perennial class clown, I was used to being the center of attention, so I felt good enough whenever I'd get up to perform in front of the other students. But once I'd start singing a standard from *The King and I*, something would go wrong. I wasn't getting booed out of the room or whatever, but I could tell that no one was really connecting with me. People were fidgeting in the front row, doodling in their notebooks, staring out the window. I was on key, my voice was like Filipino velvet, but something wasn't connecting—for my audience or for me. I wasn't the guy everyone wanted to be around in class anymore.

I wasn't being funny.

The day of our final exam arrived. We each had to perform a number in front of the entire class. Everyone else chose to perform exactly what you'd expect—songs from *The Music Man*, *West Side Story*, *Oklahoma!*—all those Broadway classics. Dancing, prancing, surreys with the fringe on top, the whole deal. It was a musical orgy of Gilbert and Sullivan standards.

Me? I decided to stick with what I knew.

I sang "Mary, Mary Quite Contrary" from Jamie Foxx's first comedy special, *Straight from the Foxxhole*.

Now, this is way before Jamie Foxx was the respected, multi-faceted actor he's known as today. He was not the Jamie Foxx of *Ali* or *Ray* or *Django Unchained*. This was Jamie Foxx in full-on motherfucking drag as Wanda from *In Living Color*. Half these musical theater students had no idea who the hell Jamie Foxx was, and the other half did know and thought I was crazy for choosing a comedy bit for the final.

Crazy, or trying to insult the hell out of their passion. Maybe both.

But here's the thing. If you've ever heard Jamie Foxx sing "Mary, Mary," you know it's not just funny—and it is funny as fuck—it's also *amazing*. His whole point is taking a nursery rhyme, something that should be silly and stupid, and putting a sexy, over-the-top R&B twist on it. So even though you're literally hearing the words "Mary, Mary, quite contrary," what it *sounds* like is Marvin Gaye doing a filthy-ass rendition of "Let's Get It On." It was exactly the combination that I needed. Smooth, sexy, and hilarious.

I got up on that stage, in front of all the cynical theatrical eyeballs who'd spent the whole semester staring at me in that class, and I felt more uncomfortable than I've ever felt in front of a group of people before. I felt good about my choice, but still—this was a risk. I was putting myself out there.

Then I started to sing—and I blew those fuckers away.

My rendition of Jamie Foxx's rendition of "Mary, Mary, Quite Contrary" was so fucking funny, so fucking hot, so fucking sexy, there were musical theater nerds having straight-up orgasms of laughter on that auditorium floor. Just giggling and wriggling and purring like some shit from *Cats*.

Turns out that when I'm really feeling a song, I can *sing*. This is only my theory, I don't have any scientific evidence or empirical data, but I think Filipinos genetically get the gift of singing from the Spanish in them. It damn well ain't from our Asian side—no one's rushing to hear the Japanese cover Luther Vandross. But the Spanish? Latinos? Those fuckers can warble, man, and they passed it on to us.

How do you think Filipino star Arnel Pineda got to be lead singer of Journey? Dude was an amazing original musician, of course, but he also *killed* those cover songs. Journey, Aerosmith, Queen, he can do it all. Every single Filipino house you visit, there's a karaoke machine in the living room, and most of us can sing better than the original. If we can't, we'll fake it—just like I did.

When I finished, the musical theater teacher's mouth dropped.

"You've gotta come audition for our next show!" she said. "This should be your major! I need you in the Musical Theater program!"

I smiled and shook my head.

"You're sweet," I said. "But I'm gonna be a comic."

It was the only college final I ever aced.

ↄ

ON NEW YEAR'S EVE, Fred and my mom decided to go out and celebrate.

"Come with us, Josep!" my mom said. "You need to get out of this apartment!"

"I'm good," I said. "I'm just gonna stay in. Thanks."

"No!" she said. "Don't be pathetic! You are a young man, you need to go out! Come on!"

"I swear I'm good, Mom! I wanna stay home!"

It was a total role reversal. My parents were going out to have a great time on New Year's, and all I wanted was to be home by myself.

"Okay, Bubba," Fred said, pulling my mom out the door. "Don't get too crazy now."

As soon as they left, I sat back on the couch and turned on the television.

Me? Crazy? Yeah, right.

We'd been in Vegas over a year, I lived with my parents, and I worked at the mall selling shoes. My girlfriend had broken up with me. And UNLV? The dean sent me a letter stating that due to my 1.8 GPA I wasn't going to be allowed to enroll next semester if I didn't bring my grades up. *Cool*, I thought, and I never went back.

My mom's hope—her dream that I'd be the first in the family to go to college—was dead, and you know what? I didn't even have the guts to tell her. I knew it would break her heart. I knew she'd add it to the long list of ways I'd failed her. Most important, I knew I'd never, ever hear the fucking end of it.

Why, Josep, why? Why are you doing this to me, ha? What have I done to deserve this horrible treatment from my son? You could've been a doctor, a lawyer, a dentist, a neurosurgeon, an astronaut, a . . .

Blah, blah, blah.

And what about *my* dream?

Since grade school, I'd told myself I was destined to be a comedian. But I'd never had the courage to tell anyone else. I'd wasted months of my life calling clubs that didn't give a shit about some young dude who'd never been onstage. Shit, the closest I'd actually gotten to performing was a "show" in my Musical Theater class!

I'd been choking on doubt and fear, losing myself in my mom's goals—not mine—and getting bogged down in my own complacency. I still told myself my dream was alive. But was that even true? Or was it all just bullshit I fed whatever was left of my ego?

Now it was New Year's Eve. Supposedly a time for fresh starts and new beginnings, and I was home doing nothing.

Except it wasn't exactly nothing.

HBO was playing a marathon of their best standup specials. I ordered a large pizza from Domino's and a two-liter bottle of Coke, and I turned to my best and oldest friend—standup. I was going to feast on comedy all night long.

I planned it as an escape, a chance to forget about everything and laugh for a while. But the more I watched, the more I got sucked in—not just by the laughter, but by the science *behind* the laughter. The comics' skill, their technique, their craft.

How could Whoopi do so many different characters just by changing the bandana she was wearing? How did Billy get from his intro to his first joke so damn fast? How did Robin channel so much physicality, so much energy, into every single word that left his mouth?

I pulled out a pad and a pen and started writing their jokes down as they told them. It was the perfect way to visualize and diagram each gag's structure: *Okay, here's the setup. Here's the punch line. Here's the precise word it all turns on, the exact moment that Robin or Billy or Whoopi goes from buildup to explosion. And here's the phrase they use to start building up all over again.*

I counted how many words each joke consisted of—how the fuck did they tell them so quick? I had to figure out how to tell jokes that fast. Had to!

As I watched, as I studied and soaked up all that standup, it took me back to my earliest experiences with comedy. Back to when I heard Richard Pryor for the first time and watched Eddie Murphy in that sick red leather suit. Back to when I first started to tape over *Superman* and *Raiders of the Lost Ark* with any special I could find on TV, watching them over and over until Jay or Johnny or Louie or Ellen was nothing but a grainy, pixelated blur.

You know what? Fuck college. Fuck working at the mall. Fuck making cold calls to strangers at comedy clubs. Most of all, fuck doubt.

I needed to get out there. I needed to get on a stage in front of an audience. I needed to stop making excuses, get off my ass, and do something real to get what I wanted. I was born to be a standup comic, and I was gonna prove it.

My mom and Fred got home at 1:30 a.m. and found me alone with an empty box of pizza and a half-drunk bottle of soda, watching TV and laughing so hard tears were rolling down my cheeks.

"Oh my God, Josep!" my mom shouted. "Get a fucking life!"

My mom didn't give a damn about swearing. She'd drop an F-bomb like nobody's business. She taught *other people's* moms how to curse.

My mom's words didn't hurt me. I might not have my own life yet, but I knew what I wanted it to be.

And I was about to get my very first shot.

7

THE **FIRST** LAUGH

The very first standup show I ever performed was in a contest called "The Biggest Fool."

I know, that probably should've told me something, right?

But I didn't care what it was called. I'm pretty sure I just randomly heard about the contest listening to the radio one day. All I knew was it was a chance to get up on a real stage in front of real people and perform comedy.

No more telling jokes into my showerhead. No more singing songs in front of music theater nerds. No more moonwalking in front of elderly Filipinos at the Knights of Columbus. This was a real comedy show at a real club on the legendary Las Vegas Strip.

It was March 1990 at an old-school joint called the Comedy Stop, right inside the Tropicana Hotel. And this was more than some little one-night competition, it was a tournament. They'd put two comics up onstage, and the crowd would pick which one got to go to the next round. Anyone could go up and tell jokes, no experience necessary, no Steve Schirripa who needed to see your tape. Whoever won the whole competition got to open for a big-name comic on April 1, April Fools' Day, to officially be crowned the Biggest Fool.

Man, I just *knew* I had what it took to be the Biggest Fool.

The week before the show I spent every waking minute writing material. Writing was a fantastic way to harness all my insecurity and turn it into something creative. Also I had to, because I'd never written a joke in my fucking life. I didn't have an ounce of material. So I bought stacks and stacks of spiral notebooks, red ones, green ones, blue ones, and I started filling them all.

I'd wake up in the morning and write in bed. I'd watch comedy specials at night for inspiration and write before I went to sleep. I even took my notebooks into work at my latest gig selling sports gear at the mall. I'd fold a few jerseys, write a joke. Stock a few shelves, write a joke. Sell a couple of pairs of shoes, write a joke. I still hadn't told anyone I wanted to be a comedian, I *definitely* hadn't told my family, so if anyone saw my crazy chicken-scratch scrawl, they probably just figured I'd finally lost it.

Instead I was writing a whole bunch of dick jokes.

☙

SERIOUSLY, ALL THE STUFF I love to talk about in my shows now—all the stories about me growing up and my mom and my dad and my sisters—I didn't write about any of that. Honestly, it never even occurred to me that those stories might be funny to anyone, especially non-Filipino people.

Ever since I permanently moved to America, ever since that little boy at the mall made the slant-eyed face at my mom, I'd been internalizing what white America thought of Asians and Filipinos. Their clichés, their stereotypes, had become my own. White audiences *couldn't* think of us as real, complex human beings; they could only think of us as clichéd, one-dimensional cartoons.

I figured the only Filipino stuff that white people *would* laugh at was all the cheap racial shit. Jokes about how we have funny accents and flip our P's and B's. Or cheesy comparisons like "When a white person goes to a restaurant, he orders food like *this*. But when a Filipino goes to a restaurant, he orders food like ***this***."

Ha. Ha. Ha.

But jokes like that were too easy, too lame—and most important, I didn't think they were universal enough. I wanted to write jokes that *everyone* would laugh at, that *everyone* would relate to, no matter their race, religion, or creed.

And *everyone* thinks dicks are funny, right?

So that's all I wrote about. Stupid shit about dicks and luxurious handicap bathrooms and really bad blow jobs—never mind that I wasn't even dating anyone and I barely even remembered what a blow job was. Everyone knew about blow jobs, everyone thought blow jobs were funny, so I was gonna fucking write about blow jobs. And people were gonna love it.

That's right. I was writing this stuff down laughing hysterically the whole time, shaking my head, hardly able to contain myself at my own comic genius.

"This dick joke is way too funny, man!" I'd laugh maniacally, all alone in the fucking stock room with no one around. "No one writes dick jokes the way I do!"

It probably seems like a contradiction—how could I have this deep-seated fear that I'd fail at standup *and* be convinced my jokes were gold? But in a strange way they're actually linked. The same fear that can be so paralyzing, if I channel it in the right way, can also be a hell of a motivator. The more scared I felt, the harder I fought it. The closer I got to the show, the louder I shouted *You gotta beat this!* Honestly, it was an amazing high.

Every day that passed, I felt more of a rush. Every minute that went by, I felt more of a buzz. Through some kind of weird chemical process, all my old doubt, all my old anxiety, all my old dread was being transformed into something—adrenaline, endorphins, comedy crack. I flunked science so I have no clue. But whatever it was, it was coursing through my veins, into my brain, and distilling into pure, liquid, glittering hope. And it was totally irrational.

By the time the big night finally arrived, I'd had a vision that I'd get up onstage, and in the middle of my set the stage manager would run to the house phone and call the biggest agent he knew and shout, "There's this kid performing right now! *Listen to him!*"

And he'd hold the phone out to the audience and the crowd would roar with laughter as the manager foamed at the mouth over how brilliant I was.

"Fuck it! This kid's the winner! Call the rest of the tournament off! It's *over!*"

He'd shove a one-way ticket to Hollywood into my hand and a week later I'd be a millionaire with my own prime-time TV show. *Yes! It was all happening! My dreams were coming true!*

Now I just needed to make it happen.

I got to the Comedy Stop, and the place was packed. Not an empty seat in the house. The energy was insane.

I stood by myself backstage, keeping one eye on the massive crowd and my other eye on my ratty spiral notebook. I was poring over every line I wrote, desperately trying to memorize it all down to the very last word.

Okay, okay, okay. **First** *I talk about the size of the dick,* **then** *I talk about the smell of the dick,* **then** *I talk about the taste of the dick,* **then** *I talk about how important all that is for a decent blow job. Right, right, right. Okay, let me read that over one more time . . .*

When my turn was up, the stage manager—the guy I thought

would fall in love with me at first sight—grabbed me and shoved me out there, barely even looking at me.

I walked to the center of the stage, stood in front of the mic, opened my mouth, spoke two words—I'm pretty sure one of them was "dick"— and time stopped.

All my confidence, all my crazy fantasies vanished—just like that. My tongue got so dry it stuck to the roof of my mouth. It was like no saliva could be found anywhere in my body, like I became a human desert. Just tumbleweed and buzzards and fear.

Fuck. Why was it so quiet? Hadn't everyone been laughing a few minutes before?

I kept smacking my lips and gulping and making these noises. *Bluh—flug—ergh.*

And I suddenly became incredibly aware of just how loud my heart was beating. Each beat was like a sonic boom in my head.

Did my heart always beat this hard? Was this normal? How the fuck did people walk around with these stupid heart things making so much goddamn noise?

My brain was a big scramble of all the words and lines and jokes I had tried so hard to memorize so perfectly, and I couldn't keep any of them straight. I looked over at the stage manager standing on the side behind the curtain.

He wasn't on the phone calling all his big contacts in Hollywood. He was motioning at me, mouthing the words *"Get off the stage! Get the fuck off!"* over and over again.

But I couldn't do it. I *refused* to do it.

I wanted to get one laugh before I got offstage. I needed it. Craved it. Just one. Just a single laugh! So I kept reciting my shitty dick jokes with my monotone voice and my sand-dry mouth and my sonic-boom heart.

But it didn't work. That laugh never came.

We were only supposed to get three minutes onstage, but I swear it must've been ten before the stage manager finally grabbed me and physically dragged my sorry ass away.

Guess what? I lost the contest.

There was no next round. No agent. No one-way plane ticket to LA. No dreams coming true.

I went home and locked myself in my room.

It was the worst feeling I'd ever experienced. Pure humiliation, pure embarrassment. I kept replaying the entire night in my head, every mistake, every miserable moment. I couldn't stop torturing myself with the feeling of sheer and utter failure.

What happened? Did I have any talent at all? All those years of dreaming, of hoping, of signing my own autograph in notebooks, was it all for nothing? Was I just a fucking loser? Would I ever be funny again?

It was like my worst nightmare had come true. All my deepest, darkest fears.

No one had ever bombed that bad before, I was sure of it. No one had ever gone up onstage and sucked *that hard* in front of so many people. No one anywhere in the fucking history of the motherfucking world. Certainly not in comedy. And then I remembered. Eddie Murphy had.

Out of all my favorite comics—George Carlin, Richard Pryor, Robin Williams, Dennis Wolfberg—I loved Eddie Murphy the most. He wasn't just hilarious, he had style. Whether he was wearing all red leather in *Delirious* or black and purple in *Raw*, Eddie didn't just get up onstage and deliver lines; he had attitude, he had swagger. He made a statement. I idolized Eddie Murphy. He was my hero.

And he had bombed, too. Not just once, but a bunch of times. I never actually saw him bomb, of course—it happened a long time before he got famous—but I read about it in an interview he gave. When Eddie started doing standup, he bombed all the time. But he never gave up.

He'd get up onstage, bomb, then get back up onstage and bomb again. And finally, one night he got a chuckle. Then a little while after that he got a laugh. Then a few more laughs. Then a few more. And it just kept growing and growing and growing, till eventually he wasn't just getting a few laughs, he was getting them in front of thousands of people.

But it all started because he refused to quit. It all started because he kept going back up onstage. It all started with that one laugh.

I just had to get mine.

⁊

THE TIME HAD FINALLY COME. I was going to tell my mom I wanted to be a comedian.

I know, my first try at standup hadn't exactly been . . . encouraging. But I didn't decide to tell her because I was already a great comic. I decided because now I knew I would never back down. I was going to prove to myself just how committed I really was.

And I was fucking terrified. Even more than when I stood on stage at the Comedy Stop.

This was a woman who'd staked all her hopes for the future on me, and she never let me forget it. I'd dropped out of college months earlier, but I *still* hadn't broken the news to her. I was too afraid of how angry she'd be, how disappointed, how devastated that I hadn't lived up to her expectations.

Being a Filipino immigrant to her wasn't just a cliché or a punch line, it meant striving. It meant having goals. It meant moving to the States and working your ass off so your kids could go to college and have a better life than you.

Now I was about to tell her that not only was I *not* going to college, I didn't even want a normal job. My long-term plan basically amounted to "Hey, I'm gonna be living with you and Fred in this cramped little apartment in Crack Alley Vegas for a long, long, long time. Oh yeah, and you're gonna be feeding me too. That is until I become a World Famous Comedian!!"

I decided to tell her the way any self-respecting adult who still lives with his parents would—by sneaking it in as we watched her favorite TV show, *Unsolved Mysteries.*

Who knows? Maybe she'd be so focused on crimes of passion and Robert Stack's gravelly voice that she wouldn't even notice that her son was throwing his life away?

"Hey Mom?" I said, my voice sticking in my throat. "I gotta tell you something."

"What?" she said, her eyes glued to the bloody reenactment on the screen.

"Um," I said, "I don't want to go to college anymore. I want to be a comedian."

Bam. It was like the world stopped turning. You could've had Robert Stack himself standing in our living room and it wouldn't have mattered.

My mom looked at me, stunned.

"What. Did. You. Say?"

"You know—like an entertainer. Like those comics I always watch on TV with the specials. A comedian."

A wave of horror washed over her face.

"A . . . a comedian? But what about college, ha?"

"I—I don't want to go to college. I'm not even in college anymore. I want to be a comedian! It's my dream!"

She burst into tears. I don't mean a little trickle here. I mean full-on, broken-down sobbing.

"I don't understand—how do you even be a comedian? What does that mean? Ha? Do you need a resume? Do you audition? What?"

I hesitated.

"Yeah, something like that. I'm—I'm figuring it out."

Her sobs just kept getting louder and louder.

"But why, Josep?" she pleaded. "Everyone in the family works! Your aunts work, your cousins work, your sisters work, I work. Everyone works!"

"I know!" I said. "I'll work, too! Being a comedian is a hard job!"

"It's not a job," she said. "Josep, you want to be a clown? Is that what you're telling me, Josep? *Ha?* You want to make your living being a *clown?*"

Now I was the one crying.

"It's not being a clown," I said. "It's my dream. I'm funny, I've always been funny. Don't you get it? It's all I know how to do."

I actually talk about telling my mom about my dreams as part of my act. In the bit, I tell my mom I think I'm funny, and she acts all offended and says, "Josep, who told you you're funny? Who?"

Then she pauses and her eyes open wide and she says, *"It wasn't me!"*

And she really did say exactly those words—years after the night I told her I wanted to be a comic for the very first time. Ironically, it became her own little bit, a joke she'd make to her friends and family whenever the subject of my chosen career came up. She'd tell them I wanted to be a comedian because I thought I was funny, then she'd turn to me:

"Josep, who told you you're funny? Who? It wasn't me!"

By the time she was dropping that line, though, the shock had long worn off. That's not to say she'd completely accepted my dreams—to this day I honestly don't think she believes comedy is a legit profession—she was just using humor to cope with what was for her a tough reality. And having a good laugh while she did it.

Like mother, like son, right?

But there was nothing funny about our very first confrontation about my comedy aspirations. I'd be lying if I told you I was expecting her to react any differently. I knew that for her it was college, followed by a respectable career or nothing else. But even though I'd known what was coming, even though I'd tried to prepare myself mentally and emotionally for my mom's rejection, still . . . her words hit me so fucking hard.

It was like getting up on that stage and bombing all over again. Except this time, instead of a bunch of strangers telling me I was no good, it was my mother. The woman who'd always taken care of me when no one else would, who'd always fed me and clothed me and given me a roof over my head. Fuck, she still was!

Yeah, she'd always given me tough love, she'd never been easy on me. But I'd still been the baby of the family, *her* baby. I'd thought that, push came to shove, she'd do anything for me. But she couldn't do this. She couldn't believe in my dream.

But you know what? As painful as it had been, telling my mom actually strengthened my resolve. Taking that leap, confronting her lack of faith, had been one of the hardest things I'd ever done. If I could get through that, I could damn well get back onstage.

A couple of months later, it was time. My second show was another contest called Star Mania, an open talent show where anyone could perform—singers, magicians, comedians, crazy pet tricks, whatever. In fact, my sister Rowena, who'd already been getting work around town as a lounge singer, decided to compete, too.

Just like my first show, the closer I got to the big night the more my anxiety turned into completely irrational comedy adrenaline. The audience would technically choose the winner, but I absolutely *knew* that before they even had a chance to cheer, the stage manager—who would totally be a much cooler dude than the first guy—would be making calls to all his big agent friends about this hysterical new talent he'd just discovered. Me.

It was that same rush, that same high, that same euphoria-induced fantasy from my first show. And I know it sounds crazy, but I honest-to-God believed with every ounce of my being that it would happen. There was no "imagine if" or "wouldn't it be funny if . . ." There was no "if" at all. It was like a superhero mentality. I *knew* I would walk through that wall without a scratch.

Was I delusional? Maybe. But it also didn't stop me from working my ass off.

I didn't leave a thing to chance this time around. The contest was gonna be at a bar and I wasn't even twenty-one yet, so to get in I used my mom's eyeliner to fill in my baby mustache. I got this sick outfit to wear—herringbone pants, a button-up shirt, and this purple and mustard tie from that super-trendy store Merry Go Round that was so huge in the nineties. No stripes on this tie, no sir—the pattern looked like a bunch of paint splotches, like one of those ties you wear that say "I'm too *cool* to wear a tie."

Most important, I practiced my material even more obsessively than I had before. I just knew I had to get my dick jokes *exactly* right, word for word, if I wanted them to land. I repeated my jokes over and over again, and if I got even one syllable wrong, one misplaced "the" or "and," I'd get so fucking pissed at myself. My delivery had to be *perfect*.

And it was. I went up that night in my fake mustache and my hip splotchy tie, right after this Lionel Richie impersonator got the crowd all hyped up with his version of "All Night Long," and I recited all my amazing dick and blow job jokes from memory *perfectly*.

I still fucking bombed. Not a single laugh. Except maybe at that tie.

Something was *not* working, and I had to figure what, and fast—or it wouldn't matter how determined I was. I'd be headed back to college just like my mom wanted.

∞

MY DAD LOVED DENNY'S.

Not so much the food—he only knows three flavors anyway, salt, butter, and A-1 Steak Sauce. No, what he loved was the simplicity, the straightforwardness of the whole Denny's experience. Especially the menu.

"You don't even have to read anything," he'd say. "You look at the pictures of the food, you pick what you want, and you point."

And that's what he'd do. We'd sit down at Denny's, he'd open the menu to a Moons Over My Hammy or whatever he was in the mood for, and he'd point.

"I want that."

Not a word more, not a word less. The perfect restaurant routine.

But today I was going to throw a major wrench into that well-oiled machinery. I was going to tell my dad about my dream.

I was nervous, of course, but deciding to tell him had a different significance than it did with my mom. I didn't crave his approval in the same way. I didn't have to work up my courage or prepare for an emotional Armageddon. It wasn't something I'd been dreading for years.

No, this felt more like an opportunity, a chance to share something special with the man I called Dad, but whom I'd barely known most of my life. Since that failed trip to the Grand Canyon, we'd been spending a lot more time together—including at Denny's. Pointing, ordering, eating, and making up for all the time we'd missed. All that stuff he'd promised about working harder to be my dad, about being responsible and supportive—so far he'd actually done it.

Honestly, I couldn't believe how much he'd changed. But this would be the biggest test. But considering our history, I wasn't expecting much better than what I'd gotten from my mom.

Shit, at least I'd get some free steak and eggs out of it.

"Hey Dad?" I said, setting down my cup of weak coffee. "I gotta tell you something."

I'd decided to stick to pretty much the same script I'd used with my mom. You know, because it worked so well.

"What's that, Jo?" he said, looking at me with those eyes that were still insanely blue after all these years.

"I don't wanna go to college anymore. I want to be a comedian."

He looked at me blankly. Not bad, not good, which was kind of encouraging.

"It's, uh, my dream," I said.

Then the most amazing thing happened. He smiled.

"You do it," he said. "Don't worry about school. Do it."

I could barely believe what I was hearing. Maybe he was bullshitting me. Maybe he knew how my mom would respond, and he wanted to prove *he* could be the good parent for once. Maybe it was all an act.

"Really?" I said. "You really mean that?"

He thought for a second, like he was trying to make up his

mind about whether to tell me something. Then he sighed, and seven beautiful words came out of his mouth.

"I always wanted to be a pilot."

My jaw dropped.

See, even though my dad had spent all those years in the Air Force, he had never been a pilot. He'd spent his whole military career loading and unloading cargo planes. It's gonna sound crazy, but he'd been obsessed with cargo planes since he was a little boy. A lot of kids went for the fighter jets, but not my dad—he liked the big planes. He had wooden models of all of them, and he was fascinated by the logistics.

How did the Army get all their tanks to Germany? How could they get six of these *massive* vehicles into a single plane, fly them through the air, and parachute them down to the ground? It blew his mind, and he turned it into a profession.

And bro, let me tell you—that dude could stack the *shit* out of boxes. I'm serious! My dad was a master packer. Any cargo plane, any warehouse, any car trunk, he could organize that thing to the very last inch of available space.

But the whole time he'd been loading and unloading those cargo planes, it turned out he'd really wanted something else. He wanted to fly them. My dad had a dream, just like me, and I'd never even known it.

"Deep down, I think I was scared of getting my pilot's license," he said, staring out of the Denny's window. "So, I kept coming up with excuses. I got married to your mom, we had kids, I got busy. I could've taken classes on the weekend if I really tried. But I kept saying I didn't have the time. And the next thing I knew I ran out of time."

I've never asked my father to explain why he left. To me that's the past, and I want to let it lie. But at this moment, I understood better than I ever had before the kind of pressure he'd felt when he'd been married to my mom. Three children to support, one of them who was violently schizophrenic, all while my dad was still in his twenties. That wasn't to excuse him for leaving us. I wasn't giving him a pass. But I got it. I really did.

To this day, my dad was still close to his dream—painfully close, working as a flight attendant, spending so much time in planes, around planes, but never actually piloting them. Never getting what he really wanted.

He looked me in the eye.

"I don't want you to be like me, Jo. I don't want you to run out of time."

℘

BUT MAYBE THE HARDEST PERSON to tell about my comedy dream wasn't my dad or even my mom. It was my hairdresser.

Now, I know what you're thinking.

You had hair?

Yes, motherfucker, I really did have hair. But by the time I was twenty, it was already falling off my head big-time, so I did the only logical thing. I decided to get it dyed blond. Shit, might as well have some fun before I lost it forever, right?

There I was, in the salon, getting my thinning hair dyed. We're talking the whole setup—one of those big smocks around my neck, foam all over my head, and my scalp burning from the bleach. And I was making my hair guy laugh and laugh and laugh.

I wasn't saying anything special. I wasn't running through my brilliant collection of finely honed dick jokes. I was just being myself, making funny faces because my scalp hurt so bad, whining about how I was losing all my hair, just having fun. But my hairdresser could *not* stop laughing. Tears literally rolling down his cheeks.

Finally, gasping for breath, he says it:

"You're so funny! You should be a comedian!"

People had probably said something like that to me a million times before, and I'd never really responded. I'd laugh a little and move the conversation along. Not that most of them even meant anything by it, you know? It was probably something they just said, just kind of threw out there in the moment—*oh man, you should be a comedian!*

But to me it was a huge deal. There was something about admitting to a random person that I wanted to be a comic—that I *really fucking wanted it*—that felt scarier and even more real than telling my own family. Telling my parents, that was private, that was personal, between me and them. But telling a virtual stranger? That was putting my dream out into the world. Like once I spoke those magic words, once they drifted off into the atmosphere, there was no turning back.

I never said it. Until now.

"Yeah," I said, hesitantly. "I want to be a standup. That's my dream."

I'm not sure what made me do it. Maybe telling my family had made me stronger. Maybe all those times I bombed onstage had given me a thicker skin. Whatever the reason, I did it—and as soon as I did, my hairdresser's eyes lit up.

"Oh my God, yes!" he said. "My friend owns a coffeehouse and they have an open mic every Wednesday. You *have* to do it!"

"Wait, what?" I said.

My head was spinning, and it wasn't just the smell of bleach in the air. I had told this guy I wanted to be a standup, and now all of a sudden, he was lining me up for a real gig? How the fuck did this just happen?

"*Yes!*" he said. "It's your *dream!* Let's go there and introduce you to him *right now!*"

"Now? But I'm getting my hair bleached!"

"Now!"

"But my scalp is on fire!"

"Now!"

"But I'm wearing a fucking apron!"

"NOW!"

And he physically grabbed me and pulled me out of the chair, tore off my bib, wiped off my semi-blond head, and dragged me out the door.

He took me to a little café called Buzzy's, on Maryland Parkway. Walked right in, went up to the owners, and got right to the point.

"This is Jo. He's one of the funniest fucking people I've ever met, and he wants to be a comedian. It's his dream."

The owners looked at me. They were a husband-and-wife team, and to them this was probably no big deal—just another dude to add to their lineup. I mean, this was a weekly open mic at a joint that sold coffee and bagels. People weren't exactly expecting Billy Crystal here. But to me, these people weren't just the owners of some generic café, they were gatekeepers. My shot at getting back onstage and redeeming myself after bombing. To me, it was everything.

"Um, hi," I said, my heart pounding. "Nice to meet you."

They didn't bat an eye.

"Cool! You around next week?"

"Yeah," I said, my voice cracking. "I'm here."

"Awesome. We'll see you next Wednesday at nine."

"Next Wednesday at nine," I said with a gulp. "Right."

As soon as we walked out the door, my hair guy cheered.

"*Yes!*" he said, giving me a big hug. "*We did it!*"

I nodded in a daze, my scalp still tingling.

I had opened my mouth and spoken my dream to my hair-dresser. I had released it into the world, and now, in one week, I'd be performing again.

✧

THAT WAS THE LONGEST WEEK of my life.

As determined as I was to follow my dream, as much as I wanted to be like Eddie Murphy and go back up there no matter what, I had to admit—failure was *hard*. Yeah, I'd get crazy confident right *before* I went onstage, but after? Bombing sucked. I needed to get that laugh, just one little laugh, to keep me going.

I went back to my notebooks and started writing again, just like before. All day, every day. At home and at work. Pages and pages of top-notch dick jokes, more material than I'd written for my other shows combined. *Fuck! I only get like five minutes—this must at least be forty-five!*

I practiced my lines over and over again, polishing my timing, perfectly memorizing every word, just like I had before.

But even as I worked so hard on my act, even as I killed myself to get it right, something was nagging at me in the back of my mind, a tiny kernel of doubt. After all, all this material I had done before—all the writing, all the practicing, all the memorizing—none of it had worked!

What if I went through all this and bombed, just like I did before?

I knew that the pros, all my standup heroes, videotaped their sets to help them hone their acts. The best of the best would watch their shit over and over again, poring over every word, every expression, every pause, seeing what the audience responded to and using that to get better.

That's what I needed—a camcorder of my own, to tape my act and help me get back on track. Of course, camcorders were expensive as hell—this was years before you could just shoot whatever you wanted on your iPhone—and I worked at a fucking shoe store, so I wasn't exactly raking it in. But I didn't care. I'd buy whatever camera I could find and do the best I could.

That weekend, I caught a ride with my mom to the mall.

In the months since I'd told her I'd dropped out of college, my mom hadn't embraced my dream. No-drama, laid-back Fred had been cool with it, of course—just a "Do what makes you happy, Bubba," I'd thanked him, and we'd moved on. But my mom had loudly and officially stated her opposition, for the record, once and for all, and she *never* changed her mind.

In fact, it had gotten to the point where it was almost like comedy didn't exist, like that part of our conversation had never even happened. Like her brain had been so traumatized by my confession, she'd blotted out the entire experience.

The only thing that changed was that now, instead of harassing me about school, she bugged me about the next-best thing. Getting an office job. Or if it wasn't in an office, at least some kind of management position at Sears. Or if it wasn't a management position, at least something with a good salary, decent benefits, and of course a 401(k). Something stable, something steady, something respectable. A *real career*.

And to add insult to injury, while I was just working a shit job at Foot Locker or Champs or whatever my latest sports store happened to be, my mother would magically transform it into a fancy profession whenever she talked to her friends.

"Oh, this is my son, Josep, he really knows a lot about tennis shoes."

"Josep, this is Mike, he likes to run. What kind of shoe should he wear?"

"Oh yes, Josep really likes sneakers, he's like a scientist of footwear really."

A government job? That was even better. If you work for the government, you *never* get fired. Everybody knows that the next-best job after nurse for any Filipino was a mailman.

"Josep, your uncles are mailmen, your cousins are mailmen. Why can't you be a mailman?"

Even Fred, who wasn't in any way Filipino, who'd retired from the military after decades of service—even *he* became a mailman after we got to Vegas.

"Fred," I asked him, "why'd you become a mailman?"

He shrugged.

"Your mama told me to be a mailman."

So, when I started looking at camcorders in the mall's electronics store, searching desperately for the cheapest, shittiest one I could find, I wouldn't even tell my mom why.

"Josep," she said, her eyes growing wide after a few minutes. "Are you going to *buy* a camera?"

"Yes, Mom."

"Why? What a waste of money!"

"I need one, okay?"

"What do you mean, you *need* one? Ha?" she scoffed. "No one *needs* a video camera."

I sighed.

"I need it for my standup, okay? To record my comedy act."

She laughed, but it wasn't a good kind of laugh.

"For your comedy? What, you're still wasting time on that?"

I shook my head. This was the last thing I needed to hear. I wanted so bad to just ignore her, to pretend I didn't care what my mom said. What she thought. But I couldn't hide my feelings. Tears welled in my eyes.

"Are you embarrassed of me, Mom? Are you just not proud of who I am?"

She opened her mouth, taken aback.

"Proud of you, Josep? Of course, I'm proud of you, I'm your mother!"

"Oh," I said, "so that's why you tell all your friends I'm some kind of shoe specialist?"

"You should be in college!" she said, shrugging. "That's what you should be doing!"

"I don't want to go to college!" I said. "I want to be a comedian. I've always wanted to be a comedian. It's the only thing I want. And it feels like you don't even care, and that sucks."

For one of the only times I can remember in my entire life, my mom was speechless.

Her eyes shining, she turned away, clutching her purse even tighter to the left side of her body. Then, suddenly, she turned back to face me and the cameras. She cleared her throat, and with an almost businesslike manner she said something that truly shocked me.

"I'm going to buy you a camera," she said.

Now it was my turn to be speechless. I wasn't the only one who was practically broke. Fred, my mom, and I still lived in our shithole apartment down the block from a dozen Vegas strip clubs. We still barely made ends meet. I finally found my voice.

"Are—are you serious?"

"I'm serious," she said. "What camera do you want?"

Ten minutes later, we walked out of the electronics shop with one of the highest-end camcorders they sold, one of those mini ones you could fit in the palm of your hand.

I stared down at the box I was holding, still barely able to believe what just happened.

"Mom," I said, struggling to find the right words to say everything I felt. "Thank you."

She smiled—then got very serious.

"You're welcome," she said. "Don't tell Fred."

∾

THE BIG NIGHT FINALLY ARRIVED.

I got to Buzzy's and it smelled like coffee and sandwiches. There was no real stage. But the lights were turned down, they had a stool and a guitar amp with a mic, and they'd brought in a big piece of paper that looked like a brick wall and taped it up. Pinned to that paper was a sign that read "Comedy Time."

There was barely anyone there, like maybe ten or fifteen people, but I talked to a few and it turned out more than half of them were local comics.

Shit, I thought. *There are local comics?*

I set up my brand-new camcorder in the back and waited for my five minutes. I flipped through page after page of dick jokes, doing my best to memorize them all, but they kept getting jumbled up in my head, the way they had before.

There were no fun fantasies about a random agent discovering me and flying me to LA. None of my usual delusions of comedic grandeur. I was a confused mess.

Fuck. And my mom actually thought I should go to college?

Then I thought of the only other college class I'd enjoyed aside from Musical Theater—Public Speaking 101. For my final speech, I'd written up an entire, detailed presentation on Bo Jackson and his career-ending football injury. I had notes, facts, and of course a bunch of carefully planned jokes—but when I got up to the podium in front of the professor and the other students, I forgot everything.

Instead I'd just riffed, talked the way I talked in normal life, casually, improvising and making conversation. And I'd gotten tons of laughs.

Sure, I probably got all the shit about Bo Jackson wrong, but still. Tons of laughs.

What the hell? I thought back at Buzzy's. *Give it a fucking shot.*

I went up in front of that little crowd of mostly comics, and I stood in front of that paper brick wall, and I just talked. I told a bunch of my dick jokes, yeah, but I didn't worry about getting every word right or which comma went where in what sentence. I relaxed, made eye contact, played to the audience, and talked like I was in front of my public speaking class. Like I was the new kid at school sitting at the end of the lunch table, trying to make new friends.

And you know what?

Someone *laughed.*

Shit, it was more than just someone. Lots of people laughed. I even got a full-on applause break. Like everyone in the place started laughing so hard at one of my jokes, they actually broke out in *spontaneous applause*!

It was fucking amazing! I was a star!

I finished up my set—that forty-five minutes I thought I had written down barely lasted four—and got offstage. A couple of the local comics came up and asked me how long I'd been perform-ing, as if I were a standup veteran. I was thrilled, but I didn't stay to talk. I just wanted to go home and watch my tape and listen to all those laughs all over again.

I got back to our ghetto apartment, sat down in the living room in front of the TV, and fumbled with the camera wires, trying to will my fingers to move faster.

I finally set everything up, pressed play, and there it was . . .

A single "HA" followed by one lonely clap.

Are you kidding me? Seriously?

I rewound and pressed play again. I must've missed something. Must've—

Damn. That was it.

Onstage it had sounded like a sold-out arena, but in real life? A single human being had put their two hands together to make one small sound.

Ha. Clap.

I sat there in my mom's living room, clinging to that one lonely laugh, that tiny little clap. I thought of my man Eddie Murphy— and I smiled.

Fuck yeah, I thought. *I got this.*

8

LIVE FROM THE

HUSTLE

Shrimp Sinigang

SERVES 2–4

INGREDIENTS

6 taro roots, peeled and medium diced

¼ cup string beans, kangkong (water spinach), or medium-sliced bok choy

1 (1.4-ounce) packet tamarind soup mix (such as Knorr brand)

½ cup onion, medium diced

1 pound shrimp, peeled and deveined

Cooked jasmine rice, for serving

INSTRUCTIONS

1. In a medium-size pot, bring 8.5 cups water to a simmer over medium heat. Each of the following ingredients requires a different time to cook, so note the progression: Add the taro and cook for 8 minutes. Add the string beans, stir to combine, and continue cooking for 2 minutes. Add the onion and tamarind mix, stir to combine, and continue cooking for 15 minutes. Add the shrimp, stir to combine, and cook for 5 minutes. Remove from the heat.

2. Serve the soup in a bowl with a side of rice.

The place we met at was pure country and western. Swinging saloon doors, frilly curtains, and big old-fashioned letters that read "Sam's Town: Hotel and Gambling Hall."

"Um, you sure *Def Jam* is happening here?" I said.

"Yeah, man," Honest John said. He talked like a jazz singer, smooth as silk. "We're all good, don't you worry about a thing."

I followed him through the corny wooden doors. It was 1996, I'd been struggling to build my career—if you could call it that—for over four years, and *Def Comedy Jam* was a smash hit on HBO. It was the coolest, edgiest, most iconic black comedy show ever created.

This casino was . . . not that.

But I trusted Honest John Basinger, a friend from the circuit who was a Def Jam regular, even though he looked very irregular compared to the rest of the Def Jam lineup. Meaning he was old, wore tie-dyed shirts, had a big bushy beard, and was white as shit.

Honest John had gotten me a bunch of gigs in the past as his opener, but nothing came close to Def Jam. We had a simple plan for getting me onstage that night, the exact same plan I relied on all the time, and that was—no fucking plan at all.

He took me backstage and I peered out at the crowd. The show tonight wasn't being taped for TV; it was a live tour spin-off from the HBO hit, which is probably why it was being held in such a weird venue—just the cheapest space the promoter could find. But the place was still beyond sold out, over 1,500 people packed wall to wall. And if you know anything about Def Jam, you know the audience wasn't exactly sitting there quietly with their hands folded and their legs crossed chatting quietly. The energy was crackling. Shit was loud, explosive. People were ready to laugh—or if they didn't laugh, boo your sorry ass right offstage.

"Jo!" Honest John called from behind me. "Come here and meet Bob!"

I turned around. The guy Honest John so casually referred to as "Bob" was Bob Sumner—*the* Bob Sumner, an institution in the Black comedy world and the co-creator of Def Comedy Jam. Wow.

Before *Def Comedy Jam* launched on HBO in 1992, only the very biggest names in Black comedy got exposure on a national platform. Heroes of mine like Eddie Murphy and Richard Pryor. White, so-called mainstream America knew nothing about Black comedy at the grassroots club level, the rawness, the unpredictability, the in-your-face style. There was a whole thriving culture there that none of the big networks had tapped into.

Bob Sumner's show changed all that. Suddenly HBO, the same premium platform of greats like Billy Crystal and George Carlin, was giving a stage every Saturday night to young up-and-coming Black voices like Cedric the Entertainer, Martin Lawrence, and Bernie Mack. Thanks to *Def Comedy Jam*, those guys have all become household names. But you know what? There were other names, too, comics like Adele Givens and Melanie Camarcho, names some of you still might not know, but they got a huge boost, too, launching careers that took them to shows on Comedy Central and UPN or movies like *Beauty Shop* and *First Sunday*.

Def Comedy Jam had taken America by storm. No one "mainstream" had ever seen anything like it before—comics so quick on their feet, sparring with the audience, so sharp with an insult or comeback. And the crowds themselves, shouting and laughing, giving as good as they got. At its peak, it was all anyone talked about at the water cooler on Monday. And here I was, about to meet the man who helped start it all.

I gulped, held out my hand nervously.

"Hi, Mr. Sumner, um, nice to—"

"This is my boy, Jo Koy," Honest John said before I could be too much of an idiot. "You gotta put him on, man. He'll kill!"

Bob eyed me warily for a minute, then shrugged.

"All right, I'll put you up," he said. "But check it out. You go out there, you stand in front of the curtains, you say your name, do your five minutes, and you get off. We're not gonna open the curtains for you, we're not gonna dim the houselights for you, we're not gonna do a thing for you. You can't even say, 'Welcome to *Def Jam*.' Got it?"

Damn, I thought. *He's gonna make me perform with the fucking houselights on?*

The whole place would be completely bright, like a movie theater before the previews even came on! People would still be finding their seats, talking to their friends. As far as the crowd was concerned, I might as well be some random dude off the street who ran in, grabbed the mic, jumped onstage, and started talking.

Which I guess I kind of was.

"All right," I said before I had a chance to reconsider. "Let's do it."

At the last second before I went out, I found the stage manager and pleaded my case. Bob Sumner was off dealing with the comics who were actually *supposed* to go onstage that night, and I had nothing to lose.

"Please, man," I said. "I'm begging you. Just lower the house-lights a little for me."

He darkened the theater for me by 30 percent. Even gave me a spotlight. I'd have to perform on the stage in front of the curtains with no Def Jam logo behind me, but it was better than nothing.

I walked out on that stage. Except for Honest John, I was one of the only non-Black guys in the whole theater. Like me, this crowd was used to being outsiders in America, but I was an outsider in *their* America. No one understood my half-breed Filipino experience, who I was, where I came from. No one knew a thing about me. I could feel all the eyes, all the skepticism, all the doubt.

Who the fuck does this dude think he is?

And I fucking loved it.

I had faced this energy my whole life, since the day I'd moved to this country, and I knew exactly how to respond. None of these people knew how funny I was—and now I could show them all.

I went right into my best dick jokes. I still wasn't doing jokes about my family onstage, but honestly? It didn't matter. I could've talked about *anything* and I would've had them that night. With a crowd like this it wasn't about the jokes, it was the interaction, the sparring, taking everything they threw at you and throwing it right back at them.

And I threw it all right. Hard. I was lightning fast off the cuff, ad-libbing like crazy, making it up as I went along. Every time they challenged me, every time they yelled something or heckled me, I shot *right* back, absolutely fearless.

I fed off their energy, thrived off it, couldn't get enough of it.

When my five minutes were up, I went back behind the

curtain—still closed before the actual show began—and found Honest John.

"So?" I asked. "How do you think I did?"

He grinned.

"You tell me, man."

He nodded toward the audience. Everyone was on their feet, raising the roof—people still did that back then—laughing and cheering. And then, from the middle of the crowd, I heard one woman's voice rise above them all:

"Yo! Put that Asian motherfucker back onstage!"

By the time I left the country-western dive later that night, I had an official invitation to tour live with Def Jam.

∽

THAT'S WHAT I DID in the early years. I hustled.

I had no plan. I had no strategy. I showed up places and talked my way onstage.

My resume? Faked it. Straight-up lied about performing at clubs I'd never even driven past.

Head shot? I couldn't afford a professional photographer, so my dad took a picture of me in a friend's apartment. We put a black sheet up to use as a backdrop, I combed my hair back, and my dad developed and printed the film himself.

I even came up with a stage name after I got sick of open-mic hosts fucking up my given name, Joseph Herbert. I know it seems simple, but no matter how many times I explained, somehow the hosts got it wrong. "Is Herbert a first name? Is it a last name? What, do you pronounce it 'Aybare,' like French? Or 'Herbert,' like rhymes with 'Sherbert'?" And yeah, it probably didn't help that I don't exactly look like a typical "Joseph Herbert."

I tried everything, even going up once as "Joseph," first-name only, like a half-Filipino Cher, but nothing took. Then one day I was with my cousin Mona, brainstorming ideas, when my auntie Evelyn walked in.

Now the first thing you've got to know is that Filipinos as a group *love* coming up with nicknames for friends and family; it's a part of our culture. And in my family, Auntie Evelyn was the queen of nicknames. She had this gift for coming up with them and making them stick. Mona was "Mona Gaye"—no sexual meaning, no meaning of any sort, she just said it one day, and from then on Mona was "Mona Gaye." My auntie Bel was "Tita Beng Beng," and my auntie Lynn was "Lingoy." "Tita" means "aunt" in Tagalog, but beyond that I had no idea where those names came from, and I didn't want to find out. Really, the names just sounded good to my auntie and so they felt right to the rest of us.

And on this particular day, for no apparent reason, Auntie Evelyn called out, "Let's go! Joe Koy, eat!" I mean, I guess because she was hungry and wanted to grab some food, but the "Koy" part? That came out of nowhere.

"That's it!" Mona said. "Joe Koy!"

Just like my Auntie Evelyn's other nicknames, something about it just felt . . . right. So I dropped the "e" from "Joe," I drew a logo with the "K" dead in the center and diamonds all around it, and Jo Koy was born.

And he worked his butt off.

I performed every chance I could; it didn't matter what the venue was. You needed someone for your birthday party? Done. Your kid was having his bar mitzvah? You got it. I did a fundraiser for a bunch of Orthodox Jews at a restaurant that didn't even have a stage, they just put some plywood on top of one of the booths and I got up and did my act.

"Hey, this is for charity!" a rabbi shouted in the front. "Watch your language!"

"You guys are making me stand on some wooden planks and talk into a karaoke machine, and you're worried about my fucking professionalism?"

I had them rolling by the end of the night, *crying*.

In a town like Vegas—which still felt small back then but was also weirdly cosmopolitan—being half-Filipino was never an issue. If anything, it actually helped with the Black shows, because they were all searching for a little diversity to add to their mostly African-American lineups.

I went everywhere, I talked to everyone, I never took "no" for an answer. And you know what? It worked, kind of.

A few years before I made it to Def Jam, I'd already landed a residency at Catch A Rising Star, a legit comedy club at the MGM Grand, doing twelve shows a week. I was a regular on a nationwide Black comedy tour that was so bare-bones it was seriously just called "The Black Comedy College Tour," and its official logo was the dot-matrix court jester you could get off Microsoft Word's clip art. I got booked a couple of times on a BET standup show called *Comic View*. I even performed in New York City at *Showtime at the Apollo*—something I'd *dreamed* of since I was a kid—and I fucking won!

I remember calling up my dad right after I got the Catch A Rising Star gig. I was so excited I could barely contain it.

"Guess what?" I said. "I—I think it just happened . . . I think I just made it!"

And in a way I had. I was getting paid to perform comedy in front of real live human beings, exactly what I'd always wanted. Shit, once I got the BET gig, I was on TV! Compared to where I had started off—a poor half-Filipino kid traveling from military base to military base and moonwalking at the local Knights of Columbus—I was fucking *famous*.

But in reality, I was still absolutely broke.

For a typical show at Catch A Rising Star I'd make maybe $75, plus free drinks—though to be fair I probably downed $1,500 in alcohol on a given night. To go out on the road for the Black Comedy College Tour, I'd get maybe $1,250, but then I'd have to cover food, the plane, and the hotel out of my own pocket. I was lucky if I made it home with $600.

The *Def Comedy Jam* live tour paid okay, but I only got to do a few of those before it finished its run—in fact, the HBO show itself finally ended in 1997. As for my TV appearances, they paid *maybe* $200. Think about it; these shows didn't have big-ass sponsors like Nabisco paying their bills. Their number-one advertiser was some chick who could read your fortune over the phone. *Showtime at the Apollo* aired at midnight, and a lot of people didn't even have BET—or if they did, they didn't care. Yeah, shows like *Def Comedy Jam* and Fox's *In Living Color* had broken a lot of barriers, but this was still the 1990s. This was the age of Jerry Seinfeld and Jay Leno. The big networks, the major studios, they all thought big national audiences just "wouldn't get it." And they'd keep thinking that way for years to come.

Of course, none of that stopped me from loving standup. My jokes bought me dinner and as many drinks as I could hold. If I had a few hundred bucks left over at the end of the month, I'd spend it on a Gucci hat or a new, top-of-the-line camcorder. I always *acted* like I had money. I always walked around like I had a million dollars in my pocket.

So what if I still lived with my mom and Fred in that old apartment on Strip Club Alley? So what if from nine to five I had to work what I called "disposable jobs" to make ends meet—jobs I could drop at a moment's notice if I got a gig. Desk jobs at hotels, retail. I even turned down a job as a valet at the Mirage because I thought it'd be too demanding on my schedule. Those fuckers wanted me to work nights, carry around a pager so I could be on call 24/7. The money was insanely good—I had valet friends who bought houses off the dough they made at the Mirage. But so what? I needed to book my shows.

So I stuck with the disposable jobs, I stayed broke, and I lived at home.

Ever since I'd opened up to my dad about my comedy dream, he'd been ridiculously supportive. The same guy who'd barely been around for my childhood was there for me all the time now, calling every week, asking what I needed. He even fronted the money for my website, maxed out his credit card to pay $2,000 for one of those HTML deals that was state-of-the-art back then. He *loved* the hustle, he *lived* for the hustle.

But my mom? She had no respect for it.

You'd like to think that once she bought me that camera—which I'm forever grateful for—she finally saw the light and got behind me 100 percent. But that's not how my mother's mind works.

She'd come to my shows sometimes, yeah, but she was still bugging me constantly to quit standup and find something practical, a real job with benefits and a pension plan. To her, comedy was a distraction, a silly hobby that someday I'd hopefully outgrow.

It was *so* frustrating—but it was logical. Why would she care that I was on BET? She cared that I was in my twenties and still living under her roof. She cared that after all these years of her busting her ass, we were still stuck in the same shitty, run-down apartment we'd been in since we first moved to Vegas. She needed me to live her American dream.

You know what finally changed all our lives? It definitely wasn't my comedy dreams.

It was Keno. The one game no one played in Vegas, because all the gamblers in Vegas think it's boring. There's no thrill, no excitement, no glamorous casino. You just pick a bunch of numbers like you're in some church basement playing bingo, and you pray you get them all right, which is about as impossible as getting struck by lightning five times in a row.

So, no one played Keno—except for Fred, who was old enough, square enough, and poor enough to play Keno.

He played the same numbers he played every week, and one night when I got back to our apartment after working at the hotel, I didn't see our Ethiopian friends hanging out on the balcony or a coke head on a bad trip. I saw the Keno guy, holding one of those big fake-looking checks you see on TV.

Except this check was real. It was for $27,000. And it was made out to Fred.

He won the jackpot. He'd hit every single number.

For the first time in their lives, Fred and my mom were able to pay all their old bills and clear out all their debt. They paid off my mom's car, and a short while later they put down money on a new house in Summerlin, a nice neighborhood on the west side of town.

No more strip clubs, no more hookers and drugs. Now there were parks and good schools and streetlights that actually worked. We finally had a home.

But as happy as this made me, the house, the money, it was also salt in my wounds. In all my fantasies about becoming a comedian, I'd always made it big. *I* was the one who'd given my mom everything she wanted. *I* was the one who'd bought her that house, paid for that car, gotten rid of all her debt. In my dreams, I had succeeded, not just for myself, but because I wanted to make my mother proud. I wanted her to respect what I did, to not be embarrassed of me in front of her friends. I wanted her to be able to point to her new house, her new car, and say, "My son bought this all for me."

And it had finally happened—because Fred got lucky playing Keno. I had nothing to do with it.

ↄ

"**WHAT DO YOU WANT ME** to bring you?" I said into the phone.

My brother paused on the other end.

"A bucket of KFC, extra-crispy," he whispered conspiratorially. "And a twenty-four pack of Pepsi. Make sure you hide it coming in."

"What?" I said. "What do you want with a twenty-four pack?"

"Just bring it!"

He slammed down the phone.

Shit. What the hell was I getting myself into?

Ever since we got to Vegas, Robert had been in Tacoma running a hustle of his own, the same one he'd perfected when I was still in high school.

Go to an institution for a few months, eat their food and sleep in their bed, take the meds they made him take, and act just normal enough—just enough like the real Robert I loved from my childhood—to get released. Then, once he got out, he'd stop taking his meds, the fake Robert would come back, and he'd hit the streets, caught up in delusions about spies and secret missions and saving the country from Russia. And then, when he got cold and hungry and sick of being out on the streets, he'd start a fight or steal something and get thrown back in the institution, where he'd start the process all over again.

My brother might've had a mental illness, but he was also a twisted genius.

He was back in the institution again. I was set to tour nearby, so I'd decided to visit. I hardly kept up with him at all anymore, only talked to him twice a year, on Christmas and his birthday. I know that sounds selfish, and I felt incredibly guilty about this, but the truth is that seeing him was *hard*.

Every time I talked to him, he'd manage to be the real Robert for two or three minutes, then just when you felt comfortable, happy to have the brother you loved back, he'd slip into all his conspiracies and paranoia. It was like this constant reminder of what we'd had—and what we'd lost.

But I was still hopeful. Maybe this time would be different? Maybe this stay at the institution had finally changed him back to the brother I had once worshipped? I know that sounds naïve, and it's not like I think a miracle is going to occur and years of history and mental illness will suddenly be erased. But deep down, as dumb as it might sound, there's always hope. As long as I have those memories of the real Robert and what we used to have, I cling to the chance that maybe, just maybe, we can find it again.

So I did exactly what he asked. I arrived at the institution in Tacoma with a bucket of extra-crispy chicken, twenty-four cans of Pepsi, and a brand-new pair of women's jeans with tapered legs from the discount chain Mervyn's. Women's jeans because Robert was very fashion-forward and got into skinny pants years before it was cool. Mervyn's because the big bag they gave me at checkout was perfect for hiding the Pepsi.

A nurse led me to the rec room, where Robert was sitting at a table waiting for me. He waited till she left and nodded at me.

"You got the stuff?"

What was this, a fucking drug deal?

"Yeah, I got it."

I started pulling the Pepsi out of the Mervyn's bag and his eyes flashed.

"Don't! Don't!" he whispered furiously. "Just slide the bag across the table."

I slid the shopping bag across the table, and in one quick, fluid motion he swooped the pack of Pepsi out and hid it under his chair, cackling the whole time.

"What are you doing?" I said. "What is happening right now?"

"They only allow diet here," he giggled. "No sugar, never any sugar."

Shit.

And just like that, right in front of me, he yanked out two cans of Pepsi and downed them, I mean *pounded* those motherfuckers like a frat boy. Two seconds and those babies were *gone*. Just gone!

"Fuck, Robert! Fuck!" I said in a panic, peering over my shoulder. "What if the nurses see? I don't want to get yelled at!"

"Don't worry, don't worry," he said laughing. "If they catch us, just tell them you didn't know."

The next thing I knew, there was a line of dudes near our table, looking around nervously, making sure they weren't attracting any attention.

"Hey man, lemme get a can of Pepsi."

"Three dollars a can," Robert said smoothly.

The money came out and the deal was done, over and over again.

"I got a dollar," one guy said. "Come on, help me out!"

"Sorry," my brother said.

"Wait, wait—I got a *Playboy* back in my room. Yeah, I can get you a *Playboy*!"

Robert considered.

"Bring me that *Playboy*, then maybe you can have the Pepsi."

"Um, Robert," I stammered as he sold can after can after can. "I really think we should, uh—"

But it was too late.

Cans started cracking open everywhere, and these dudes fucking lost it. Guzzling this stuff, just shoving it down their throats. Like imagine the thirstiest man crawling across the Mojave Desert, getting an ice-cold glass of water after hours of desperation. That's how this was—Pepsi just pouring down their faces, spilling everywhere. What, you want a sip? Fuck a sip!

They'd burp these loud burps, like the loudest burps you ever heard, like frat-house burps.

Gurgle, gurgle, gurgle! BURRRRP!

Soon patients were *screaming*, running down the halls, throwing shit everywhere. That soda was straight-up cocaine to these guys.

Fuck! I'm thinking. *What the fuck did I do??*

Nurses ran into the rec room, saw all the chaos.

"Who the hell brought in the Pepsi?!?"

One of them points at me.

"It was the guy with the Mervyn's bag!"

By now I am cowering in the corner, whimpering.

"I didn't know!" I cry. "I didn't know!"

But somehow, in the middle of the haze, in the fog of all this war, I realize two things:

First, no one's even touched the fried chicken. So at least I've got my dinner covered.

Second, as frustrating as he could be, *no one* could hustle like my brother.

℘

IT WAS 1998 and I was working the front desk at my latest disposable job, a big resort on the Strip without gambling. Like, that was the owner's actual concept! "Hey, what if I build this huge expensive hotel in the heart of Las Vegas, the Capital City of Gambling, and—wait for it—you absolutely *cannot gamble there*! So all the people who want to gamble in Las Vegas, which is everyone, have to go spend their money *everywhere else but my place*. Brilliant idea!"

Yeah, horrible idea.

But that was the beauty of the disposable job. I didn't care if this business was good or bad. Even if I lost the job, I'd just find another equally disposable job at the mall or somewhere else on the Strip. As long as I got a paycheck and nights off to do my gigs, that was all I cared about. Most of the time.

When your whole life is a hustle, you never know where your next opportunity might pop up.

"Hey, man, you guys cool with all cash?"

I looked up. A young guy was standing in front of me wearing a sick black hat fitted tight to his head with a small curved brim in the front.

"Um, yeah," I answered. "We're cool with all cash."

When people paid cash, they'd have to pay a lot up front. Without a credit card on file, we'd want an advance deposit on incidentals, on any damages that might occur—you name it, we'd charge you. You'd get the deposit back after your stay, of course, but it could add up to thousands. But that wasn't a problem for this guy. He just nodded and started pulling out money. Stacks of it.

"Cool," he said. "I reserved nine rooms for the week."

This dude dropped $5,000 on each room. Cash. I looked at the reservation, and it was under Dada Supreme—the same logo on his hat. Fuck. Now I understood.

There was a men's apparel convention going on at the hotel, and Dada Supreme was the absolute peak of men's urban apparel at the time, which is a fancy way of saying that Black dudes loved this stuff. Dada, FUBU, Karl Kani—in the mid-1990s, urban brands that had been part of the niche hip-hop scene just a short while earlier were suddenly going mainstream. Now Macy's, Bloomingdale's, JCPenney, all the major retailers wanted to stock this gear. That might've explained all the cash—a company like Dada Supreme could be raking it in from big vendors while still being so small and underground it didn't have company credit cards. I'd known about Dada Supreme long before they made it big, first heard of them years ago when I saw the Notorious B.I.G. wearing one of their hats in a music video. I'd been a huge fan ever since.

"Hey, man," I said. "How you like working for Dada?"

"I don't work for Dada," he said with a grin. "I own it."

"What?"

Turned out the dude was Dwayne Lewis, the founder of the company. Putting cash deposits on ten rooms is a process—it took more than thirty minutes to draw up all the receipts—but that meant he had time to tell me his whole story. He designed his first hat while he was working for Pan Am as a baggage handler in New York City. Spent his own money to get hundreds of them made, went to an apparel convention in Vegas just like this one, and personally handed out his hats to every vendor there, along with one of his cards. By the time he'd flown back home, he had 40,000 orders.

If anyone understood the hustle, this guy did.

"Bro, I *love* Dada," I said. "I wear your stuff all the time!"

"Here's the card for my LA marketing guy," he said before he took off. "You give him a call, tell him you talked to me, and he'll hook you up with whatever you want: sweatshirts, shoes, whatever you need."

But I had a lot more in mind than sweatshirts and shoes. After years of working every angle I could to get booked on other people's shows, I wanted to start a show of my own.

Even for a guy as shitty at math as I was, the numbers made perfect sense. When I did shows for Catch A Rising Star, they didn't only expect me to perform, they expected me to sell tickets—literally. They'd give me a stack of orange "two-for-ones," buy-one-get-one-free tickets, and it was on me to sell a certain number every week. Half of the people at those shows were friends of mine! And for all that, I got $75 plus free drinks.

Why do all that work for them if I could do it for myself? If I put on my own show, I could sell my own two-for-ones and keep all the money myself.

I had the whole thing planned out. I wasn't just going to do a little open mic in someone's living room. I was gonna go big, do an entire live event with a DJ and dancers to warm up the crowd for a full lineup of big-ticket comics.

I'd even already found the perfect venue, this old run-down building on the corner of Charleston and Maryland Parkway called the Huntridge—a historic movie theater built in 1943, long abandoned but recently renovated and now rented out for private events. It had eight hundred seats and an amazing, classic marquee, but the neighborhood was a mess, legitimately dangerous. But the price was only $600 for the whole night, and for that kind of deal I figured I could put up with some broken glass and a possible run-in with a junkie or two. There was just one little problem. I needed someone to front all the money, not just to rent the theater but to market the show, pay the comics, hire security, and more. I needed a sponsor.

In Dada Supreme, I thought I'd finally found one. But it wasn't easy.

I chased after Dada's LA marketing head, Carlos Parrott, for over a year—seriously, a year—and he dodged me at every turn. *I'm busy. I'm busy. I'm busy.*

I wore their hats and shirts on BET to try to get his attention. *I'm busy. I'm busy. I'm busy.*

I called and wrote every single week. *I'm busy. I'm busy. I'm busy.*

Finally, I decided to straight-up ambush the dude. I got a friend of mine to sneak me into another apparel convention, where I staked out the Dada booth for a week, until on the very last day I managed to schedule a meeting the following month to pitch my show to Carlos and another owner named Lantz Simpson, who headed up their footwear division and happened to be a big standup fan.

The day of the meeting I drove to their office in the garment district in downtown LA. In my car I had a massive portfolio I'd put together with a friend of mine. This thing had graphs, it had charts, it had a cover page, it had a long list of potential (fake) radio sponsors. I put more work into this presentation than I put into my entire college career at UNLV.

My friend and I argued for *days* about how much money to ask for.

"What about $7,000?"

"Are you fucking kidding me? They'll kick us out the door!"

"Okay, $5,000?"

"I don't know—five still feels like a big number to me."

"Okay, $4,500—not as intimidating as $5,000, but still bigger than $4,000."

"I guess . . ."

"*Fine!* Fine, $4,000!"

I finally got to the Dada office, and after an hour-long wait that felt like a day, at last the owner walked through the door. Lantz ran the company along with Dwayne Lewis, whom I'd met at the hotel. And I'm telling you, this dude looked like a multimillion-dollar hip-hop angel from the heavens. Powder-blue sunglasses, a matching powder-blue sweatshirt with the Dada logo on the front, and a seventies-style Afro that was so big and smooth he might as well have had a pick on the side. This guy looked like *money.*

Lantz sat down across from me, cool and smooth like he had all the time in the world.

"Hey, man, I love your work," he said. "So, what kind of ideas you got?"

I handed him my portfolio, this masterpiece of business planning and vision I'd put so much blood and sweat into, chock full of details that I had obsessed over, including the amount of money we'd decided to ask for after debating for *days* so as not to appear too greedy or too amateur.

And this dude didn't even look at the first page.

"Okay, cool, when can we do it?"

I should've asked for ten grand!

I'd walked into this place without an ounce of confidence. Now this big, beautiful man was not only giving me every penny I asked for, he told me he was a fan before I barely opened my mouth. A fan! I didn't even have to sell myself! I might not be rich—yet—but it felt like all my hustling, all my back-alley shows and late-night TV appearances were finally starting to pay off. People, important people, were finally starting to know my name.

My show was on—almost. Thanks to my own, timid-ass business plan, I still needed to scrape together a little more cash to help pay for things like airfare and hotels for my comedians. I wasn't going to treat my talent like other tours had treated me—I was gonna do right by them.

Guess who went to work finding my last few sponsors? My mom.

Now, I know what you're thinking. *Did she support me or not? Did she want me to be a comic or did she want me to find an office job with benefits? Why couldn't she pick a side?*

But life is complicated, and so is my mom. Don't forget—we're talking about a woman who could happily drive me home drunk from a 7-Eleven one week and then threaten to disown me when I stole a few bus passes the next. A woman who'd worked at a bank for decades but started out as a manager for a rock band back in the Philippines. She was a woman of contradiction who lived in perpetual tension between two forces—a mom's natural desire for her talented kid to be happy, and an immigrant's desire to be safe and secure. As crazy as she thought my comedy dream was, she did *want* it to happen. I always say that I got my talent from her, no question. And she's an incredibly vibrant, charismatic personality in her own right. But thanks to her immigrant's mentality, she *had* to be practical. It was almost impossible for her to believe my dream could happen. She wanted me to play by her rules.

So, of course she'd wanted me to go to college. She was crushed when I dropped out. But once that option was gone, she still wanted me to succeed in life. She still wanted a son who made it. And she'd fight for me every step of the way.

When she found out I needed more sponsors to put on my *own* show—a show that could make me real money—she busted her ass, talking to every small business owner she knew. If she shopped at your store, if she'd ever bought some of your flowers or tried on one of your dresses, you were fair game.

"You know my son Josep is a famous comedian . . ."

"Yes, he's putting on a *huge* show . . ."

"It's already sold out, many, many times over . . ."

Of course, I hadn't even started selling tickets, but my mother and I followed the same philosophy when it came to marketing— create your own reality. Build buzz. Even if it is total bullshit.

She landed me my two biggest sponsors outside of Dada. The first one was her optometrist. The second was her mechanic. The optometrist put up cash and bought ten tickets for his staff. The mechanic paid me to have oil-change coupons printed on the back of all my tickets. What the fuck did I care? It was $800, enough to cover all the hotel rooms I needed, and the fans got a great deal on their next oil change. Win-win!

My mom found sponsors, she sold tickets, she even let me use the garage at her house for storage. That thing looked like a Foot Locker warehouse, there was so much Dada gear packed inside. The tickets she sold? I got sheets of them printed out at Kinko's and spent all night cutting them out myself, one by one.

Finally—finally—after years of scheming and pleading, planning and preparation, the big night arrived.

The Huntridge Theater looked like a million bucks even though it cost me six hundred. "Jo Koy's Comedy Jam" was up in lights on the old-school marquee. I'd hired a team to sweep up the broken glass in the parking lot, and even had security on hand to keep watch on everyone's cars.

A buddy of mine was the house photographer for Cirque du Soleil, so I asked him to take photos during the show. I hired a local DJ and brought in some local kids to dance when the curtain came up. I would act as the host and the headliner—I wasn't just putting on a show to make money, first and foremost I was promoting my own career—but I found a lineup of top-flight comics to appear with me. Jay Lamont was a talented comic I'd met on tour. He'd done *Def Comedy Jam*, he'd done *Showtime at the Apollo*, and he could crush it with impersonations of rappers and R&B singers. Pierre was a dude I met through Dada. I hadn't worked with him before, but he was another Def Comedy Jam alumnus, acted in movies like *B.A.P.S.* and *How to Be a Player*, and I knew he would kill it. And of course I had to have my old friend Honest John.

I didn't just hire these comics, I treated them right. I covered their rooms and travel, I promoted the hell out of the show and got them major exposure in Vegas, and none of us made much money, but I always made sure they got paid before I did.

We actually sold out nearly all of the eight hundred seats—with my mom accounting for *half* those sales—but I left fifty singles open to sell at the gate. And I knew exactly who I wanted working the ticket booth.

My mom got there with Fred a couple of hours before the show started. There they were, this tiny Filipino immigrant lady and her big white Vietnam-vet husband—both *dripping* in Dada. Shirts, hats, shoes, jewelry, the whole deal, like middle-aged billboards for the thug life.

"Okay, Josep! Let's do this!"

I put my mom in that booth, right under that marquis, and she sold the last fifty tickets and ripped the stubs for everyone else. She even gave out a free Dada key chain with every purchase.

The night was a bigger success than I could've ever imagined. Sponsors had covered most of our expenses, which meant I got to pocket almost $5,000 from our ticket sales. That was a hell of a lot better than my usual $75.

Best of all, though, it cemented my relationship with Dada, and yeah, even with my mom's optometrist and mechanic. That one show became the first of many. They became a regular occurrence, featuring major comedy talents like future star of *Curb Your Enthusiasm* J. B. Smoove, the *Bad Boys of Comedy*'s Michael Blackson, and more. And Jo Koy became known as *the guy* in Vegas—both as a performer and as a promoter for hip, edgy, urban comedy shows. That rawness, that realness, that energy, you couldn't find any of that at the local Vegas comedy clubs. But you could get it from me.

But that evening wasn't about the big picture, not right away. That night was about celebrating everything I could accomplish with my friends and my family when we flat-out refused to take "no" for an answer.

After the show was over, my mom sat in her booth, poring over the receipts from the final fifty tickets she'd sold at the gate. Suddenly she looked up, stunned.

"Oh my God, Josep. You made $800! You're practically rich!"

I felt like the King of Vegas. But it wouldn't be long before a whole new city cut me back down to size.

Los Angeles was calling my name.

9

KING NO MORE

In 2001, I finally moved out of my mom's house. I was thirty years old, a grown-ass man, and I'd lived with my parents almost my entire life.

My mom cried.

"Josep—Josep, are you sure you're ready for this?" she said between sobs. "Do you—do you really think you have what it takes to survive? Ha? Out in the real world?"

And then, her voice suddenly growing firm:

"Because I don't think you do."

Now, to be fair, I wasn't just moving out of her house. I was moving to Los Angeles.

By this point I had become the King of Vegas. It had been about three years since I put on my first show, and now it was a regular event. I knew all the right people, and I could make anything happen. It was mafioso-style. Favors were traded, commodities were bartered, you scratch my back, I'll scratch yours. *Hey, I need to feed my comics—you let them eat at your casino's Sunday breakfast buffet and I'll get you ten third-row tickets to the show, cool?*

My mom had always been a hustler, a scrapper, building a life for herself from scratch in a brand-new country, working her butt off, selling *lumpia* egg rolls out of her purse on the side, and I was taking after her in every way. Even Steve Schirripa would've been proud. I wasn't cold-calling fuckers and using made-up names anymore. I was an operator.

But it was starting to feel too easy. I was getting too comfortable. Yeah, I performed at my own shows, but they were such big events, so involved with so many working parts, that I spent most of my time just producing them. But my dream wasn't to be a promoter or a producer. My dream was to be a comic. I wanted to make people laugh at the highest levels of entertainment. To do that, I had to move to LA.

So, I saved up tons of money, and not just what I was making from putting on my shows. I'd never stopped hustling. I was still working a day job at a hotel—and this hotel had the number one live show in Vegas. It always had a wait list, it always had a huge demand for tickets that were very hard to come by—unless you knew me.

As an employee, I could buy tons of tickets in advance at face value and then sell those babies at a nice markup, $25 a pop. That might not sound like a lot, but I was selling thirty or forty tickets a day. Yeah, I could've charged more, but I didn't want to attract the wrong kind of attention, and keeping my price reasonable meant my customers were still getting a bargain compared to what they'd pay a scalper on the street. But I was still making money hand over fist, man. Was it legal? I doubt it. Ethical? Who the hell cares.

After a couple of years, I'd saved up $27,000, all in cash bills. I literally had a bag of money in my bedroom.

I figured it was enough to get by in Los Angeles for two years. I could get a cheap place, live off Taco Bell, and focus entirely on performing. The city would be mine.

Then I got to LA. Pretty soon, I was the one being owned. It took everything I had not to call my mom back up, squeaking in a little-boy voice.

"Hello? Mommy? Um, yeah. Maybe you were right."

My lifestyle took a major hit. I'd spent the last few years living in plush middle-class luxury, but now I was back to nothing. Stuck in a dangerous part of the Valley, miles away from the action, drifters hanging out on the streets, I was sharing a house with a couple of friends from Vegas who'd made the move with me. These guys were b-boys who made money producing and selling their own dance videos, so that meant our house was this crumbling, practically condemned mess on the outside, and a fucking movie studio on the inside. High-end electronics, professional-grade lighting, and digital cameras. I couldn't believe no one broke in and robbed us.

There were ants everywhere, linoleum on the living room floor so the guys could practice their moves, and a giant pit bull that basically owned the house and crapped all over the floor. I had this big-ass aquarium in my room, empty—no fish, no water—and to this day I have no idea where it came from. Home, sweet home.

But if anything, the state of my career was even more desperate.

Overnight, I'd gone from being King of Vegas to King of Who the Fuck Are You? None of the big clubs in LA even knew my name. No one cared that I'd put on some big show three hundred miles away. It was meaningless. The *Def Comedy Jam* live show had ended its run, so that was out of the picture. I could still tour with the Black Comedy College Tour, and I even popped back to Vegas to perform every now and then, but those were all sideshows now as far as I was concerned. I'd moved to LA to make it big, and my career was anything but that.

Worst of all, for the first time in my career I was running into racism like a fucking brick wall.

The racism I encountered when I moved to LA in 2001 was systemic in the most literal sense of the word. There was nothing overt, no one calling you racial slurs, no signs on the club doors that read "Whites Only." I don't think the big club owners were even consciously aware that they were being racist. The racism was simply baked into the system. It was the way business had always been done, the way attitudes had been shaped over years and years in Hollywood, in America. That was just how it was, and we all accepted it.

Weekend shows, for example. Or what comedians of color called "the white room." Those were the shows where the audiences were biggest, where they paid the most at the door, where they ordered the most drinks. In other words, those were the money nights. The crowds they drew at the biggest clubs were also almost entirely white—tourists from out of town, people driving in from the suburbs for a night out.

And in the early 2000s, the natural assumption that all big club owners made was that white audiences wanted to watch white comics. White crowds just wouldn't "get" nonwhite humor. Or at the very least they wouldn't pay money for it. Sure, there were your couple of exceptions—Eddie Murphy, Chris Rock (though even Chris Rock was a relative nobody until his HBO special *Bring the Pain* showed white people how great he was). But they were just that—exceptions. It was simply a given that white customers wanted to laugh at jokes told by people who looked like them, about subjects they could relate to, about material they could "understand."

When I say "people who looked like them," I mean white dudes. Period. If you were anything else, you were out. Black, Latino, Asian, female, gay, whatever. Oh, there *were* nights for the rest of us—they were just the nights no one else wanted. Guys like me were shoved into ethnic theme shows during the week, like "Chocolate Sundaes" or "Mo Better Mondays" for Black people or "Refried Tuesdays" for Latinos or "Wonton Wednesdays" for Asians or whatever. I kid you not—these were all real shows, and some of them continue to this day.

Just like the weekend "white rooms," it was all baked into the system. No one would ever say, "Hey you! Asian guy! You go up Wednesdays only!" right to your face. As a nonwhite comic, you simply knew ethnic shows were the way to get your start, your only way in. Or if you pitched starting your own show to the owner of a small club, there might be a short, awkward pause before they said something like, "Well, Thursdays are a light night for us. Maybe you could put on some kind of theme show. . . ." That was code and I knew what it meant.

In a weird way, for years the system had worked to my advantage as I put on my own show in Vegas. How do you think I was able to get all those high-profile Black comics to perform for me on Fridays and Saturdays? It was because the major clubs never booked them for prime time.

Now I was facing the same thing in LA.

I didn't want to be known as the Filipino comic. I didn't want to be pigeonholed as the guy who told cheap ethnic jokes, no matter what Hollywood wanted. And that's not because I was ashamed of my background or my identity, not at all. I just wanted to appeal to everyone—white, Black, Asian, Latino, Arab, Indian. *Everyone.*

I wanted my comedy to be universal. So I still wasn't doing material about my family. I still wasn't telling any stories from my life. I know it sounds weird, because that's such a huge part of my act today. I talk to fans now, and the first thing they bring up is my mom. But if you saw my set in the early 2000s, you wouldn't have even known I *had* a mom. Honestly? I didn't think anyone would get it.

It's funny. Because as hard as I was trying to not be pigeonholed as the Asian comic, to not become a Hollywood cliché, in a way I had internalized exactly what the club owners thought. I had taken on their own racist attitudes. How could white audiences laugh at stories about my Filipino mom? Wouldn't they be confused if I talked about our food? Didn't they want jokes that related to their own lives instead of mine? So I kept my humor broad. I stuck to all my dick jokes. Blow jobs have no race! Doggy style doesn't discriminate based on creed or color! We all love getting laid!

To prove my universal appeal—and because they were honestly the only shows that would let me on—I decided to do *every single ethnic night I could find*. Hell, I already knew my material killed in front of Black crowds. Now I'd go crush everywhere else.

I did the Black shows, I did the Latino shows, I did the Asian shows. I even did a Filipino show, "Pinoyz in the Hood," at an LA casino, and I *still* stuck to all my dick jokes—and got a standing ovation. I was nothing if not committed. I got booked on a Saturday night at a Black club in south LA—the only kind of club that *would* book me on a weekend—and I did so well the owner let me put on a few shows of my own. I figured if I could do it at the Huntridge in the Vegas hood, I could do it here, and I did. Packed it every time.

I was now living the quintessential standup life. I stayed out all night at the clubs and slept during the day. If I made fifty bucks here or there, I was good, that paid for dinner, because I lived off my savings from Vegas. I had all my cash, *all my money in the world*, hidden in my closet in this sketchy house—so fucking stupid—and every day I'd wake up and peel off a hundred-dollar bill from my stack. I drove everywhere in this piece-of-shit Honda with a broken taillight. When I say "broken" I mean there was a giant hole in it from when I ran into an armored car, and you could literally stick your hand in and reach my trunk. My driving skills hadn't improved much.

And you know what? I loved every minute of it. There was just one problem. After almost a year in LA, I still felt like I wasn't getting anywhere.

Yeah, I was booking a lot of gigs during the week. Yeah, I was making a lot of connections in the industry. Edwin San Juan, a Filipino comic who was a fixture on the local scene and organized "Pinoyz in the Hood," got me access to tons of shows once he saw how funny I was. Corey Holcomb, a comic I met at one of the Black shows, also took me under his wing. Corey had done *The Tonight Show, Last Comic Standing, Def Comedy Jam*, and he introduced me to all of LA's up-and-coming Black comics. We'd finish our shows at midnight and hit the Mel's Diner on Sunset with guys like Godfrey, who'd already done Comedy Central; Ian Edwards, who'd written for MTV; and Kevin Hart. This was Kevin Hart back when he still drove an old Ford truck, a long time before he became the biggest name in comedy.

Most important to me at the time, Corey let me open for him when he headlined shows. That could mean $150 in a single night, and I was incredibly grateful.

But after working the theme nights for months, after proving to local promoters and audiences just how funny my incredible dick jokes were, I felt like *I* should be the one headlining, you know? I felt like *I* should be finding young comics to open up for *me*.

One night Corey and I were driving back to LA from a nightclub in Palmdale—that's how cool this guy was, he gave me rides so I wouldn't have to drive my Honda with a hole in it—and I finally decided to ask him.

"Corey, what do I gotta do?" I said. "I feel like my material is killing, but it's not enough. I'm thirty years old, man. I'm not getting any younger. What do I gotta do to be a headliner?"

"All right, you wanna know the truth?" he said. "You're not telling me anything about *you*. You get offstage and people are laughing and thinking you're funny, but they don't know who you *are*. Who are you? You gotta talk about *that*."

Later that night, I lay in my bed in my room with the empty aquarium, and I stared at the ceiling. Maybe Corey was right. Maybe by trying to appeal to everyone with the broadest jokes possible, I was holding too much back about myself.

I still didn't think I could pull off telling stories. My mind honestly didn't even go there. I was a comic. I told precise, perfectly paced jokes that made people laugh. That wasn't going to change, at least not then. But maybe I could make some of those jokes about me and my background?

Maybe I could let audiences in—just a little. Just enough to tell them who I was without scaring them off—also because of who I was.

All right then, who the hell was I? Well, I was half-white, half-Asian. What did that mean? Everyone knew what that meant—it meant my dad was in the military.

Bam. Joke one.

Who else was I? Well, the truth was that growing up no one ever really knew. I'd tell them Filipino, and they'd look at me and go off about some Asian but totally not-Filipino food—like orange chicken.

Bam. Joke two.

I came up with both of those jokes that night. They'd go on to become two of the cornerstones of my act for the next twenty years, iconic fan favorites I could tell time and again both to make people laugh and to tell them who I was.

They also helped me break into one of comedy's most prestigious clubs—and through the white wall that had been keeping me out.

☙

THE HOLLYWOOD LAUGH FACTORY WAS one of the biggest, most legendary comedy clubs in town. It featured huge names like Tim Allen, Jim Carey, and Dave Chappelle—one of those rare Black-comic exceptions who proved the rule—and it was incredibly hard to get into. *But* it had an Asian Invasion night.

Was it the main stage on a weekend? No. But it was a foot in the door.

I'd been in LA a little over a year. Everyone knows that the entertainment industry is all about relationships, all about connections, but at the Laugh Factory I had none of those, so I started with a name—Amy Anderson. I later found out she'd been born in Seoul, then adopted by American parents and raised in Minnesota, hence the all-American name. She started and hosted the Asian Invasion show, and if I wanted in, I had to do it the old-fashioned way—not by smooth-talking my way onto the stage, not by showing up and begging until they let me on, but by submitting a tape of my set. I had to prove I was funny enough.

Now, not only did I have video of me performing my classic dick jokes—which still killed, by the way—I also had the new material inspired by my conversation with Corey Holcomb. Just like Corey had predicted, audiences had been *loving* my autobiographical jokes. But this was going to be the biggest test yet.

Tape in hand, I went to the club one night looking for Amy.

"Sorry, bro," the guy at the door told me. "It's $25 to get in."

"Twenty-five bucks!" I said. "Are you kidding me? I'm a comic, man! I just want to drop off my tape to Amy Anderson!"

"And you can do that," he said. "But first you have to pay me $25."

Fuck. I had to give them money just for the chance to get potentially rejected. But I did it—what choice did I have? And by the time I found Amy, I made sure I was all charm and smiles. She watched my tape later that week, and just like that I was in.

Pretty soon I was a theme-show regular. That was fantastic, of course, but that wasn't the goal. The goal was to get on during prime time, on the weekend nights, on what we called "the white room." To do that, I had to get attention of the club's owner, Jamie Masada.

Jamie was a legend in his own right. An immigrant himself, born in Iran, he'd founded the club in 1979 and worked with everyone from Richard Pryor to Jay Leno to David Letterman. He could make you, he could break you, he always wore the same light blue suede jacket whenever he came to the club—and he was very, very hard to pin down.

I'd see him at the back of the club—I'd see him!—watching my act during the Asian Invasion night, laughing. I'd go up to him after, all nice and polite, and say "Hi, Mr. Masada, did you happen to catch my show?"

And this motherfucker would look me in the eye every time and say in his soft Persian accent, "No, buddy, sorry. I walk in at the last second. Maybe next time."

I swear this happened twenty times.

Till one night a friend of mine, the amazing comic Ralphie May, who went on to do *The Tonight Show*, *Last Comic Standing*, and a couple of specials on Netflix—and tragically died of cardiac arrest in 2017—finally cornered Jamie after one of our shows.

"Jamie, this dude's a beast!" he said. "Quit acting like you ain't see him! You *know* he's good! Give him a shot!"

Literally the next day I got a call from Jamie Masada. Next thing I knew, he was putting me in all their other theme shows, college night, Latino night, every night you could imagine. I was making a name for myself. A few months later, he invited me into his office, offered to be my manager, and gave me carte blanche to appear every night of the week.

That meant I could go up anytime I wanted. I wouldn't even have to call in advance. Just show up, and they'd put me on, it didn't matter when. And for the first time ever, I could do the big show. Fridays and Saturday nights.

Holy shit. It was on.

The lineups they'd have were insane. Dane Cook, Jon Lovitz, Bob Saget, Tiffany Haddish. The lines of people waiting to go in would go down the street—literally all the way to Laurel Canyon Boulevard, a block away. After I parked my piece-of-shit car, I'd walk that extra block just so I could walk along the crowd, just to hear that energy. Every now and then I'd hear someone say something like "That's Jo Koy! I saw him last week, he's amazing!" and my heart would swell with pride.

I'd get to the door, and now I was high-fiving the same dude who once charged me $25 just to submit my tape (and every time I'd think "Motherfucker, I *still* can't believe you charged me that $25"). And the excitement inside? The electricity? The anticipation?

That place was packed wall to wall every night, man. We're talking people stacked on top of each other, bodies on top of bodies on top of bodies, upstairs, downstairs, in the VIP room behind the balcony, everywhere. That space is supposed to hold 300 people, and I bet we had 450 packed in there, easy. All those crazy fantasies I had when I first started in Vegas, back before I even got my first laugh—about crowds exploding and cheers echoing off the walls and people calling friends and saying "you gotta see this!"—it was like that times a thousand.

And honestly, even though I know my story is unique, I think that process is how a lot of us nonwhite comics finally broke in. How the face of comedy in Hollywood finally started to change. It was the theme nights, acting as a door that we could sneak our way through.

Not only did the theme nights give us a venue—a platform for Black comics, brown comics, female comics, gay comics—but it also allowed the club owners to see just how funny we all were. A guy like Jamie Masada—an immigrant who came from nothing—wasn't *trying* to favor white comics on the weekends, he was just doing what he thought the business required. But on those theme nights, he could see people like me making everyone in the audience laugh—including white customers. Funny was funny. When he and other owners started to understand that, they started to change—slowly, yes, but surely—and the scene changed with them.

Eventually we all started to mix, brown comics, Black comics, gay comics, you name it. We all started playing each other's "nights," blending and crossing over. That includes white comics, too. I don't know how many times I saw Dane Cook or Bog Saget playing Asian Invasion or Latino shows. Audiences became more sophisticated as well, more open to acts that didn't fit in the traditional "mainstream." I know because I was one of those acts. I was one of those names that drew all those crowds to the Laugh Factory every Friday and Saturday night. I was finally hitting my stride.

But on the way, something happened that changed my career—that changed my life—forever.

I met a girl.

10

THE TINY
GAME-CHANGER

This was my very first time doing stand-up, circa 1972.

My brother, Robert, looking like a young Bruce Lee, and my Auntie Lynn looking like a young Robert.

My brother, Robert; me; and my sister Rowena. Guess which one is half white!

Me and Lola Tinay, circa 1980. That green bow tie was made out of toilet paper. This is also the last time I wore white pants.

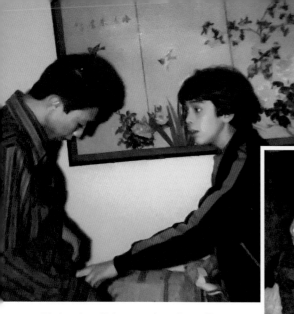

My brother, Robert, and me in my Puma jacket because I was an OG B-boy, and that's what B-boys wore!

My mom always made me do impersonations of Michael Jackson at EVERY event. She also made me the glove to go with it. "Josep, do the Michael Jackson!"

Gemma, Dad, Mom, me. This wasn't long after I fell on a rock and broke my two front teeth.

Love my uncle Ray Portugal, aka The Filipino Santa.

My cousin Monah, Gemma, me, and Mom. I don't know why someone didn't tell me that there was a piece of paper on my feet.

My freshman high school yearbook photo. Rockin' my Sally Jessy Raphael glasses.

Left to right: Auntie Bel, Lolo Loveless, Lola Tinay, Mom, my sister Rowena, Uncle Ric, Auntie Malou, Auntie Evelyn, Cousin Michael, Cousin Monah, my dog Sissy, me, and my sister Gemma. This is proof that I've been a sneakerhead since day one. Rockin' the '90–'91 Air Alpha Force 2 Barkleys!

There's always fish sauce on the table at a Filipino birthday. Find the patis!

Mom and Sergeant Fred Harrison's wedding day. So happy this man came into our lives.

My mom, Gemma, me, Rowena, Robert, and my dad. The Herberts. Look at me with the Cinelli bike hat, and I didn't even own a bike. Swag!

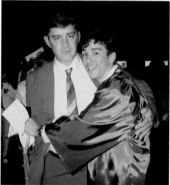

Graduation day with my stepdad, Fred. Proud of myself passing with a 1.7 GPA, but the future looked bright!

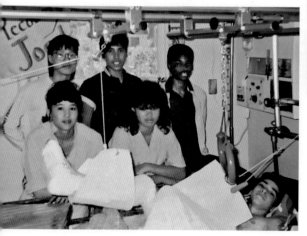

Compound femur fracture. Fractured tibia and fibula. Six surgeries. Man, I should've listened to my mom.

Sagging my pants at the Huntridge Theater.

JO KOY

My dad said he was a photographer, and took my very first headshot. Thoughts?

Mom & Fred
Thanks for the food! Can I wash my clothes?!

-Love-
JoCoy
"Comedy Jam"

A letter to my mom and Fred. I was producing shows at the Huntridge Theater, but still washing my clothes at my mom's house!

Onstage at the La Jolla Comedy Store. Still rockin' the classic V-necks to this day.

Shoutout to Dada Footwear for sponsoring me in the early days. Love you, Lantz, Dwayne, and Carlos. You helped a young kid make his dream a reality.

My Showtime at the Apollo artist credentials. Thank you, Rudy Rush, for this dream come true. I got to perform AND WIN Showtime at the Apollo.

My Def Comedy Jam artist credentials. Thank you, Bob Sumner, for giving me the chance, and Honest John for opening the door for me.

February 2, 2001. The day I opened for Snoop Dogg and Ludacris at the Blaisdell Arena in Hawaii. Seventeen years later, I taped my second Netflix special in the same arena.

This is the actual ticket I made for Jo Koy's Comedy Jam in Las Vegas. I would print these tickets at Kinko's, and stay up all night cutting them.

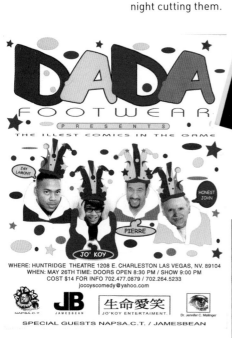

I still remember standing right next to Lantz Simpson, the owner of Dada footwear, and watching him design this flyer for me.

One of my first business cards that I made in 1997. How do I know that year, you ask? Just look at my '97 Nike Air Max shoes. OG sneakerhead.

It's cool looking back and seeing where both of our careers went. Who would've thought Michael Blackson and I would be where we're at today.

When my son was born, he became my world. This dude changed my life.

Little Joe's second birthday, 2005, at a fun little place called Chuck E. Cheese.

Big Jo in 1971 and Little Joe in 2004. Like father, like son. Some things never change.

My first national TV appearance—*The Tonight Show with Jay Leno* in 2006. The next day, I was back to slangin' shoes at Nordstrom Rack.

Always so much fun on the *Chelsea Lately* panel. This lady changed the game. Not only for TV, but for the cats that she shared the panel with. (Photo courtesy of E! Entertainment Television)

One of the coolest moments of my career was shooting the promos for my first Netflix special with my son. By the way, this was the special that Netflix wasn't going to give me, so I had to make it myself. My son saw his dad bust his ass to get to this point.

The day Adam Carolla ate $4,000 of Wagyu beef at my restaurant, but I didn't charge him, because this guy is a big part of my career.

Thirty years in the game, and I got to sell out two shows at the legendary Forum in Inglewood, California. The first show sold out in minutes. Shoutout to Tisha Campbell, Eric Hernandez, Wanya Morris, Tommy Lee, and Gabriel Iglesias for showing up for this amazing moment. Oh! Anita Baker was there too. (Photo courtesy of Josh Adams)

Seventeen years ago I was holding this kid in my arms, thinking about quitting comedy. Thank God I didn't, because he would've never seen his dad sell out these arenas.

Me, Rowena, Mom, and Gemma. Love these three ladies; no matter what obstacles life throws at us, family still sticks together.

Eighteen years later, Angie and I may not be married anymore, but we are the best parents our son could have. I love her and Little Joe with all my heart.

What an amazing night! Winning Stand-Up Comedian of the Year 2018 at the Just for Laughs festival in Montreal. I started out with a lot of these cats, and to receive this award in front of my peers was such an honor. If you could've seen Tiffany Haddish and me seventeen years ago at the Laugh Factory, well, we only dreamed that something like this could happen.

My son and I got our *GQ* on moments before I received my star on the Philippines Walk of Fame in 2020. This was my first time ever in the Philippines with Little Joe. What an awesome memory.

I remember watching Lakers games on TV, when they used to play at the Forum. Thirty years later, my name is written on the wall there, with a "2X" next to it. So surreal. (Photo courtesy of Mike Miller)

I treasure this moment, and I wouldn't have wanted to share it with anyone else.
Hugging my son onstage at the Forum as he witnessed me selling out two shows
there. He said he had the chills, and so did I. (Photo courtesy of Josh Adams)

All my life I'd only ever dated white girls.

Not for any real reason, you know? Like I wasn't walking around telling people, "Sorry, no Asian girls for Jo Koy. It's a light skin tone or nothing at all. The more prone to sunburns and skin cancer, the better!"

Shit, I had no game. I was lucky if I got dates at all. It just so happened that the women I was mostly around in Tacoma and then Vegas were white.

That all changed one night in 2002.

I was doing a show, emceeing an event in downtown LA sponsored by my old friends at Dada. After my set, as I was walking around the club, a friend of mine came over and grabbed me.

"Hey, I came with this girl, she says she wants to meet you."

In the year or so I'd been in Los Angeles, I'd been so obsessed with standup and my career I'd barely even *talked* to any women, forget about dating. But as soon as I saw Angie, I could tell she was different than anyone I'd ever gone out with—literally.

*She's definitely a mixed **something***, I thought. *I don't know what that mix is, but this girl is absolutely a half-breed.*

I was right. It turned out that in addition to being a singer, Angie was really into the street car-racing scene, like *Fast & Furi-*

ous stuff—modeled for the car magazine *DUB*, worked in a pit crew, even raced herself. And she did it all under the name "Mestiza Driver." Guess what "mestiza" means in Tagalog? Half-white, half-Filipina.

Jackpot, baby.

Now, don't get me wrong, it was more than that, too. Angie was smart, pretty, funny, the whole package—I mean, she literally raced cars for fun. But there was something about our shared background that really sucked me in and made me want to know more about her.

Here I was, living in the middle of a huge, sprawling city that still felt new, even foreign to me, fighting to break into an industry that still only saw me as an Asian. With Angie, it felt like I'd *finally* found someone who could accept me exactly as I was—no asterisks, no hyphens, no special theme shows.

I called her, and we went on our first date, and the most amazing thing happened.

I told jokes about my mom, and we were both laughing. Then Angie told jokes about her mom, and we were both laughing. We clicked. We spoke the same language.

The clutching of the purse on the left side, the stealing of ketchup at McDonald's. The constant love and the guilt and the judgment and the obsessive devotion, all swirled together in one weird cohesive but contradictory mess.

And beyond that, the push and pull of coming from two different cultures. A mom from one place, a dad from another. A country that we called home—but which constantly made us prove we truly belonged.

It was all there, it was all so right. I didn't have to explain where I was from, I didn't have to make my jokes "universal" or whitewash everything I said. Angie and I had a connection more real and intimate than anything I'd ever experienced. I was in love. Really, truly, madly in love.

So naturally I thought, *I gotta get this girl pregnant ASAP.*

All right, all right. So maybe that's not exactly what I thought, but it might as well have been—because that's exactly what happened.

It felt so fast. One second, I was a struggling standup on the rise whose biggest care in the world was whether I'd have Wendy's or Burger King for dinner that night.

The next second I was a dad.

Little Joe's birth was the greatest day of my life. He was gorgeous, the most beautiful thing I'd ever seen. I'm an emotional guy, a total crier, but even for me this was intense. I was in the delivery room bawling, man, crying buckets; it was all incredible.

But I was also scared as shit. What was I supposed to do? What came next? How would I take care of Angie and my son? I had no idea what a baby I was until I had a baby of my own.

I was thirty-two, so technically I wasn't so young, but I had the maturity of a twelve-year-old. Think about it—except for that brief fiasco with my friend after high school, this was my first time living on my own! I had roommates who were break-dancers, an empty aquarium in my bedroom, and a dog that shit all over the floor. Now I was a father?

Plus, it's not like I had my own wholesome childhood to draw on for lessons. My own dad had barely been around at all until I graduated from high school and my mom basically shamed him into stepping up. Before that, my strongest father figure was Fred, a great guy who protected my family and loved sports as much as I did, but who also had a drinking problem.

I wanted to do the right thing, but I didn't know where to begin. It all happened so fast my family and Angie's barely had time to react. It went from "meet this new person I'm dating, aren't they nice?" to "guess what, we're pregnant!" in what felt like a week. But generally everyone was supportive, even thrilled. Filipinos love a new baby, man.

As for my mom, her own youngest son had just given her a grandson. For once in her life she was so happy, she didn't judge my life choices at all. Whether I wanted to marry Angie or not, she said she'd back me all the way. Mostly she was just excited that I was going to be a dad—and she wanted me to be a good one. Maybe in part, though she never said so initially, to make up for my own father's failings.

"As long as you're a great father, Josep," she said, "I'm happy."

And that was fantastic. But as much as I needed support, I also needed advice. I needed guidance on what to do now that I had a kid of my own. So I turned to the person my mom probably wanted me to emulate the least. I called my dad.

"Do the right thing, Jo," he said. "You gotta marry her."

At the time, I was a little confused by this statement. I mean, my father was not someone I would instantly associate with the sanctity of marriage. But thinking back on it now, it makes sense. Part of him knew he'd let me down by not staying married to my mom, and he wanted to make sure I didn't make the same mistake.

I took my dad's advice, and Angie and I got married.

Turns out, that was a mistake, too.

❦

AFTER WE GOT MARRIED in a small ceremony that my mom paid for, Angie and I moved in together in a small apartment near Marina del Rey, and I got to work.

With Little Joe in our lives, I needed to make more money. I couldn't just live off my Vegas savings anymore—all the diapers and formula weren't going to pay for themselves. As exciting as weekend nights at the Laugh Factory were, they barely paid anything—just $20 a show. You read that right. Twenty bucks. I'd actually wait a couple of months just to collect my paychecks all at once so I could go "Whoa, $300!" Appearing at the Laugh Factory was about the prestige, the exposure, about building an audience—it was about the long-term investment, not about the short-term payday. So, I went on the road, building off the foundation I'd laid in Vegas and some of my new LA connections, because touring was the best way to bring in fast cash.

When I wasn't touring, I was working three part-time jobs in LA. They were classic disposable jobs, so I'd have the flexibility to travel, but I was still *constantly* on the move, *constantly* hustling, *constantly* trying to make an extra buck for my kid. I was a family man now.

I got one job stocking and selling shoes at Nordstrom Rack—back to my roots—and that was from 1 p.m. to 9 p.m. four days a week. Before *that* job even started for the day, I was already stacking books at Border's at 7 a.m. Then, on weekends, I had a gig in Marina del Ray cleaning up for a catering service that held private events on yachts. I'd go from 6 p.m. to 11 p.m., scouring those boats after rich people had partied on them. When I was done with that I'd hop in my car and race back to the Hollywood Laugh Factory in my busboy uniform.

And I didn't stop there. I had tons of side hustles going on.

At Borders, they didn't just sell books, they also had a CD section. The store would get sample CDs from the record labels, and they'd dump the extras in a big bin in the staff room. We're talking tons and tons of free CDs, just sitting there for employees to take home!

Guess what Daddy did?

I'd rummage through those bins and grab whatever I could, then take them right down to Amoeba Records. To this day, Amoeba Records is an institution in LA, practically a landmark. But back before digital streaming took over, it was absolutely insane—this gigantic two-story hub of entertainment that had *everything*. Albums, movies, posters, action figures. Of course there were CDs and DVDs, but they also had every record you could imagine—from the 1960s, '70s, '80s, '90s, the Beatles, Michael Jackson, even classic comedy albums from Richard Pryor, Lenny Bruce, and more. And there's just something about the smell of a record store, you know? There's a throwback vibe. If you love music, if you love pop culture, you're in heaven.

Amoeba wasn't just where you went to buy new stuff—you went there to sell and trade, too. And now I had plenty of free Borders samples to sell. I figured they'd pay the most money for the popular stuff, Beyoncé and Mariah Carey. But Amoeba was already swimming in contemporary artists. I'd barely clear a buck off *Dangerously in Love*. But bring in music they didn't have— especially classical like Bach and Mozart—and suddenly I was pulling five dollars a CD.

All the other employees would be grabbing for Black Eyed Peas, and I'd be like, "Um, can I please have that dead German dude?"

With enough of a haul, maybe some of those box sets with five or six CDs inside, I could pull an extra $200 a week! Whatever it took for Little Joe.

But even with all that I was still barely keeping up.

As supportive as my mom was of me being a dad, she also had new ammunition for her old demands about finding a job and settling down. Okay, so maybe I didn't want health care, but what about my son? Why not start working at Nordstrom Rack full-time and move my way up to manager for some decent benefits? Of course I only wanted the best for my son. But I also knew that in the long-run, becoming a successful standup was the best way to provide for Little Joe. I'd come way too far to squander my momentum on a full-time job selling shoes.

But I gotta hand it to my mom—when she found out we were still driving Little Joe around in my shitty old Honda with the busted taillight, she bought us an Acura LX so he'd be safe. Thanks to her, my son was out of danger—and a new side hustle started.

No distributers were even making DVDs of my few TV appearances on *Comic View* or *Showtime at the Apollo*, so I decided to do it myself. I sat down in my bedroom and literally recorded reruns of my old act straight off my TV, burning stacks and stacks of my own DVDs. I scored the cases from a friend of mine who worked at Blockbuster, so my costs were almost nothing. Then I'd fill up the trunk of my new car with all my officially bootlegged Jo Koy DVDs, and sell them in the parking lot after my shows for five bucks a pop. The audience may not have arrived that night knowing they needed a lo-fi Jo Koy DVD in their lives, but I used my act to convince them. And if the crowds at a club like the Laugh Factory weren't buying, I'd just give them away for free— better to build my fan base by handing out free merch than to hold out for a few extra bucks.

All the work started taking a toll on my relationship with Angie. I was never home, constantly scraping and scratching to make a few bucks and trying to build my comedy career.

And let's be real here.

Sure, in some ways getting married was the "responsible" thing to do, but Angie and I had no idea how to actually live with each other. Shit, we'd known each other for less than a year! It didn't take long to realize that as much as I loved her, Angie and I were better as friends. And yeah, it probably didn't help that I was as emotionally evolved as a teenager.

After a few months of marriage, we got divorced. Angie moved in with her mom a couple of hours north in Bakersfield. And she took Little Joe with her.

❧

MY MOM SIGHED on the other end of the phone.

"Josep," she said, "do you remember how you felt when I'd be arguing with your dad about extra money?"

"Yeah," I answered. "So?"

This was weird. I'd just had a big fight with Angie over money, so I called my mom to complain about how unreasonable my ex-wife was acting for wanting more. My mom was so fiercely protective of me, I knew she'd take my side. She always did. Until now.

"And you remember when we couldn't buy you shoes or go places because of money?"

"Yeah."

"Is that how you want your son to feel about you?"

"No," I said sheepishly.

"Then do the right thing," she said. "Take care of Angie. Don't let your son say he has a bad dad. Let him be proud of you."

I wish I could say that after the divorce I was the perfect dad and ex-husband. I really do, especially considering everything I experienced myself while growing up. It was the one thing my mom had really wanted for me when we had Little Joe—to be an ideal father. But I wasn't, far from it.

The divorce hadn't been acrimonious. What did we have to

fight over? We were both virtually broke. We hadn't even hired separate attorneys to represent our respective "interests"—we just found a dude to write up a simple contract, done and done.

But once the ink of that paper was dry, once we started trying to make it work, I started acting selfish, petty. I started being stingy with what little money I had. In fact, even after that talk from my mom, I didn't change.

Don't get me wrong. I wasn't a deadbeat. I covered all the basics, maybe even a little more. I paid Angie child support every month. I gave her enough money to buy a little Ford Escort so she and Little Joe could get around. And after a while I even paid for her to move back to the Valley, so I could be close to both of them—covered the U-Haul, the first and last month of rent, the whole deal.

But beyond that, I was cold, unfeeling. If Angie said she needed more money to get something for Little Joe, I didn't give it to her, or even have a conversation about it like a responsible, reasonable parent. My knee-jerk response was, "Fuck that. If she wants more, she can go through a lawyer. She's not getting another fucking penny."

My entire attitude was poisoned, because I was acting out what I knew. When I was a kid, all I ever saw was my dad fighting with my mom about money. If she got a dollar out of him, it didn't come easy. And when he saw us struggling, it never felt like he stepped up and helped us out. It felt like he just ignored the problem. Ignored us.

Deep down, that, to me, was what being a dad meant. Because it's what I grew up with. Yeah, I had Fred as an example, too, but he'd come later in my life, when I was almost out of high school. He'd helped me heal. My earlier experience with my dad was what had molded me. Taught me to never give an inch, that fighting was the only way. As crazy as it sounds, in the haze of my resentment, it actually felt like *Angie* was being the selfish one.

Like here I was, working my butt off, and all she wanted to do was take, take, take. The truth was she was working hard, too, as a property manager and as Little Joe's mom, but I didn't care, I only focused on myself. Who cared if we fought? Who cared if Angie didn't get exactly what she wanted? This was my money—*mine*. I was entitled to every cent I earned, and she was lucky she got what I gave her.

It was bad. I needed something to wake my sorry ass up, once and for all. Something undeniable, something I couldn't possibly ignore.

That something was Angie herself.

I arrived one day at her apartment to visit Little Joe, and she was sitting at the kitchen table with a piggy bank in front of her. It belonged to Little Joe.

"What are you doing?" I said.

"What am I doing?" she said. "*What am I doing?*"

Crying, she stood up and broke the piggy bank open, dumping all the change on the floor. Quarters, nickels, dimes, pennies scattered everywhere.

"This is what I need to do to buy your son something to eat. *This.*"

Then she got down on the ground on her hands and knees and started picking through all the change, searching through the pile for anything silver.

"This is how I'll get us dinner, this is how I'll buy gas for the car to get us home. By going through your son's piggy bank."

I turned, and Little Joe was standing there, watching the whole thing.

My heart broke. In that moment, my pride, my ego, my stubbornness—it shattered. I flashed back to all the times I'd watched my own parents fighting over money when I was a kid. I remembered just how miserable I'd felt, just how torn. Now here I was putting my own son in the same situation.

This was the mother of my child. She was a good mommy, and my boy loved her. Why was I fighting her? Why *shouldn't* she have everything she needed to take care of him?

My son deserved better than I had growing up. His mother deserved better than my mom. I didn't want to repeat the mistakes my dad had made. And yet I was, over and over. I felt ashamed. More ashamed than I had ever felt in my life.

I'd already been working so hard, busting my ass to make it in comedy—but now I was going to work even harder. I was going to do whatever it took to make sure my son and his mother only had the best.

I got down and helped Angie up, tears in my eyes.

"You'll never have to worry about money, ever again," I said. "When I make money, you'll make money. When I do well, you'll do well. You won't even have to ask."

And you know what? She never has.

&

"ALL RIGHT," I SAID. "He's asleep right now, so you totally won't have to do much."

"It's cool, man."

"And the diapers are right here, but he just got changed so he should be good for a while."

"All good, I got this."

I was up in the balcony of the Laugh Factory with Little Joe and Tiffany Haddish, my friend, an amazing comedian, and now my temporary babysitter.

"And if he starts crying, he really likes it if you carry him and kind of hum—"

"Jo! I know the drill! I'm cool with babies, man. Now go do your set!"

"All right, all right!" I said. "I just don't want him to scream during the show!"

I ran downstairs and sprinted backstage to do my act. Thank God it wasn't too crazy that night, the crowd wasn't that loud. Tiffany was another one of Jamie Masada's favorites, so she was at the Laugh Factory about as much as I was. On nights I had Little Joe, she'd look after him while I was doing my set, then Little Joe and I would watch Tiffany do hers.

After the show, we'd head out to the sidewalk and grab hot dogs from one of the street vendors. Those things were so good—piled high with onions, relish, ketchup, mustard, the works. Every now and then Tiffany would ask me to spot her for a second dog. Of course I'd say yes—what's a couple of bucks for a hot dog for my friend?

Years later, after we'd both made it and she was one of the biggest comics in the nation, she told me that she'd take those extra hot dogs and eat them back in her car, which she was living out of. I had no idea at the time. But I guess we were all helping each other out in our own special ways. Me, buying her dinner, and her, keeping an eye on my son. I was doing the best I could to balance my career and parenthood, but without people like Tiffany it would've been impossible. Even with her, it almost was.

I was desperate. It had been three years since I'd made the move to Los Angeles, but I still needed that big break. Sure, I'd made progress in my career. I was performing weekends at the Hollywood Laugh Factory regularly, I was touring nationally, I was slowly but surely building an audience.

But I was still a long way from true mainstream success. Network TV, movies, or massive sold-out shows—I was light-years away from that kind of career.

I needed both the success and the money. For my family and my sanity.

Just like I'd promised Angie, I was working harder than I ever had in my life. I still had all my side jobs—shoe sales at Nordstrom Rack, stacking books at Border's, cleaning yachts on the weekend—*plus* all the Laugh Factory shows, *plus* a touring schedule that was insane.

Touring was still my best way to make money, so if I could book a show somewhere, I would. I never said no to a gig, never, and it started to feel like I was on the road *all the time*. Fly out Wednesday morning, fly back the following Monday, then do it all again two days later. So many airports, so many cabs, so many diners, so many motels.

I don't want to complain, because I loved it. I was getting paid to make people laugh. This was my dream. But it also meant I was missing some of the best moments of my son's childhood. Christmases, birthdays, watching him take his very first steps, hearing him say his very first words, those moments you never get back.

People would always say to me, "Oh, just take a couple of weeks off, spend some more time with your son." But I didn't have those full-time Nordstrom Rack benefits my mom thought were so important. I didn't have any paid vacation.

As a comic, if I wasn't working, we weren't eating. If I turned down a few hundred bucks to work some club in Maryland, that was money I was never getting back. If I stopped stocking books at Border's and cleaning yachts on my weekends at home, I didn't have money for Angie and Little Joe. A single comic might be able to take it easy, hang out with friends, spend his days auditioning for movies or TV and building his entertainment portfolio, but not me. I had a family to support. I had to work. I had to tour.

Sometimes I wondered if I'd moved to LA too late. Sometimes I wondered if by staying in Vegas so long I missed out on my best opportunities. I'd met the comedian Bobby Lee at a small club in La Jolla, California, in the 1990s, years before I moved to Hollywood. Bobby is Korean, and back then he was one of the only Asian comics on the scene. I saw him perform that night with his big bouffant hair, and I thought two things: (1) This guy is funny as hell, and (2) Holy shit, there are other Asian comics out there?

Bobby was my same age, he was already based in LA, and he told me I had to leave Las Vegas if I wanted to make it big. He *told* me. But I'd just started producing my show at the Huntridge Theater, I was making decent coin, so I decided to hold back.

In 2001, Bobby ended up being cast on *MADtv* the same year I finally pulled the plug and relocated to Hollywood. He'd become the face of a major network TV show—his Kim Jong-il was one of their most recognizable characters—just when I was starting from nothing.

Sure, I'd made progress since then, a lot of progress. But it was impossible not to second-guess myself. Not to wonder what could've been if I'd moved out when Bobby told me to.

In 2004, I thought I finally had a chance to break out of my holding pattern—in a show costarring my same friend who'd passed me by years earlier.

A manager and producer named Barry Katz got in touch with me about a TV project after he saw me at a few clubs in LA—I don't even know how the guy got my number. Barry is from out east, but he always wore this cowboy jacket, this leather deal with tassels on the arms, and he spoke with a little drawl. He'd repped some big comics, people like Dave Chappelle and Whitney Cummings, and he was putting together a special for Comedy Central.

It was an Asian-themed special called *Kims of Comedy*, and it would star Bobby Lee, Ken Jeong, Steve Byrne—and me, if I wanted it.

"You guys will be coming out of a Chinese takeout box," he told me. "That'll be the poster!"

Fuck, man. I loved and respected the hell out of all those guys. This could finally get my career to Bobby's level. But I was pissed. Just because we were Asian we had to get stuck on a theme show? I thought those days were behind us. We were all objectively amazing comics. We deserved our *own* specials.

"You know what, Barry, I think I'm going to pass."

"What?" he said.

"I want my own special, not a theme special."

"But if Comedy Central sees you in this, they'll love you and give you your own special."

Play the ethnic game to get a foot in the door, in other words— the same kind of bargain I'd made to get on the Laugh Factory stage. But I was tired of making those kinds of bargains. I was tired of compromising. I wanted my big break, and I wanted it on my own terms. I wasn't busting my ass on tour with my three day-jobs to do another theme show.

"Sorry, Barry," I said. "I want my own special. Not this."

"This is going to be huge," he said. "You're making the biggest mistake of your life. No one says no to Barry Katz! No one!"

He hung up the phone.

The next year, they did the special—with Kevin Shea as the fourth comic. Part of me was jealous. It was real money. And at the time, Comedy Central was *the* place to be for successful comics. They had *Chappelle's Show*, the *Daily Show*, *Reno 911*. They'd revolutionized standup with their show *Premium Blend* and their half-hour specials, providing the first national platform devoted entirely to comedy and comedians. Other than *The Tonight Show* and maybe *The Late Show*, Comedy Central was it for standup comics. But my gut told me I'd done the right thing. I needed to hold out, needed to find an opportunity that was right for *me*. That was the only way I'd break big.

Until then, I had to keep grinding it out alone on tour, away from my son.

Ever since I'd started pursuing my dream, all the way back to my first time onstage in Vegas, I'd faced adversity. My first few bombs, my mom's lack of faith in me, club owners that wouldn't give me a shot because of who I was. But I'd always pushed on. I'd always made it work. But now, juggling three jobs and touring, with a baby boy I barely got to see, for the very first time I was wondering if it was all really worth it. Maybe my mother was right. Maybe I should get a normal job, a desk job, something steady with health care and a 401(k). A job that would allow me to both take care of Little Joe and be present as he grew up.

I wasn't ready to quit. Not yet. Not after everything I'd been through. Not after coming so far. But I didn't know how much more I could take.

❧

THE JUST FOR LAUGHS FESTIVAL in Montreal is one of standup's biggest, highest-profile events.

Every year, all the top agents and bookers go there, hoping to discover the next big thing in comedy. Jimmy Fallon, Amy

Schumer, my old buddy Kevin Hart—they all got discovered by performing in JFL's prestigious New Faces show. They'd gone from being comics who had solid careers to booking big TV shows to eventually becoming household names. If there was one way for me to finally smash my way into the major leagues, this was it.

But for three years, they'd turned me down. I'd performed at one audition after another, and the organizers kept passing on me. They were always very nice about it. *Yeah, we love your stuff, we think you're fantastic, but we went with someone else. The timing's just not right.*

These guys were Canadian, but they took the infamously indirect "Hollywood No" to the next level. Not only did they never say the word "no," but they practically made it seem like I was the one rejecting *them*.

Then, in 2005, I finally got a spot in the lineup.

I wish I could tell you why I made it that year instead of all the others. I wish I could tell you it all came down to a new joke or the way I tweaked a line in my act or even a brand-new lucky jacket. But I don't really know. That's part of what's so humbling about entertainment. You can do everything right, you can be the funniest guy in the room, and there are still no guarantees. All I could do was have faith in my talent, faith in my dream, and work harder than everyone else put together. The rest was in the hands of God and the JFL organizers. Hell, if you asked them why I finally got in, they'd probably say something about the timing being right.

All I really knew once I got my chance was that I couldn't—I *wouldn't*—fuck it up.

I got to Montreal that July, and the festival was insane. Imagine an entire major international city putting all its focus, all its energy, all its love, into nothing but comedy for a week. There were big stages where you could see huge names like Dave Chappelle and Craig Ferguson and the iconic cast of *The Kids in the Hall*, and small side theaters where you could see names like Patrice O'Neal and Brian Regan, insanely funny guys who went on to do specials on Showtime and Comedy Central but hadn't quite broken big yet. There were huge shows in front of thousands at 8 p.m. and tiny gigs in front of twenty or thirty people at 3 a.m. It was like a Canadian comedy Coachella. And I was at the heart of it all.

My big night finally arrived, the night I'd been striving for for three years—and my good buddies, the show's organizers, wanted to put me on first.

Every comic knows that going first is the worst position in a lineup. The crowd's still getting settled, no one's had anything to drink yet, no one's in the mood to laugh. They haven't been warmed up yet. And that's exactly why the producers wanted me to go up.

"Oh, we just *love* your energy! It's so infectious! It would be so good for the night and the other comics if you went first!"

So nice and friendly, like always. And I went through with it, too—at least for our first show of the week. But when I saw my name in first position on the set list before our second and final show, I exploded.

"That's bullshit, guys! I'm not someone else's warm-up! I don't have an agent, I'm working at Nordstrom Rack, I've got a little kid! Fuck that, I'm here to be discovered!"

They moved me to fifth. It was exactly the spot I needed.

I got onstage and opened with the joke I'd created years ago, staring up at the ceiling that night in my bed, trying to figure out a way to connect with audiences by telling them something about myself—without being *too* unrelatable, *too* other.

"Living in this country, you get the worst compliments when you tell people you're Asian.

"'Oh, you're Asian? I *love* orange chicken!'

"What are you *talking* about? That's not a compliment, that's an insult!"

Then I gave the kind of sarcastic response I'd always wanted to give whenever people made assumptions about my identity. The kind of thing I'd always wanted to say to everyone who questioned whether I belonged when I was growing up in Tacoma. The kind of thing I wanted to scream at all the big club owners who hadn't given me a shot because of who I am. Except now I delivered it in front of an audience as a bit.

"What do they expect me to do when they say that, like I'm supposed to go '*Oh-ho-ho! Sank you! Sank **you**! O-ran shicken very, very good! Okay, bye-bye, o-ran shicken!*'"

I did the most over-the-top, clichéd Chinese impression imaginable, turning the racist Asian stereotype on its head—and into an indictment. It was offensive. It was subversive. It was bold. And it brought down the house.

I crushed, man. Had the set of my life. People roaring with laughter from beginning to end. When I told the crowd good night, for a moment I didn't even move. I just stood there and bowed my head. Soaking in the moment, my eyes welling with tears.

I got off the stage, walked two hundred feet, and two guys came up to me. I had no idea who they were, had never met them before in my life. And what did these two strangers say to me?

"You're going on *The Tonight Show*."

I was stunned.

"I'm sorry, what?"

"You heard us. Out of all these new faces up here tonight, you're the one who's making *The Tonight Show*. Congratulations!"

It sounds like a fairy tale, I know, and I guess it kind of was. Their names were Bob Read and Ross Mark, and they were the bookers for the show.

The tears welled up again.

Like I said, I'm an emotional dude, but—*The Tonight Show*? Wouldn't you cry?

This was it. A spot on the one television show that could get me the mainstream recognition I had been working for. That could help me build a massive, nationwide audience. That could help me turn my standup into a real career making real money. Enough to both support my son *and* allow me to watch him grow up.

I'd been dreaming of this moment ever since I started studying Richard Pryor videos. Ever since I pretended to do comedy in the shower and practiced my autograph on our phone book. Ever since I got my very first laugh at Buzzy's Café in Las Vegas.

Now it was happening. At last. All it took was years of constant running, and the decision to embrace my identity instead of running away from it.

When I finally managed to untangle myself from the crowd, my mom was the first person I called.

"Hey Mom!" I yelled into the phone. "I got *The Tonight Show*!"

"Okay, good," she said, completely nonplussed. "You know your aunt is coming to Vegas next week, right?"

I couldn't believe it.

"Did you hear what I said? I said *I'm doing* The Tonight Show*!*"

"I know, Josep, I heard you," she said impatiently. "Why are you shouting? Ha?"

I sighed. Who knows? Maybe someday I could work this into my act.

11

YOU'RE THE FUCKING MAN

Halo Halo

&

"Halo halo" *means "mix mix" in Tagalog, and that tells you a lot about this tasty dessert—the only real rule is that you mix whatever sweets you like together in a glass along with some shaved ice, and voila! You've got your halo halo.*

The following recipe is my own favorite blend of sweets. You can buy them all pre-prepared at your local Asian grocery store, which is what I do.

SERVES 1

INGREDIENTS

1 tablespoon sweetened chopped banana

1 tablespoon sweetened chopped jackfruit

1 tablespoon sweetened sweet potato

½ tablespoon of sweetened garbanzo beans

½ tablespoon sweetened red beans

1 tablespoon sweetened coconut strips

Shaved ice

2 tablespoons leche flan, scooped from the container

1 scoop ube ice cream

¼ cup of sweetened condensed milk

INSTRUCTIONS

Place the sweetened fruits and beans at the bottom of a tall glass. Fill the glass with shaved ice, then add the leche flan and scoop the ube ice cream on top. Pour the condensed milk over the *halo halo* and enjoy!

It was January 2006, I was backstage at *The Tonight Show* waiting to go on, and I was bouncing up and down like a boxer, up and down, up and down. I wanted to punch someone.

The someone I wanted to punch was Joaquin Phoenix.

Now, I'm sure Joaquin Phoenix is a great guy. Or maybe he isn't. I barely knew who he was, and to be honest I didn't care. What I *did* care about was that he was Jay Leno's other guest tonight, and he was up before me, and he was running long.

For one sweet, blissful moment earlier that day it had actually looked like Joaquin might be too sick to go on at all. He'd come in coughing, not feeling well, and if Joaquin canceled, that meant Jay would need to fill his time with more of me—not only doing my standup, but actually *sitting down on the couch* across from Jay Fucking Leno and having a whole conversation in front of millions of people everywhere.

Oh shit, the very idea of it was *amazing* . . . and it put me in the slightly awkward position of really, really hoping that Joaquin Phoenix was really, really sick.

I mean, not a *bad* kind of sick. Nothing fatal or painful. I didn't even really want to punch the guy. I'm actually a very nice, warm person. I just wanted him to be sick enough to not do the show, and then after the show he could be totally healthy and happy again.

But I wasn't fine. Not at all. Because somehow Joaquin Phoenix not only miraculously healed, he apparently felt so damn healthy that he was going long with Jay and stepping on *my time*.

My interview with Jay, sitting across from him on the couch, that was already gone. Over. No chance it was happening. But if Joaquin Phoenix kept talking, I could get bumped altogether. Sure, I'd get rescheduled eventually, but I was ready now. I needed this to happen *now*.

I kept bouncing, breathing, shadow boxing.

I had a patch of the Filipino flag sewn right onto the front of my jacket in honor of Manny Pacquiao, a Filipino boxer who was pound-for-pound the greatest fighter in the world and who had a huge bout coming up against Erik Morales. I was channeling Pacquiao's energy. Focused, unbeatable, ready to strike, just waiting for that bell to ding.

I looked over at the backstage security guards, and they were bouncing, too.

"Why are you guys bouncing?"

"We're bouncing because you're bouncing!"

The stage manager grabbed me.

"Are you ready?"

"I've been waiting my whole fucking life for this."

He gave me the nod, and out I went.

I stood in the middle of the stage with the Filipino flag on my chest for the world to see, I smiled, I soaked up the moment. And from that second on I had blinders on. Nothing mattered—not Joaquin Phoenix, not the conversation with Jay that wasn't going to happen, nothing. I channeled all my energy into my standup. The show had told me to do the same set I'd done at Just for

Laughs, so that's what I did, and as soon as I got that first applause I knew I had 'em.

I responded to everything the crowd gave me. They gave me their energy, I gave it back times ten. They laughed, they cheered, and I took my set to a whole new physical level, moving my body, turning around, running back to the wall.

When I finished my set, I stood there smiling as the whole audience burst into applause, and then one after another everyone got to their feet like a massive wave sweeping over the studio.

A standing ovation.

"Get over here! Get over here!"

I look over at Jay and he's waving me over.

I was going to the couch.

I sat across from Jay and his amazing, piercing blue eyes. He set me up perfectly for the newest addition to my act. My son.

"I know you have a little boy now," he said. "How old is he?"

"Yeah, a little boy, he's two and a half. It's weird, though, he doesn't know how to talk yet, and he's all 'Ba! Ba! Gaw! Daba!' And this is how I know girls are smarter than boys, because I got a friend, name is Stella, she's got a little girl, two and a half, same age, she's already talking. She's articulate, too, like 'Mommy, can I have a sandwich?'

"And I'm like, 'Wow . . . there's a "d" in "sandwich"?'"

It still wasn't storytelling. I was still sticking to my tried-and-true setup–punch line joke format, but my material was slowly evolving. I'd finally started talking about a family member—the safest, most relatable one. I never even had to bring up his ethnicity, because it didn't matter. He was a baby! Who doesn't love funny babies?

Jay grinned as the audience burst out laughing.

"Jo Koy, everybody! There's a 'd' in 'sandwich'!"

The crowd erupted. My segment was over. As we went to commercial I turned to Jay.

"I thought there wasn't enough time for me to sit and talk at the couch!" I said.

"You got a standing ovation," he said. "I wasn't going to let you stand out there. You deserved this."

My dad and my two sisters had come to watch the taping. My mom had been so unimpressed when I told her *The Tonight Show* news, I figured my dad, the man who'd always dreamed of being a pilot but had never learned to fly, would enjoy the experience a bit more.

Jay called them out, and we all took a photo together on the stage as the audience looked on.

"You're the fucking man, Jo Koy!" someone in the crowd shouted.

I grinned.

For the first time in my life, I kind of was.

സ

MY BREAKTHROUGH ON *THE TONIGHT SHOW* dovetailed perfectly with the biggest innovation to my act since I wrote my very first punch line. After sixteen years of standup, I finally got onstage and told a story about my mom.

Took me long enough, right?

In a way, it was the result of a slow, steady evolution in my comedy. I started out with the most universal, most anonymous material possible—the dick jokes. To help audiences get to know me better, I added some jokes about my background—but I still kept them quick and simple. They were jokes, nothing more. Then I branched into bits about my son. Still punchy, still not authentic storytelling, and I avoided his Filipino heritage altogether, but the jokes were getting more complex, more layered. I was adding more personal detail about my life and Little Joe's.

My understanding of comedy—as a craft, as an art—had been evolving as well. A couple of years after I moved to LA, once I'd already broken into the Laugh Factory, I opened one night for the comedian Joe Torry at another local club, the Comedy Store. Joe was an institution in the world of Black comedy and beyond. He'd hosted *Def Comedy Jam* on HBO for three years, he'd done Conan, he'd even costarred in the big Tupac and Janet Jackson movie, *Poetic Justice*. This guy was the real deal, and I wanted to prove I could hang.

So I went up before him and *destroyed*. Told all my best dick jokes, all my dirtiest stuff, and the crowd ate it up. Laughing and laughing, they could barely even pause to catch their breath.

After the show I went up to him, and I'm not gonna lie—I was feeling pretty good about myself. Don't get me wrong, he'd killed, too. These were his fans, they were there to see him. But I'd come in hot for what was supposed to be a warm-up act, and I knew it.

"Hey, man," I said, shaking his hand, "it was an honor working with you."

He looked at me.

"Yeah, you were great," he said. "But I'm gonna give you some advice. You go for those big jokes, the big laughs with all the applause breaks, and I get that, that's cool. But don't be afraid of silence. Just because your crowd goes quiet sometimes doesn't mean you lost them. It means they're listening. They're with you. You got them. Don't be afraid of that. Don't run from those silent moments."

The first thing I thought was "Fuck that! He's just jealous!"

But the more I thought about it, the more I realized Joe Torry was right. I'd always been so good at making people laugh, it had never occurred to me that there might be something more. I was the funny guy. Funny guys told great jokes. I'd grown up literally studying people like Eddie Murphy, George Carlin, Billy Crystal, diagramming their jokes on paper to figure out how they got to their punch lines so quickly, all so I could make my own bits tighter, more efficient. All so I could get to that laugh as fast as possible, then move onto the next. But maybe in my hurry I was missing out on something deeper, potentially more valuable?

It was a natural extension of what Corey Holcomb had told me shortly after I moved to Hollywood—if you want to build an audience, you have to do more than make your audience laugh. You have to help them connect. You have to inspire them to listen to what you're saying, to truly engage on an emotional level. You have to embrace the silence.

But even with all that—the evolution of my act, my deeper understanding of comedy—for years I continued to avoid talking about my mom onstage. I wanted to tell compelling stories, yes, but I also didn't want to get bogged down in detailed explanations of Filipino culture, which I thought would be too much for an audience to handle. At the same time, I also didn't want to reduce my mom to some kind of cartoon Asian cliché. My mom is complicated—you've probably figured that out by now. I wanted to portray that complexity, but also stay accessible for people who didn't know a thing about Filipino moms. I needed a way in.

That Christmas in 2006, just months after Jay Leno had introduced me to America, I finally found it. And it came in a box Santa left under our tree.

"A brand-new Wii!" Little Joe shouted. "Thank you, thank you, thank you!"

That's what was so great about the Wii. Little Joe was almost three years old, but it was so simple, so intuitive, he got it immediately. Nintendo had just released it a month earlier, and the whole nation had gone insane. Hook it up to your TV, start swinging around your controller, and you could play virtual tennis right there in your living room. People loved it, it was the hottest gift around, and "Santa" had decided to splurge—even if it meant booking a couple more gigs or selling a few more Beethoven CDs at Amoeba, it was worth it for my son.

CRASH!!! came the sound of the virtual bowling balls. *"Nice throw!"*

Bowling was Little Joe's favorite. Wind up, let that ball go, he had a blast. I knew he'd love it. But then I noticed how closely my mom was watching him play.

"Mom," I said. "You wanna try?"

"No," she said. "Video games. It's silly."

Silly, my ass. She totally wanted to do it.

"Go on! Give it a try!"

"Okay," she fake-sighed. "Maybe I'll play a little."

Watching her go head-to-head with my son, seeing her get more and more excited as she competed with a three-year-old, basking in her joy as she laughed and jumped up and down after every strike, it suddenly hit me. This was my way in.

There was nothing innately foreign about this scene. This was a grandma playing video games with her kid! It was universal, something everyone would understand, especially now that everyone wanted a Wii. I *had* to try.

I performed at the Laugh Factory all the time, even during the holidays. So later that night, I did.

"Guess what, guys? I just bought a Wii . . ."

I barely put any thought into it, just riffed about my mom, this tiny little lady, who was so into virtual bowling with her three-year-old grandson. And wasn't it funny how moms always had this way of signaling to you whenever they wanted you to buy something? Then came my next innovation, the one thing that really made it all come together.

Instead of explaining my mom, instead of talking about where she was from and what her culture was like, I simply *became* my mom. I did her voice, I did her mannerisms, I embodied her whole character exactly as she'd been just hours earlier, trying to get me to buy her her own Wii.

"Josep, this is such good exercise, don't you think?"

"Yeah, Mom."

"And the doctor, he says I need exercise, for my heart."

"Yeah, Mom, you should definitely start getting out more."

"Well, I don't like walking outside, Josep. It's not safe. People might rape me."

"Oh my God, Mom! Do you want a Wii?! Just say so!!"

The audience just got it. She was a mom. And they were *dying* laughing.

It was only a small snippet of material, not too much. I just wanted to try it out, get a feel for how the crowd would respond. And it killed.

When I got off the stage, Jamie Masada came right up to me.

"From now on, I'm only putting you up if you tell stories about your mom."

My jaw dropped. But he was being serious. He liked the stories about my mom so much, he wouldn't even let me tell my classic orange chicken joke on the weekends anymore. He wanted more about my mom, my son, my family. And he was right.

I still kept the stories pretty "universal" at first. Barely even mentioned the fact that my mother was Filipino. But over time

I added in more and more context, until eventually it became a little less "can you believe moms do this" and a little more "can you believe Filipino moms do this." I realized I didn't have to be so afraid of people not understanding my background.

By talking about my Filipino family and all their quirks, I wasn't shutting my audience out, I was bringing them in, building bridges between our cultures and showing how much we all have in common. I wasn't being a token "Asian comic" in a theme show, and I wasn't doing cheap ethnic jokes. I was telling stories. I was showcasing my complexity, I was embracing the silence. I was being human.

I finally learned that the best way to entertain tons of people, to transcend categories and even race itself, was by simply being my mixed-up, half-breed self.

It all clicked for me, just like that. It had taken more than fifteen years of performing, fifteen years of trial and error, lots of advice from other comics, and gaining the confidence I needed to finally be myself—completely and entirely me—onstage, but I was finally there. I understood exactly who I needed to be as a comedian, as a storyteller, as an artist. I felt no frustration that it took so long. It was all part of a process, I'd been growing, and I loved every minute along the way. But now that I finally got it, now that I'd found my voice, it was on. I was ready to go.

Eventually I added a tagline to the story about my mom playing the Wii for the first time. How after spiking a virtual tennis ball on me *and* making me promise to buy her a Wii of her own, she smiled triumphantly and said two words: "Game. Over."

But the truth is, it was just beginning.

కు

THE ONE-TWO PUNCH OF MY *Tonight Show* appearance and my new mom-centered approach to comedy transformed my career.

It's not like it happened overnight, don't get me wrong, but gradually I started getting more and more TV spots. Soon after I appeared with Jay Leno, I finally broke onto Comedy Central when they featured my standup on their iconic show *Premium Blend*, the channel's showcase for young breakout comics. In 2007, I did my first call-in to Adam Carolla's extremely popular radio show, which led to a long friendship and years of contributing to the show and then his podcast. Then, at the beginning of 2009, I got my biggest TV break yet when I started appearing regularly on Chelsea Handler's groundbreaking show, *Chelsea Lately*.

I first met Chelsea a few years earlier when we were both performing at the Laugh Factory, before she'd even launched her show, but she already had a lot of buzz. Her comedy had this incredible authenticity, this frank, insightful wit that could be both brutal and playful. It was like nothing anyone had seen before. She and I hit it off immediately.

We had this natural chemistry, this connection, I think because I had that same appreciation for honesty and authenticity. We could go at each other one second with the most hilarious, almost vicious insults, and the next second we'd be having a heart-to-heart about our families. This is one of the ways that changing my act to focus on my mom had a huge impact. Chelsea *loved* hearing about my mom. And not just onstage.

Whenever we'd talk she'd ask me for a full report—my mom's latest visit, our latest conversation, our latest argument. I'd tell her a story, and she'd laugh her ass off, but I could tell it was more than just the comedy for her. She'd get a look in her eyes like she was truly touched by our relationship, and she'd always end our conversations by saying, "Awww, I love your mom." I found out her own mom had just passed away in 2006 after a long battle with breast cancer, and even though she never said so, I always felt like that loss made her feel a connection to my own mother. Chelsea had a soft spot you might not expect, and I loved it.

She and I got along so well that before she started *Chelsea Lately*, she actually invited me to be her permanent sidekick on the show, her Ed McMahon—playing the role that Chuy Bravo ended up occupying. This wasn't just a thing she mentioned and dropped. We had multiple meetings, brainstorming ideas, coming up with bits, you name it.

But at the last second I ended up passing. Yeah, I needed the money—hell, I was still selling shoes at Nordstrom Rack—but I also knew that once you became the sidekick, you could never go back. Ed McMahon will always be linked with Johnny Carson. Andy Richter will always be linked with Conan O'Brien. Chuy Bravo will always be linked with Chelsea Handler.

Those guys are all insanely talented comics in their own right, but that life wasn't for me. In part, for the same reason I turned down *Kims of Comedy*—I wanted to be my own man.

So I had my agent say no. And the next day I got a call from Chelsea.

"Are you fucking stupid!?" she shouted. "This show is gonna be the shit! You just made the worst decision in your life! Good luck with that!"

This went on for about forty-five seconds. I don't think I got a word in. She hung up, and I remember looking at my phone and thinking, *Holy shit, that sucked.*

And in a sense Chelsea was right. The show was a huge hit. An instant cult classic. Just like with her comedy, no one had seen a panel show like it. There was that same authenticity, that same realness. Nothing was off-limits—pop culture, sure, but also gender and race. I'd get home from selling shoes, turn it on, and think, *Man, I fucked that one up.*

But a few months later I got a call from my agent. They wanted me on the show—not as the sidekick, of course, but to appear on the panel. I said yes in a heartbeat. Appearing as a panel guest would mean national exposure without the risk of being permanently typecast as Chelsea's sidekick. At the same time, though, I was nervous.

I hadn't even spoken to Chelsea since the blowup. What was she gonna do when she saw me? Was I gonna get another forty-five second blowup?

I went to the studio the next day, saw Chelsea, and immediately started babbling.

"I'm so, so sorry about everything! Thank you so much for—"

She was hugging me before I could finish. As far as Chelsea was concerned, it was like our argument had never even happened. That thick-skinned honesty, it wasn't just part of her act—it was her. She was the real deal.

Before I knew it, I was appearing on the panel every week. Now that I was part of the show, I gained even more appreciation for what made it so special. The chemistry we had couldn't be faked. It felt like friends talking to each other. Before the show, we'd always go over jokes we wanted to tell, then when it started we'd forget it all and just banter. She helped launch other comics, too, people like Heather McDonald and Josh Wolf and Ross Matthews, and we all developed this shorthand with each other on the show, we all knew how to click. Heather told stories, Josh was high energy, Ross was great with zingers. Chelsea set the tone, we followed with our own organic give-and-take, and audiences love it.

For a comic like me, TV appearances—whether they're on

Chelsea Lately, *The Tonight Show*, or *Premium Blend*—aren't really about the paycheck. They're about the exposure.

My television success helped me book bigger and bigger rooms when I toured, attracting not just more people, but different types of people. Suddenly I had moms coming up to me after shows saying, "This is the first live standup we've ever seen! We didn't even know this club existed!" And I'd think *There goes a Chelsea fan.* College kids, middle-aged, white, Black, Latino, Asian—thanks to TV, I was pulling in everyone imaginable, all over the country. No more two-for-one ticket giveaways. I made sure clubs charged full price, and I demanded a percentage of ticket sales at the gate. Because now, I could.

I'd been touring a lot before, but that was nothing compared to what I was doing now. If I wasn't in town shooting *Chelsea Lately* or another TV gig, I was on the road. Now that I was finally making big money, I wasn't about to take my foot off the gas. I knew that TV shows didn't last forever—not even *Chelsea Lately*—so I was gonna build my audience and rake in every dollar I could for me and my family.

I understand that that might sound materialistic, but put yourself in my shoes. For someone like me who'd grown up with so little, earning good money wasn't about greed—it was about security, about peace of mind. I knew what it was like to go hungry. I knew what it was like to scrounge for change so I could buy a cookie at school for lunch. I swore to myself that Little Joe would never experience that kind of want, that kind of need.

And to be clear, I was making much better money, but I was still far from rich. Maybe I wasn't selling shoes at the mall anymore, but I was still hawking my homemade Jo Koy DVDs after every show, still scraping for every dollar, still trying to grow my audience.

So I stayed on the road, never seeing him, missing out on so much time with my son for the sake of his own well-being.

The week of Little Joe's seventh birthday, I got an offer to do a few shows in St. Charles, Illinois. We're talking about a town of thirty thousand people, like forty miles west of Chicago. I'd have to be there the whole week.

It devastated me to miss his birthday, absolutely ripped my heart out. It felt like the same kind of shit my dad had pulled so many times. But we needed that money—at least I felt like we did—so I choked back my guilt and went.

My first night in St. Charles there was almost no one there, maybe five or six people. But this guy and his wife showed up thirty minutes early, and they grabbed seats right in the front.

Shit, man, I thought. *You could've shown up whenever you wanted. You got the whole fucking place to yourself.*

Then I realized they were Filipino. I spent my whole time on-stage just joking around with him and his wife, playing directly to them. After the show I was selling my DVDs as usual, and he and his wife walked up.

"How much?" he said.

"Come on, man," I said. "It's yours. I'll give it to you for free."

"No way," his wife said. "He's been waiting to buy this for years!"

Somehow, I don't know how, this guy had discovered me, and he'd been following me since the early days in Vegas.

Now, in case you couldn't tell, we Filipinos take a lot of pride in each other's accomplishments in America. Tell us any line of work, anything at all, and we can rattle off the name of the Filipino who made strides in that industry. NBA? *Aw, man, you see that Jordan Clarkson? I'm a Cavs fan for life!* Wrestling? *Fucking Dave Bautista, he's gonna be bigger than the Rock!* Dentistry?

Oh, you hear about Dr. Fernandez? That guy can fill a cavity like a champ, bro!

But I'll be honest, this dude in St. Charles, Illinois—he was devoted even for us.

He came to another show later that week. At the end of the night, I was tired and hungry, so I decided to ask the local for advice.

"Hey, man, you know where to eat around here?"

He looked at me and smiled.

"You want Filipino food?"

Damn fucking right I wanted Filipino food. My boy and his wife had me back to his place, and they cooked me one of the best dinners I'd ever had in my life. We're talking thin-sliced beef steak, stewed onions, and soy sauce with a hint of lemon. So delicious, and right there in the heart of the Midwest. A true home-cooked meal.

But as amazing as that show of kindness was, I couldn't help but think of my actual home back in Los Angeles. I thought of my son and all the meals I was missing with him, every day, every week, every month, I spent on the road or at work. I thought about his birthday, this magical moment that was gone now, which I'd never be able to recapture.

What the hell was I doing?

As I saved more money year over year, I was able to finally cut back on my touring schedule. Eventually I stopped doing Wednesdays, then I stopped doing Sundays. That meant I could be home four or five days a week, sometimes more. It was hard saying no to some gigs, at first. They'd put a big stack of money in front of me and I'd just have to turn it down, try to make it up by selling more merchandise at the shows I still took, taking more pictures, shaking more hands.

But it was so worth it, because it meant I was getting closer to my one true goal—being a better dad to my son.

⁓

MY PHILOSOPHY AS A FATHER was pretty simple: I wanted to make sure Little Joe had a happier childhood than mine. My parents were good people who meant well, but they made a lot of mistakes, and I wanted to make sure I learned from those mistakes.

I never saw my dad, so I wanted Little Joe to see me all the time. I never got much from my dad for Christmas or my birthday, so I gave Little Joe gifts whenever I could. I never got the support for my dream I wanted from my mom, so I supported Little Joe in everything he did.

Little Joe went to a private grade school, and he never had to worry about paying for lunch the way I did. But that wasn't enough for me. When I was a kid and I couldn't afford lunch, I wasn't just hungry, I wasn't just poor—I was lonely. My mom was working constantly to support us, so much so that she didn't even have time to pack me a sandwich. My dad was never standing at the door in the morning to ask me if I needed a few bucks for a slice of pizza. I was on my own, fending for myself.

Being broke was never really about the money, it was never about the possessions—it was about the fear, the vulnerability that came with it. I wanted Little Joe to know that his life was going to be different. I wanted him to know that I'd always have his back.

So, the first time I took a Monday off from touring, when Little Joe was in the third grade, I decided to bring him lunch myself.

I literally drove up to the school's front gate with his favorite fast food, Taco Bell, and I waited until the bell rang for lunch. As his class walked to the cafeteria, he and his friends spotted me and came over to the gate. He was a late bloomer, so he was always a couple of inches shorter than his buddies, even at that age.

I handed him his lunch.

"I love you, Joseph," I said.

"Thanks, Dad!" he said. "Love you!"

His friends shouted, "We love you, too!"

So I started buying them Taco Bell, too.

Soon I was bringing Joe and his friends fast food *every day* I was home from touring, sometimes three days a week. It became our thing, our tradition. We kept it up in the fourth grade, the fifth grade, all the way through eighth. It got to the point where other parents started to get irritated. Not because I was feeding their kids a steady stream of junk food, but because they started liking me *too* much.

"Why the fuck do you bring your son lunch every day?" one of the moms asked me. "You're making all the other parents look bad!"

To be fair, the mom was Heather McDonald, my hilarious friend from *Chelsea Lately*, but still—I'm pretty sure her son Drake liked me better than her.

But who could blame him? Taco Bell for lunch?

I bought annual passes to Universal Studios, and we'd go to Six Flags Magic Mountain two or three times a week, pop over in the afternoon just because we felt like it. We started taking yearly two-week-long vacations to Hawaii, and I'd bring along Joe's eight cousins, so they could enjoy some time together without any adults around. Why no grown-ups? Because back when I was a little kid in Tacoma, the older generation at the Knights of Columbus always managed to get caught up in drama and gossip—in *tsismis*—and it always drove wedges between the different families. So I wanted to give the cousins two weeks in paradise that were only about them. Not about their parents, not about their grandparents, not even about me. Just kids being kids, having fun, growing closer, and cementing their bonds as cousins.

I was doing everything I could to make sure Little Joe wasn't my son in the formal, technical sense, but my son in the sense that we had a friendship. I didn't want any of the guilt, the anger, the manipulation I'd experienced with my parents to enter into our relationship. I didn't want anything to come between us. I wanted him to feel like he could tell me anything, and he did.

We talked about life, we talked about sports, we talked about sex. There were no barriers, no boundaries. And that started to present its own complications.

One day when Little Joe was in junior high, he said he had something to tell me.

"Dad, I hate it when I get out of the pool and my pubic hair is tickling my butt."

I immediately thought three things: (1) Awww, my son has pubic hair, he's really growing up! (2) Wait, I think he's just saying that he has a single pubic hair, and it's so damn long it tickles his butt when he gets out of the pool. (3) I cannot wait to put this story in my act.

A few weeks later I took my son, my friend, to one of my shows. He'd been coming to my shows since he was a baby, of course, back when Tiffany Haddish would babysit him in the balcony of the Laugh Factory. But now that he was a little older, it was more fun, more fulfilling. He could learn more about my work, meet the other comics, and feel special with his backstage pass.

I finished up my set, closing with my newest addition—the story about Little Joe and his single long pubic hair tickling his butt. The joke *crushed*. People were laughing their asses off.

I went backstage, saw my son, and asked him how I did, just like I had a million times before.

"Um, great, Dad," he said. "Yeah, you were funny."

But even though he said it was great, I could tell something was wrong. Something in his eyes told me I'd hurt his feelings. In his mind, he knew it was a joke, he knew I didn't mean anything by it, but that's not how he felt. He didn't say so—I just knew.

As a comic who specializes in personal stories, I was aware that my "characters" were real people, usually family members, who could hear everything I said. But it generally wasn't an issue. My mom had come up to me after one show saying "I don't remember it that way!" I just shrugged and told her I *did* remember it that way. The next night, she was back in the front row with twenty of her friends—all gladly covered by me—laughing louder than anyone else. I felt like all my family members implicitly accepted a basic trade-off—I'd get to tell my stories, which were just as much mine as theirs, and they'd get to share in my success. So far, that had worked fine for everyone.

But those were adults. They could take it. They knew it was an act. This was my kid, my son. I didn't want to raise the issue with him directly—he was almost a teenager, I figured that would just embarrass him more. Besides, I knew he'd never just come out and tell me to take him out of my act. That wasn't his style. He'd want to show me he could take it, that he could be a man.

But I still wanted to do something to make him feel better, make him feel protected, help him understand it was all a stupid joke. From then on, I decided that anytime I told a story about Little Joe, I'd make sure *I* was the real butt of the joke.

If I talked about something crazy he did, I'd bring it right back to "but that's *nothing* compared to how nuts I am." If I talked about him masturbating, it would only be through the lens of how much I did it. If I talked about how he wanted to grow an Afro, it would only be after I made fun of how bald I was. Or in the case of the pubic hair story, I started ending it with a zinger about me—and just how small my dick is. By the time I got done ripping myself apart, anything I said about Little Joe would pale in comparison.

Years later, I was getting ready to shoot my second Netflix special, *Comin' in Hot*. In all this time, I'd never told the classic pubic hair story for TV before. I'd done it for other shows, but not for television. It was hilarious, it killed. But something about that look Little Joe had given me the first time he'd heard the joke made me hold back from sharing it with the entire world.

Minutes before showtime, Little Joe found me backstage.

"Dad, are you gonna do that joke about my pubic hair?" he asked me.

"Um," I said, hesitating. "I really don't think—"

"You *have* to do it," he said. "Close with it. It's the best you've got."

I was so blown away by his maturity. His mother and I always said he was an old soul. In a way he handled the situation better than I did.

It had been one of the first times I really understood that I couldn't treat Little Joe exactly like a buddy of mine. Some boundaries weren't just healthy for our relationship, they were necessary. Being father and son *and* friends wasn't an easy balancing act; it would require constant evolving, constant give-and-take. But I knew that as long as we communicated with each other, as long as we continued to respect and love each other, we'd get it right.

That night, with Little Joe behind me, with his support, I went out there and crushed.

☙

"MOM, WHAT DO YOU WANT for Christmas?"

It was December, and for the first time in our lives we weren't counting change. I wanted to spoil my mama.

"Josep," my mom said. "As long as our family is healthy and the children are healthy and I am healthy, that's all I want for Christmas. Everyone to be healthy."

"All right, cool," I said with a shrug. "Looks like everyone is healthy."

"And maybe a Louis Vuitton purse—so I can put all my healthy pictures in it."

Oh, sorry. That's a Louis *Buitton* purse. "Buitton," with a "B." For some reason, every Filipino mom wants one; it's considered the ultimate status symbol. My mom was using the exact same tactic she had used that night she played the Wii for the very first time—those not-so-subtle hints to let me know what she *really* wanted. All so she could clutch it to her left side, and turn it into the most expensive lunchbox in the world, carrying little bags of oyster crackers and other random-ass snacks to nibble on wherever she went.

But you know what? I loved it. I *wanted* to buy my mom fancy things, wanted her to splurge—not because I really cared about a brand-name purse, but because of what it represented. How many times had she sacrificed for me growing up? How hard had she worked to make sure we had enough to eat each night? Sure, I had never had the luxuries some of my friends had—the Nintendos, the sweet sound systems, the Polo shirts—but she always made sure we had what we needed. Now that I was finally making money, finally achieving my comedy dream, I wanted to show her and the rest of my family how much their support meant to me.

For Fred, I finally paid him the hundred dollars I lost to him when I bet him Kirk Gibson would blow it for the Dodgers in the World Series in 1988. I also paid him back for the car I wrecked, and I paid off the mortgage on the house he bought for my mom with his Keno winnings in Vegas.

I gave my dad a Ford Expedition, the least I could do for how much he supported me when I first got started as a comic—not to mention those incredible head shots he took.

For years, my sister Gemma had been helping me in her own ways, too. Back when I first started touring with the Black Comedy College Tour, she was a flight attendant with United, and she'd give me her buddy passes so I could fly around the country for free. Once my career took off, I noticed that whenever I had an assistant who screwed things up, Gemma was always there to clean up the mess and make things right. She was smart, she worked her butt off like everyone in my family, and I could trust her with my life. So she started working on my management team.

As for Little Joe's mom, Angie, the better I did, the better she did, just like I promised. Once I'd gotten past all my initial jealousy, once I'd embraced everything Angie meant to Little Joe, we'd turned into a real-life version of the TV show *Modern Family*. She and I were like the best married couple who were no longer married. There was nothing romantic between us, we both saw other people, but we were the best of friends, we hung out all the time, and we raised our son together, as coequal parents. So, the more money I made, the bigger my child support checks got. Every time I moved into a new place, I'd move her, too. I got a condo, she got the condo next door. I got a house, she got the house next door. All so we could keep being a real family for our son.

For myself? I bought a very expensive mask, and it probably saved my life.

I'd been sleeping like shit for years. I honestly don't know how people let me up onstage, because I looked like hell. Rings under my eyes, walking like a zombie, my breathing labored and ragged.

I have sleep apnea. And after I'd arrived in LA it started to get *really* bad. When I fell asleep it sounded like I was choking, because I really was.

Ackkkkkkkkk! Aaaackkkkkkkkkkk!

I was single and I never wanted to have women stay over, because whenever I fell asleep they thought I was dying a violent death, so it wasn't exactly great for my sex life.

I was so tired, I started falling asleep behind the wheel all the time. Whenever I came to a stop—literally anytime I'd stop my car for more than thirty seconds—I'd doze off. My foot would drift off the brake, and my car would start moving forward while I slept. I rear-ended so many cars. I hit a truck at a stop sign and another guy in a parking lot. On the highway I rear-ended a Volvo with Little Joe in the back in his car seat.

A few weeks after that one, I was headed to an audition at Fox when I came to a stop on the way into the parking structure, and it happened *again*. Pulled off to the side to explain to the other driver what happened, and the lady I hit gave me a funny look.

"Are you the comedian from the Laugh Factory?"

"Yeah!" I said. "Jo Koy! Have we met?"

"Yeah," she said. "I'm Bob Saget's assistant. This is his car."

That's Bob Saget, comedian and star of both *Full House* and *America's Funniest Home Videos*, worth approximately one billion times as much as I was.

Oops.

Lucky for me, his assistant did me a *huge* favor and promised not to tell Bob what I had done. I got the feeling she wasn't exactly supposed to be driving his car herself. But it worked out for me because he never found out I crushed the entire bumper of his car to the tune of $2,000.

(Hey, Bob, if you're out there, I owe you two thousand bucks. I really hope you're not out there.)

Shit was bad. I mean, I'd always been a bad driver, but not *this* bad. This was frightening.

When I could finally afford it, I practically raced to a sleep clinic. Luckily, no crashes on the way. To run their study, they hooked me up to a mask and stuck tons of wires to my fingers and chest. I was supposed to sleep through the whole night so they could do a thorough diagnosis, but five minutes after I conked out the dude ran in and woke me up.

"Holy fuck," he said. "It's been a long time since I've seen one this bad. You have the breathing of a four-hundred-pound man!"

So, I bought myself an oxygen mask for sleeping, called a C-PAP, and it changed my life. It was like I went from seeing in black and white to seeing everything in the brightest, sharpest color. I took that thing with me everywhere, even on the road.

Didn't improve my sex life, though, because now when I went to bed I looked as appealing as Bane from *Batman*.

෴

ONCE MY CAREER TOOK OFF, my life started changing in other ways, too. Comics I'd grown up watching on television, guys I'd *idolized* my entire life—I got to meet them. I got to become friends with them. It was as if I was invited into the club I had always wanted to join.

Everyone from *Def Comedy Jam*'s Cedric the Entertainer, who I got to open for, to Dave Foley from *The Kids in the Hall*, who sat next to me at the Just for Laughs festival. I even got to solve a

mystery that had been haunting me—eating away at my soul!—
ever since I'd seen the movie *Deuce Bigalow: Male Gigolo* in 1999,
when I finally got a chance to hang out with Hollywood's other
half-Filipino comic, Rob Schneider.

I know—strong statement about *Deuce Bigalow: Male Gigolo*.
But I'm not exaggerating, and every Filipino reading this book
will understand when I say why. During the movie, Deuce Bigalow's dad, pretty much out of nowhere, says his wife used to make
him the best raspberry *bibinka*. Now, *bibinka* is an iconic Filipino
dessert, delicious baked rice cakes, and when I heard one of our
native foods mentioned in a mainstream movie, I was so proud.
And everyone sitting around me in the theater knew about it: *He
said "bibinka," that's a Filipino dessert! Trust me, it's so good, you'd
love it!*

But there was one problem. There is no such thing as "raspberry" *bibinka*. The flavors simply don't go together. It's like saying meat loaf ice cream. It makes no sense. There's no way Rob
Schneider wouldn't know this—so why would he allow it? Why
would he put in a reference to our culture, only to get it so incredibly wrong?

I loved the reference, and I hated it. And it had been burning
a hole in my brain for more than a decade when I finally got a
chance to ask him after a night at the Laugh Factory.

"Rob, why raspberry *bibinka* in *Deuce Bigalow*? Why? There's
no such thing!"

"Aw, man," he sighed. "Originally it was just *bibinka*. I put it in
because I wanted people to know my mom was Filipino. But the
writers made me add the 'raspberry' because they thought no one
would know what it was. At least with raspberry, it would kind of
sound like a dessert, right? I didn't want to do it, but I knew why
we had to do it."

It all made sense. And in a way it was reassuring. We all had to make our sacrifices when it came to being accepted in America. Even Rob Schneider. Even *bibinka*.

"Man," I said. "That's such a relief. I hated you for so long."

But by far the biggest impact on my life was made by another *Saturday Night Live* alum, Jon Lovitz.

I was hanging out at the Laugh Factory after a show one night with a few other comics when the door opened and he walked in. It was like Elvis walking into a Vegas hotel. The crowd just parted for this guy, that's how much the comedy community worshipped him.

Growing up, I'd watched *Saturday Night Live* religiously. Other people might've had plans on a Saturday night, but I was staying home watching my show. And Jon Lovitz was one of my favorites. I did impressions of all his biggest characters—Annoying Man, Harvey Fierstein, and Tommy Flanagan, the Pathological Liar. "Yeah! That's the ticket!" And I was good, too. Put me next to the TV, close your eyes, and you would *not* be able to tell the difference between Jon Lovitz and me.

Now here he was, standing just a few feet away.

Jamie Masada, the owner and the same guy who forced me to start telling stories about my mom, came over and introduced us. I was starstruck, hoping Jon Lovitz would be a warm, encouraging, enthusiastic guy. Like "Oh, it's nice to meet you! You do comedy? How amazing! Give me a hug!"

Not so much. He barely looked at me.

"Oh. Hi."

And then he walked away without another word.

Now, Jon was an improv guy; he'd never really done standup. Jamie was trying to convince him to go up onstage and give it a try. But Jon is naturally hilarious, so pretty soon, he wasn't just trying standup, he was doing it two or three times a week and headlining his own show on Wednesday. But with me he was never anything but standoffish.

Until one day I got a call.

"Hi, Jo Koy. It's me, Jon Lovitz."

This living legend, calling me up on the phone! Why?

"Hey, Jon!" I said. "How are you?"

"I just want to say you're really funny, and I love watching you."

"Thank you, man," I stammered. "You watch me? I didn't know."

"I watch you from the balcony."

Turned out motherfucking Jon Lovitz would sit in the shadows watching me perform all the time. He liked my act so much he invited me to start opening for him on Wednesday nights. Of course, I accepted.

Wham. Next thing you know, I'm best friends with Jon Lovitz.

I was hanging out with him, shopping with him, eating dinner with him, going out at night, on weekends. He went on the road and took me with him. I opened for him in Hawaii. I was on the beach with Jon Lovitz.

He'd introduce me to people, tell them I was great, then make me do my amazing Jon Lovitz impersonation. So, I'd stand there impersonating Jon Lovitz for Jon Lovitz and his friends.

One night in LA, he called me up.

"I want you to come to a restaurant with me," he said, pausing dramatically. "I own it."

Which meant he owned a small percentage of it, but I wasn't going to argue with my best friend, Jon Lovitz.

We got to the place, and right off the bat our table was bombarded. Random people and celebrities alike, including Nick

Lachey, and Jose Canseco and his wife, who sent over two apple martinis, which was weird because (1) apple martinis, and (2) neither of us drank.

"See this, Jo Koy?" Jon Lovitz said to me. "This is what happens when you're famous."

I thanked Mr. and Mrs. Canseco very politely for the apple martinis. Then suddenly Jon's jaw dropped.

"Oh no," he said.

It was Andy Dick, the notoriously crass, unpredictable comic who's been in a lot of things, but is mostly famous for being Andy Dick.

It was well known around Los Angeles that Jon and Andy did *not* get along. Jon blamed Andy Dick for the death of his dear friend Phil Hartman. Rumor was that Andy got Phil Hartman's wife back into drugs after she'd gotten sober. Her drug use eventually led to that horrible moment when Phil's wife killed both Phil and herself. Andy denied it all, but everyone knew Jon couldn't stand him.

The night had just taken a sharp turn from very cool to incredibly intense. Because right now Andy Dick was shit-faced, obnoxious, and loud as hell.

"Hi, Jon!" he said. He was with three other dudes, one of them was his brother, and they looked like they didn't want any part of this interaction.

"Just go away!" Jon said. "I don't like you!"

"Ooooh!" Andy said, flapping his hands in Jon's face. "Jon, you're so loud!"

Jon stood up. This was starting to feel like it was going to turn into a real fight. I just wanted to have dinner at the restaurant that my best friend Jon Lovitz only partially owns.

"Get out of here!" Jon shouted.

"Or what," Andy said. "Are you scared I'm gonna put the Phil Hartman hex on you?"

Jon exploded.

"Get the fuck out of here! Get the fuck out!"

The three guys Andy Dick were with grabbed him and actually picked him up, I mean physically hoisted him off the ground like he was a wet log, and while they were struggling, Andy Dick somehow grabbed our goddamn apple martinis from Jose Canseco and downed them both.

"Looks like you won't be drinking these!"

Andy Dick was flailing and squirming and slopping apple martini all over himself, and these dudes were trying to carry him through the restaurant toward the door. And that's not easy, you know? This was a whole human body they were hauling away like a big old Persian rug, bumping into chairs and tables with Andy yelling the whole time.

"Ooooooh! Ooooooooooh! I'm putting a voodoo curse on you! Ooooooooooooh!"

For a while it almost felt like Andy Dick was following Jon around, trying to provoke him.

He even came to the Laugh Factory one time, and Jon shoved him up against a wall after Andy got in his face. I actually had to get in there to separate them.

It was surreal being in the middle of all this, but also very hard to see Jon in so much pain. He wasn't just a comedy legend anymore, he wasn't just a celebrity on TV. He had legitimately become my friend. And whether it was my good company, my spot-on impression of him, or my ability to break up his fights, I endeared myself to Jon, too. He gave me an amazing gift after I opened for him one night at the famous Cobb's Comedy Club in San Francisco.

"I have a special friend at the show tonight," Jon told me in the greenroom. "He's coming upstairs right now."

I turned around and who did I see but Dana Fucking Carvey. One of the greatest comics and impressionists of all time.

Me being me, I got all choked up.

"Thank you so much for inspiring me," I said, hugging him. "I grew up watching you, man. You're one of the reasons I do standup."

"It's cool, man," Dana said, patting me on the back. "You're great!"

Jon, however, was livid.

"You never said that about *me*, Jo Koy!" he shouted. "What. The. Fuck."

I got my emotions under control and patted my best friend Jon Lovitz on the shoulder apologetically. Then I handed him my camera.

"Jon, could you please take a picture of us?"

Jon Lovitz snapped the shot.

"You son of a bitch."

⁊

WHEN LITTLE JOE HIT HIGH SCHOOL, it was clear I'd entered a new era of fatherhood, one with even more challenges to our relationship—and more struggles to define the boundary between fatherhood and friendship.

I knew everything was going to change the day before he started the ninth grade.

"So, I'll see you at lunch tomorrow, right?" I asked. "Bring your favorite Taco Bell?"

"Nah," he answered. "That's cool, Dad."

I looked at him, horrified. This had been our tradition for six years! This was our thing!

"Are you sure?"

"Yeah, I'm sure," he said. "There's open campus. I'll just go to McDonald's with the guys."

He didn't even need me for fast food anymore! Even when he was home, his bedroom door had always been open to me before, but now it was closed.

All. The. Time.

He'd be on his phone with his friends, playing video games with his friends, texting with his friends. And I'd be sitting outside his room, devastated, pathetic, pawing meekly at his door.

"Hey, uh, wanna go to the mall? Wanna—wanna get something to eat? I'll buy!"

I'd hear his muffled voice from inside his room:

"Can't! Playing video games with my friends!"

And I'd practically break down sobbing.

"But I thought *I* was your friend!"

I still don't question my overall approach to raising my son. A lot of parents try to forbid their teenagers from drinking. My own mom didn't "allow" me to drink when I was in high school. But that never stopped me. Sure, sometimes if I needed a ride when I'd been drinking, I'd call her, like those nights at the 7-Eleven, and she didn't get too mad. But if I was at a party and didn't want to deal with one of her guilt trips, I'd get in a car with my drunk friends instead. It's a miracle I never got hurt.

I didn't want to take any chances with Little Joe. I told him that when I was fifteen I drank with my friends, so there was no reason to lie—I knew. I didn't condone it, but I also knew there was no way I could realistically stop him from doing it. It might make me unhappy, but I'd be a lot unhappier if he drove with his drunk buddies or took an Uber and passed out in the backseat of a sketchy car. So if it happened and he needed a ride, he was to call me, no matter the time, no matter the place, and I'd pick him up. No questions asked.

And it's worked. There've been times when he's called me from a house party—doesn't even say he's been drinking, just asks for a ride—and I've picked him up, just like I was picking up a friend. I don't interrogate him, don't give him a hard time. I just want to get him home safely.

But honestly? Those times are few and far between. I think a big reason teenagers drink is that they like rebelling, they like breaking the rules and trying to hide shit from their parents. But if you take that stigma away, if you show them you trust them, they respect that. Little Joe knows he doesn't have to prove anything to me by breaking the rules, so he doesn't.

Mostly.

There have been moments when my philosophy didn't work. In the ninth grade, my son got caught shoplifting from Macy's. *Shoplifting.*

"What the fuck are you doing?" I yelled at him when we got home from the store. "We're so fortunate! You don't need to steal!"

He sat there shaking his head.

"Man," he said, "I should've ran."

I couldn't believe my ears.

"What did you just say?"

"When the security guy saw me, I should've ran!"

"What the fuck?" I exploded. "I'm *glad* you got caught! Do you realize how stupid this is? You know I'll buy you whatever you want! I'm so disappointed right now. So disappointed."

Of course, I shoplifted all the time when I was Little Joe's age. Shit, I stole when I was even younger than him. But I felt like I didn't have a choice. We were poor as fuck! He had everything he wanted and more. He had no excuse at all. Maybe I'd been going too easy on him? Maybe I was too soft?

After all, I'd dealt with a lot of shit growing up, but that shit also made me who I was. In a way, my dad's absence made me a stronger person. My mom's doubt made me work harder to achieve my dreams. Hell, some of my funniest material came from my darkest days, my deepest disappointments.

Then I thought about how my own parents punished me when I'd been caught stealing. Like *for real* punished.

That first time I got caught shoplifting, when—I swear—I was only following my sister Rowena's example, and I got busted swiping a Michael Jackson album, my dad didn't give a shit about my excuses. He was so mad, he made the military cop take me back to their jail and book me, just to scare me. When we finally got home, as we were unloading our groceries he threw a gallon of milk straight at my chest. It exploded all over me, leaving me in tears.

And my mom? She never hit me when I was growing up, but if I fucked up she'd use straight-up psychological warfare. When I got caught stealing those transit passes from school, she made me feel like the lowest life-form on the face of the earth. She never let me forget that day.

But what did all that punishment really achieve? Yeah, it gave me some funny jokes. But mainly it just made me resent my parents. It drove us further apart. It didn't earn my respect. And it definitely didn't stop me from stealing again.

Little Joe knows there's a line he can't cross. He knows that even though we're friends, he can't argue with me like we're friends. When I'm angry, he listens. The rule is that he gets one chance to really fuck up. One. I'll yell at him, maybe take away his phone for a few days, and then it's over. But if he does the same thing a second time? Then there will be real consequences.

Honestly, I have no idea what those consequences will be—but that's because so far there hasn't been a second time.

Sure, he messes up the way boys his age do. Sometimes he takes what I give him for granted. Sometimes I wish he'd work harder, think more about his future, the kind of stuff all parents wish about their teenagers. But I'm proud to have him as my friend. He's a good kid. He's grounded. Like I said, he's an old soul.

In fact, in lots of ways he reminds me of myself when I was younger. He looks like me—back when I still had hair, anyway. He wears the same kind of glasses I wore when I was his age, schoolboy Sally Jesse Raphael specs. He even sucks at math like me. You know what he got caught stealing?

Polo.

The exact same brand *I* used to steal back when I was in high school.

It's like he's mirroring me. In fact, the older he's grown, the more I've seen him mirroring me in another way, too.

He's funny.

Not just funny the way kids are, you know? He isn't making his friends laugh by making fart noises. He has a real sense of timing. He's witty, able to improvise and think on his feet. When he walks into a room, he owns it. Even if it's packed with people he hardly knows, he wins them over, and the next thing you know they're all standing around him, laughing. Just like I'd won new friends over when I was a kid, moving from base to base.

The closer he got to graduating from high school, the more I hoped. Maybe someday he'd find that same passion, that same fire I had when I was young. Maybe someday Little Joe would take that natural gift and channel it into comedy just like his dad.

e⁄ɔ

THEN AGAIN, MAYBE I WASN'T exactly the best role model.

As grateful as I was for all my success—and I was incredibly grateful—I started to feel like my career was plateauing.

I was still hungry, I was still doing the work, trying to be funnier. Some comics will put together a single set and then use the same material for a few years. Not me. I was constantly honing my act, constantly evolving. If I had a big show coming up, I'd workshop my set for weeks in advance. Put me up in some café in front of seven people with all the lights on and a fridge humming in the back—if I can make those fuckers laugh, I can make anyone laugh. I loved the art, I loved the discipline. It was, and is, my passion.

But I was hitting a wall.

I'd developed a solid fan base, and I could play bigger venues than I'd ever been able to play before, not just clubs but full theaters. But my fan base had stopped growing, I wasn't bringing on new people. When I toured, I might be able to sell out one show in a major city like Miami or Toronto, but I couldn't sell out a second. I couldn't sell out abroad. I couldn't fill a stadium. My momentum had stalled.

And television? I felt like I kept getting close to the kind of revolutionary vehicle that would capture all the nuance of my story, my comedy, my identity. Something light-years beyond an ethnic-themed show.

But every time I got close, I ran head-on into the same racial ignorance I'd experienced when I first moved to California.

In 2008, I partnered with a couple of TV producers, Mike Clement and Tom Werner. Tom was the genius behind *The Cosby Show, Roseanne, Third Rock from the Sun*—some of the biggest, most iconic sitcoms of all time. So, the dude knew what he was doing, and he loved an idea of mine, an animated TV show all about my dysfunctional family life.

We pitched the show to all the major networks, ABC, CBS, NBC, FOX, you name it. We'd get into the room with these TV execs and tell them that this show was the future. It was "diverse"—the catchphrase that basically meant "not-white"—and it was relatable, it was authentic, it represented the real face of America instead of some airbrushed, whitewashed bullshit.

And one by one these suits would give us this blank look.

"I just don't know if Middle America will be able to, uh, get this . . ."

"So, um, with the whole Filipino thing, what I'm trying to wrap my head around is . . ."

What the fuck was there to wrap their heads around? It was a family comedy, just like *Roseanne* had been, just like *The Cosby Show* had been, just like *Full House* had been. This family just happened to be Filipino. I had stories about my mom playing Nintendo Wii with my son. You couldn't get any more universal than that. What was the issue here? Did they want my mom to speak without an accent? Because it was just as hilarious either way.

"Uh-huh," the execs would say. "I just think we might, uh, have an issue with relatability . . ."

At one of the meetings Tom jumped to his feet.

"This story needs to be told! It's the funniest thing I've ever seen!"

My fans all over the country, from Nashville to Seattle to Miami, would've agreed with Tom. Audiences everywhere, people of all colors, were eating up my material, but the entertainment industry was clearly way behind the viewers they were supposed to cater to. Even with all my mainstream success, even with one of the biggest producers in entertainment *history* backing me, I still couldn't get past Hollywood's prejudice. We got nowhere.

Feeling more and more depressed, I was walking into the MTV lobby to take yet another meeting that would amount to absolutely nothing, when guess who popped out of the elevator?

My old buddy Barry Katz, the guy I turned down for *Kims of Comedy*, wearing his trademarked leather jacket with a fringe, and walking with all-star magician Lance Burton.

Of course, having cut my teeth in Vegas, I was most excited to see Lance Burton, who performed for thousands of people every week at the Monte Carlo, and who looked absolutely mesmerizing in a black tie–less tuxedo.

But Barry made sure the focus stayed on him.

I was holding an unopened Diet Dr Pepper, and Barry walked up, reached out, and took it from my hand. Then he cracked it open and took a long, deep sip.

"That's what you get for saying no to Barry Katz," he said. "A Diet Dr Pepper is the least you can do."

Then he walked out of the lobby with Lance Burton floating majestically behind him—my soda in his hand.

"Who was that?" a bewildered MTV assistant asked me.

"Barry Katz, man," I said. "Barry Katz."

Then, in 2009, I thought I had my vindication. Comedy Central gave me my own hour-long special, *Don't Make Him Angry*— "him" being a reference to my son, who by this point was as big a part of my standup as my mom. I'd been dreaming of a special like this for years. No theme show, no sharing the stage with other comics. Just delivering my best material about my life, my family, and my background for an hour.

But after it aired, Comedy Central buried it.

They showed it once, but a network like Comedy Central

doesn't live off premieres, it lives off replaying its content on a regular rotation. They'll take their specials and replay them dozens and dozens of times, in prime time, during the day, in the morning, whenever. And that's how you, as a comic, get your exposure. That's how you grow your fan base.

But after Comedy Central first aired my special, they didn't show it again until three months later in the middle of the night, and after that barely ever again. I did another special with them three years later, and they buried that one, too. I had no idea why. They wouldn't even give me clips to promote on my YouTube channel. They just weren't talent friendly. It started to feel like the iconic Comedy Central of old was gone. Like they weren't hungry anymore, like they'd stopped innovating, like they were dying a slow death. None of which was helping me.

"It's like you're right there at the hump," my manager told me, "but we just can't get you over."

A couple of years later, I finally had a solution.

It definitely wasn't Comedy Central. It wasn't HBO, the premium channel whose comedy specials with Eddie Murphy and George Carlin had changed my life growing up. It was a whole new platform with an international reach that blew everyone else out of the water.

It was Netflix.

There was just one little problem. If I wanted a special with Netflix, I was gonna have to hustle the exact same way I had for my first show in the run-down Huntridge Theater back in Vegas.

I was going to have to do it all on my own.

12

IMMIGRANT
REVOLUTION

It was a Saturday night, and I was up onstage in front of three hundred people at the Hollywood Laugh Factory, the crowd was laughing, and I was feeling good, so I decided to let everyone in on a little secret.

"You guys, you guys!" I said. "I gotta tell you something, okay? You gotta get ready . . . for my Netflix special!"

The crowd erupted.

What I didn't tell them was that my Netflix special was such a secret, not even Netflix knew about it.

Yeah, I was lying my ass off. There was no Netflix special. None of their executives had even seen my show. But that's how bad I wanted that special. That's how bad I *needed* that special. If I kept lying about it, maybe it would come true. If I kept saying it was happening, maybe it would happen. I'd will it into existence.

But nothing was working. Nothing.

Ironically, I knew I needed Netflix thanks to my old friends at Comedy Central. They'd done virtually nothing with the first special I'd shot with them in 2009. Then, a few years after it first aired, almost as an afterthought, they licensed it to Netflix.

Bam.

Suddenly I was getting tweets from all over the world. South

Africa, Dubai, the Netherlands. Black people, white people, brown people. All commenting on my family. My comedy had truly become universal. I'd gone worldwide.

And here's the crazy part. Netflix hadn't promoted my special, either. They hadn't pushed it out at all. They'd just posted it along with all their other content, and my audience—my *brand-new* audience—had found it all on their own.

Then, just as suddenly as it started, it stopped. Comedy Central pulled my special off Netflix and decided to license it to Amazon instead. Now, don't get me wrong—Amazon is a great company and all. But I didn't get any Amazon Prime customers messaging me about how they loved watching my special while they were getting diapers delivered for free.

Instead, I got people all over the world tweeting me, "What the fuck happened to your Netflix special?" "I'm trying to find your special on Netflix, and it's gone!"

So, I knew that if I wanted to get over that hump, if I wanted to go from drawing passionate but medium-sized crowds in America to selling out giant arenas worldwide, I needed to get back on Netflix. If I could reach that many people around the world with a special no one even advertised, imagine what would happen if Netflix actually promoted it? Netflix was the answer to all my comedy problems.

I was in luck, too, because in 2015 Netflix was in the middle of a major shift in their standup strategy. For years, they'd focused on simply licensing specials like mine that had been originally produced for other networks like Comedy Central, Showtime, HBO. They'd let those guys do the work, shooting the specials, marketing them, airing them first, then Netflix could come along, pay a fee, and redistribute the content for a set period of time. Easy. But now Netflix wanted skin in the game. They wanted to finance, produce, and own their own comedy specials. The ownership part was key, because as simple as licensing content was, eventually they had to give it back to the owners. Netflix wanted to distribute this comedy forever.

They'd started slow, putting out a few specials in 2013 and 2014 from fantastic comics like Nick Offerman and my friend Chelsea Handler. But now they wanted to come on strong. They wanted to show the world that from here on out Netflix was going to be *the* destination for premium, high-profile standup.

And 2017 was going to be their coming-out party. They were planning a lineup of specials from the biggest names in comedy—Jerry Seinfeld, Amy Schumer, Jim Gaffigan, Tracy Morgan, Sarah Silverman. We're talking living legends, artists at the peaks of their powers.

So I knew two things. I had to be on Netflix. And it had to be 2017.

For the next few years, I was wearing blinders. Netflix, Netflix, Netflix. I had to get on Netflix. Comedy Central even offered me a third special of my own, claiming that this time they wouldn't bury it. My manager wanted me to take it. Money on the table, he said. But I wasn't falling for that trick again. Besides, Netflix's new standup strategy was already paying off. Fans, comics, agents, producers—*everyone* loved Netflix. I'd sensed that Comedy Central was dwindling years earlier, when they wouldn't even help me promote my own show, and I was right. They were over. Netflix was the new king of standup comedy. For me, it was Netflix or nothing else.

There was just one small problem. Netflix didn't want anything to do with me.

Actually, no—it was worse than that. In 2015, the execs at Netflix said they *might* be able to fit me into that treasured 2017 lineup, but they wanted to check out my act first, in person. They promised they'd come to my next show . . . and then they stood me up.

Then they did it again. And again. Four times, five times, six times.

It was like they were taunting me.

I did everything I could to sweeten the pot. You guys wanna fly to my show first-class? Great! It's on me. You want dinner? Cool, it's covered. A limo to the theater? Done.

Thanks! they'd say. We'll be there. Can't wait.

Each time this happened, I'd get all hyped up. Pacing back and forth in the greenroom before I went onstage. Maybe this'll be the time. They said they'd come, they promised they'd come, they have to come.

But they didn't.

Every time they failed to show up, I'd flash back to all the times I'd been rejected throughout my career, all the times people hadn't believed in me. I'd stand in the greenroom, minutes before I was supposed to go out onstage, and I'd remember the Hollywood producers who didn't think anyone would "get" my story. I'd remember the big club owners who refused to give me a shot on their big weekend stages because I wasn't white. I'd remember everything I'd been through to get to this point, all the shoes I'd stocked, all the DVDs I'd sold in parking lots, all the time I'd missed with my son traveling on the road. I'd remember all that, and I'd seethe.

Sure, maybe I wasn't performing in giant arenas in front of tens of thousands of fans—yet—but I knew that Netflix would be impressed if they bothered to show up. I was still selling out club after club. Maybe my audiences were only in the hundreds, but they were passionate, devoted, electric. I put everything I had into my performances, I poured all my energy into my act, and the crowds were giving it back to me. What more could I fucking do?

I'd choke back my tears, I'd hide my frustration, and I'd put on my game face for the crowd. No matter what happened before the show, I always delivered for my fans. I'd take all that negative energy and use it, channel it into my set. I had to be at my best. Night after night after night.

Then, I finally got a break. One of Netflix's newest executives was Robbie Praw, a pro from the Montreal Just for Laughs Festival. Robbie knew me and loved me from way back in 2005, when I'd performed in JFL's New Faces show and earned my first spot on *The Tonight Show*.

Robbie showed up. He had a great time, but even he couldn't get me a concrete answer. The slate was full for 2017 by then, he said, but there might be a spot in the 2018 lineup. Maybe. Or maybe 2019. It felt like a consolation prize.

By then I had a new manager. Joe Meloche was a former comedy promoter who I had known for years. He had an idea.

"Do you believe in yourself?" he said.

"Yes," I answered.

"All right then," he said. "Let's go. Let's shoot it ourselves."

It was decided that quickly. If Netflix wasn't going to come to my show, I'd bring my show to them.

I'd shoot my *own* special. I'd create something so awesome, so undeniably Jo Koy that Netflix would have to take it, promote it, and distribute it worldwide. I really would will my Netflix special into existence—not by lying about it to my fans, but by doing it my way.

Back when I'd put on my first show, *Jo Koy's Comedy Jam* at the Huntridge Theater in Vegas, I needed all the help I could get. Dada Supreme put up cash and supplied free clothes. My mom sold tickets and got her mechanic and optometrist as sponsors. I called in favors from every friend I had, hiring photographers, DJs, even break-dancers at amazing rates. I spent my nights posting flyers, I printed our tickets, and I cut them all out by hand. That show was my vision, my willpower, my dream, but it was a total team effort.

This time I wouldn't have that kind of assistance. Sure, producing and filming a major comedy show always takes a ton of teamwork—the stage manager, the cinematographers, the gaffers, the editors—it really does take a village. But this time was different.

This time I'd be paying for everything with my own money, and it wasn't going to come cheap. I was blowing my son's fucking college fund! Well, assuming he even went to college, given his math skills, but that's beside the point. It was a lot of money and it was frightening. But more than the money, it was the principle. I'd been doing comedy for more than twenty-five years, I'd built a following all over the country, and now I had to finance my own special because Netflix wouldn't be straight with me.

It was infuriating. But once I decided to go in—man, I was *all in*.

We booked the classic Moore Theater in Seattle for April 2016. It's the oldest theater in the city, two blocks from Pike Place Market, and with eighteen hundred seats, it is massive. Being from Tacoma, thirty miles away, I had been claimed by Seattle as its own. The Moore was the first major venue I'd ever sold out, but for this shoot I'd need to sell out *twice*.

That's right, to get all the footage we needed to edit the special, I had to do two live shows. I'd never sold out two back-to-back shows in my life. It only felt right to risk it all on my home turf.

We hired two fantastic directors, and I told them my special had to feel premium. From the time I was a kid, I'd always bought—or shoplifted—the most fashionable, high-end brands. Polo, Ralph

Lauren, Dada. Now I'd moved on to Gucci, Prada, the best of the best. That's what I wanted for my special. I'd done my research; I'd seen what happened when other specials cut corners.

"See this comic?" I told my team as we watched our tenth special together. "I've seen him live, and he's a thousand times funnier than this. I can't even hear anyone laughing; they didn't mic the theater. I want our special to look and sound like a million bucks!"

Well, they took me literally.

Up until then, I had no idea what the title "Executive Producer" meant. It sounded like a cool credit to have on a TV show or movie, but yeah—once I took on the EP role, I found out the truth. Every single extra cost had to be approved by me. And each approval was painful.

"Okay, so the stage *could* be a wood floor, which is kind of rustic, or we can lay in this amazing black flooring . . . for an extra $7,000."

"We *could* just mic the stage, or we could mic every inch of the theater . . . for an extra $11,000."

"We *could* get some of these guys to handle your lighting, or we could hire this dude who did all the lighting for Bruce Willis's projects . . . that's $80,000."

I said yes to everything, because I wanted the quality, but deep down I was freaking out. What if I spent all this money, and Netflix didn't want to buy my special? What if *no one* wanted to buy it?

I guess I could always go back to selling DVDs out of the trunk of my car.

I was so desperate for everything to go absolutely perfectly at the tapings, I didn't even invite my family. At my Comedy Central specials, everyone had ended up bickering about shit. At my first special, *Don't Make Him Angry*, my mom got upset because my dad was seated a row or two behind her in the audience. Normally this might not have been a big deal, except she knew the camera was going to get a shot of her during the show. The last thing she wanted was for this man who'd left her on her own for so many years to appear with her—even in the background—smiling and laughing on national TV.

I got it. I really did. I'd suffered through that past myself.

But that night shouldn't have been about the past. It should've been about putting on the absolute best show possible for my very first special.

I asked my dad to move to a different section so he wouldn't be in the shot, and he said no problem. Issue resolved. But the whole thing had been a huge drain on my energy. Instead of focusing on getting ready to go onstage, I'd been resolving a minor family crisis. Of course I still put my game face on before showtime, just like every time the Netflix executives failed to show up. If you watch that special, you won't be able to see a thing wrong with me. You'll just be laughing your ass off.

But I didn't need that kind of drama in Seattle. This time, I didn't want any distractions, any negativity from last-minute arguments. This time, I needed pure positivity.

This time, nothing could go wrong.

The shows were set for March and Seattle came through for me. Like a miracle, I sold out both shows, every single seat. But most of the ticket sales went to pay the directors, so my ass was still on the line in every single way.

And guess what?

The whole time leading up to the taping I'd still been grinding on the road, touring hard, and the day before the first show, I came down with walking pneumonia. I don't normally get sick like that, but I was coming off eighteen shows all over the country. And more than that, there was the unique pressure of this moment, this all-or-nothing show. So much stress, so much exhaustion, so much riding on everything going right. And here I was with red eyes, a scratchy throat, congestion. I was a barely living, barely breathing Nyquil commercial.

Plus, it was Seattle, so of course the forecast for the day of the first show was nothing but rain and storms. Not only did that suck for my health, it meant the theater would be sticky and wet, and the whole audience would have raincoats and umbrellas. On a technical level, that meant it would be hard for the editors to intercut shots of the two crowds—the first night's crowd would be in raincoats and soaking wet, and the second night's wouldn't. But more important was the mood. My mood, the audience's mood— who wants to have fun when it's gray outside and they're wet and miserable? Suddenly I remembered why I'd been so happy to move to the sunshine of Vegas all those years before. So much for nothing going wrong.

I crashed as soon as I got to my hotel room, slept a groggy, fitful sleep, and woke up the next morning to film the first show in a pitiful state.

"Uh, I think I need medical attention."

A doctor came to my hotel room and shot me up full of steroids and B$_{12}$, and then the most amazing thing happened.

Someone opened up the curtains, and it was sunny outside. Blue skies, 72 degrees with a nice breeze. The most perfect Seattle day I'd ever experienced.

Okay, I could do this!

There were lines around the corner at the theater, no umbrellas necessary, and I knocked the first show out of the park. Like I'd never been sick a day in my life. I was Superman.

The next night, for the second show, I struggled. My throat was killing me, even though I did my best to hide it. I hoped we had enough great footage to make the edit work. Besides, we had no other option.

I got back to LA and spent three straight days in an editing bay, poring over every shot, every angle, from the first joke to the last. This thing had cost me so much, but it was incredible seeing it all captured on tape. That Bruce Willis lighting guy was worth every penny. There was light in every balcony, every crack, and every crevice. And the sound? We had mics everywhere. We had laughter from the lobby, laughter from the dude buying popcorn, laughter from the people waiting in line outside. There was so much laughter, it almost sounded canned.

Once it was done, I could barely bring myself to watch the final cut of *Live from Seattle*. That's how terrified I was.

We sent the special out to anyone who'd consider it, every network, every studio, every distributor. The more people who wanted it, we figured, the more leverage we'd have when it came to the sale. Except no one bit. Comedy Central passed—probably angry that I'd turned down their earlier offer. Then a small company offered us about half of what we'd paid to produce the thing.

Is this for real right now? I thought. I was gutted. This couldn't have all been for nothing.

Then Netflix finally got around to watching it. As soon as they did, they called.

"Don't take this anywhere else. We'll make an offer."

Suddenly, 2017—the year I'd been told was full, the year Netflix was releasing all their best, most prestigious standup— miraculously opened up. They bought my special and released it in March, between specials from Amy Schumer and Louis CK.

And just like that, everything changed.

The day Netflix posted my special, millions of people watched it around the world. Everyone started pulling clips and posting them everywhere, all over the internet, going viral. Watching, sharing, watching, sharing, the view count growing and growing and growing.

Almost overnight, my entire tour sold out for the next six months. I sold out Australia, I sold out Amsterdam, I sold out around the world. Not just clubs, but huge, massive theaters. I sold out 23,000 seats in Hawaii alone.

The first live show after the special aired, I knew. There was an energy in the air, a crackling. These weren't my die-hard fans who were seeing me for the second time, the third time, the fifth time. These were first-timers. They were here because they had seen my special. They were new fans. They wanted to be a part of something big, something fresh.

That something was me.

The risk had paid off.

∞

EVEN AFTER ALL THESE YEARS, even after everything I've accomplished, I still feel like my mom doesn't really get it.

Don't get me wrong. She's supportive and proud of me in her own way. She loves bringing tons of people to my shows, and she's very thankful when I donate seats and merchandise to the Filipino charities she works with. I mean, shit, at this point I don't just mention her in my act—she's *part* of my act. I release videos starring the two of us, trying Filipino food, searching through her Louis Buitton purse, on a regular basis. They rack up millions of views, people can't get enough.

But part of her still thinks of my comedy career as a hobby. Like entertainment can't be a real job, doesn't require real work or real sacrifice. She thinks when I do standup or appear on TV, I get picked up by a limo, say a few funny things, eat some lobster, and go to bed. Even after all these years, my mom still has a skewed view of what I do.

"That's your life, Josep! You're funny, that's what you do! What's the big deal?"

She doesn't understand the hours, the days, the weeks of preparation that go into every one of my bits. All of the time I spend workshopping my act in front of tiny audiences for no money at all, honing my timing, perfecting my delivery, making sure that when I go on TV in front of millions of people I'll give them the best fucking show they could possibly ask for.

It's like no matter how hard I work, no matter how much I sacrifice, somewhere deep down she'll always think of what I do as "being a clown." And yes, she still thinks I should find a regular job with decent benefits.

"Sure, you got money now, but what if you get sued? You need something to fall back on!"

It hurts. Even after so many years, and the success, my mother's attitude hurts. This isn't just happening to me. I *made* it happen. But I also know that I wouldn't be the man I am today without my mom—without her own sacrifices, without her own hard work and love. She had talent, too, she loved music and the creative work she did back in the Philippines, and she gave it all up so she could work in a bank, sell *lumpia* on the side, and raise her kids in America. Even after I broke her heart by dropping out of college, she still let me live under her roof for years, got her optometrist to sponsor my first big show, bought a car for my little family so her grandson would be safe. That stubbornness of hers? That inability to take no for an answer? Where do you think I got the strength I needed to fight my way to the top in an almost impossible industry? My mother is a contradiction. I have made peace with that. Though at times, she still drives me absolutely crazy. I pick up the phone, hear her say *"Josep!"* and I think "Uh-oh, what's coming next."

I'd be nothing without my mom—and I wouldn't have half of my best stories.

⁋

THEN THERE'S FRED—solid, dependable, tell-it-how-you-see-it Fred, my mom's husband and my strongest father figure in high school—he's a little different than my mom. He's still evolving. He still surprises me.

A few months ago, I was watching a documentary about Desert Storm, and a soldier who'd fought in Iraq talked about his experiences there, describing what it was like to come home and try to manage all the trauma, all the strain, all the memories. He'd starting drinking, doing drugs. He'd become abusive in his relationships. He was suffering from PTSD.

It made me think of Fred—not because Fred had been like that guy, but because he hadn't. Fred had gotten shot up and injured twice in Vietnam, but he'd never seemed crazy or out of control to me. Sure, he drank, but a lot of people drank. He was always cool, always fun, and he definitely never said anything about PTSD.

Was he just wired different? A stronger kind of man? I didn't know.

A couple of days later, I was standing in the parking lot of a Best Buy with Fred. We'd just finished shopping, and he turned to me. He's a hard-looking man with a tough, intimidating face, but for once his face looked soft, frightened.

"I never yelled at your mama," he told me. "I want you to know that. But I seen some shit back in the war, and I want you to know that, too."

"Okay, Fred," I said, listening, taking it in.

"I been trying to deal with it on my own, Bubba. I didn't want to take those drugs they give us, those antidepressants. Those drugs make me a bad person. But I need to start talking to somebody. I gotta see a therapist. I need to talk to somebody about what I saw."

And it all made sense to me. Fred's drinking, the way he'd buried his feelings, the few things he'd said when we watched those old Vietnam movies together. Fred *had* suffered from PTSD. He'd just been suffering silently.

Years ago, when I'd paid off their mortgage, I'd hugged Fred and told him I never wanted my mother and him to worry about money again.

"You just worry about yourself now, Fred," I said. "You take care of yourself."

It was the first time I'd ever seen him cry. The parking lot was the second. To this day, all I really want is for Fred to take care of himself. I don't know why he chose that moment to open up to me the way he did. But I'm so grateful for it. I'm grateful that I can give Fred the kind of support he gave me when I was a kid, when I needed it most. I can be a son to him, just as he was a father to me.

❦

MY BROTHER, ROBERT, IS STILL in and out of a Washington institution, playing the same game—getting "better" by taking his meds, getting released back to the streets, then getting himself reinstitutionalized when he gets tired of living life on his own.

I still almost never visit him. It's selfish of me, I know, and I feel guilty. Life gets in the way, not just for me, but for my sisters and my mom, too. We try our best to keep in touch, to at least call every now and then, but a lot of times we don't even do that much. Honestly, it's just too painful dealing with his complete disconnect from reality.

You know who does visit him?

My dad.

My dad, who doesn't even live in Washington. Who's not even Robert's biological father. Who put up with years of Robert's physical and mental abuse.

He's the only member of our family who still visits Robert on a regular basis, whenever one of his airline's flights takes him to Seattle. He brings him clothes, he brings him shoes, he brings him cigarettes. He does *not* bring him Pepsi.

No one knew he was doing this. I only know because I looked at the visitors' log one of the very few times I went to see Robert myself, and there, next to Robert's name, was my dad's signature. Hundreds of them.

I called my dad after I found out. My eyes were opened, and I understood that he was more family to Robert than any of his "real" family, including me.

"What you do for Robert," I told him, "that makes up for everything else."

My dad has made so many mistakes. He would admit it. I spent years of my life being mad at him, and for good reason. But he was young, he was in over his head. I understand that now. Now I can forgive.

My father didn't have to start being a better dad to me. He didn't have to support me as I fought to break into comedy. He didn't have to keep visiting Robert, year after year. But he did, and I love him for it.

ᴄ⌇

I COULDN'T SLEEP THE OTHER NIGHT.

I tried to take some melatonin, but nothing worked. I couldn't stop thinking. I was stuck in my own head.

We'd just arrived home from the trip we take to Hawaii every summer. Little Joe and all his cousins, loving life for two weeks. It is a tradition now, pure vacation mode, and so much fun.

At the airport, Little Joe had come up to me.

"Dad, you know what I realized? I'm seventeen years old now. I'm just about to start my senior year. You know what that means? Next time we go to Hawaii, it'll be my last time as a kid. Next summer will be my last summer as a kid. My last childhood vacation."

He stood there, surrounded by his family and friends after we'd just finished one of the best trips of our lives.

"Man," he said, "I'm probably gonna cry."

Part of me was proud. Little Joe isn't little anymore. He's growing up, starting to appreciate what he has and understand how much I love him. It's amazing to watch him become a man.

But part of me was sad. Sad because I was watching his childhood slip away.

"Enjoy every minute," I told him. "Because the minutes go by fast."

Later that night, back at our house, I got into bed and started thinking about all the moments of Little Joe's life I'd missed. Everything I hadn't been around for because I was too busy touring on the road. Five birthdays. A couple of Christmases. Who knows how many smiles, how many laughs, how many hugs.

I can't go back in time. I can't rewind. I'll never get those back.

Once I started thinking, I couldn't stop. I tossed and I turned,

I took my melatonin, but I kept asking myself the same questions over and over again.

Did I have to do that show in St. Charles, Illinois, on his birthday? Why did I have to take that gig on Christmas Day? Why didn't I cut back just a little? *Just a little?*

But as painful as those questions are, as depressing as thinking about it can be, I know the answer. I did it for him.

I get to give my son a life I could've only dreamed of as a kid. At his age I didn't know how I'd pay for my next school lunch. I didn't know when I'd next see my dad. I didn't know how my story fit into this country, whether I'd be able to achieve my dream, what my future would be.

But Little Joe doesn't have to experience any of that anxiety, any of that fear. He'll never have to worry about money. I've learned from my early mistakes as a father, and his mom and I are both constant, loving, supportive parts of his life. And as for his place in America, because of pioneers in entertainment like his dad, he sees people like him on TV and the internet, hears people like him in his music. Not just different kinds of Asians, either, not just Japanese or Koreans or Chinese—but Filipinos. Half-breeds, full-breeds, whatever-breeds. We're everywhere. Little Joe feels accepted, like he belongs. This is *his* America.

A few days after my sleepless night, I took Little Joe with me to the Hollywood Laugh Factory to watch me perform.

It might be hard to believe, but this was the first time he'd been there since he was a baby. I've taken him to other shows of mine, interesting locations on my tours, but never to the Laugh Factory, where my LA journey began. The club is located right in the middle of the Sunset Strip, so he'd driven by with his friends dozens of times, seen the giant neon sign and the glowing marquee, but he'd never gone inside.

I took him up to the balcony, showed him where Tiffany Haddish would watch him while I went up onstage. I brought him backstage so he could see where all the comics hang out, showed him the light that would turn on when you hit a minute left in your act, let him study the set list, with names like Tom Green, Ken Jeong, and, of course, mine.

Little Joe was in awe. I loved watching him soak it all up. I loved seeing my two worlds, my comedy and my son, come together.

I've talked to him about being a standup like me. I even told him he could open for me at one of my own shows. I'd put him up in front of my own fans, the friendliest crowd he could possibly imagine. If he's serious about comedy, he'll still have to do all the open mics, build his own audience, pay his own dues. He'll have to grind just like I did. But I can open that door for him. I can give him the kind of help I never had when I was his age, and my mom was trying to force me to get a regular job. He can have what I always wanted.

I know he has it in him. Some people can be funny if they say the right things, tell the right jokes, work on it long enough and hard enough. But some people just *are* funny. It comes naturally to them. I was lucky enough to have that gift, and my son has it, too.

Of course, he has other talents, other interests. He likes design, he's creative. He's good with people and bad at math. He's curious about entertainment, but he hasn't pursued anything seriously yet. If only he made up his mind to focus on comedy, if only he committed himself to standup, I know he'd be great.

But you know what? This is his life, not mine. Maybe I'll let him write his own story.

☙

THIRTY YEARS AGO, I was sitting in my mom's living room, cold-calling random comedy clubs and begging to get onstage. Now I'm speaking to people of every age, color, and background. Not just in America, but around the world.

As hard as my journey has been, it feels like it's finally paying off. I've done not just one Netflix special, but three. I'm working with Steven Spielberg—Steven Spielberg!—to develop a movie based on my family. I was recently inducted into the Philippines Walk of Fame. I played the legendary LA Forum, a dream of mine, and sold out both of my shows to a total of twenty-five thousand screaming fans. And Montreal's Just for Laughs Festival—the same show that turned me down for three years only to finally give me by biggest break—named me 2018's Stand-Up Comedian of the Year, at the same ceremony where they honored my friend Tiffany Haddish as Comedy Person of the Year. When she received her award, she told the entire audience about our days back at the Laugh Factory and how grateful she was for my support. And yes, for those extra hot dogs I'd buy her. I cried like a baby. We've come a long, long way since then.

My family's story is the immigrant's story. My mom brought us to this country and worked her ass off to provide for us. I'm sure she didn't want to be slaving at the office all day and night to make a few bucks. She didn't want to live in some shitty apartment in Vegas or scrounge for money to buy us food and clothes. But she wanted to provide for us. She wanted her kids to have an opportunity she never had—to go to college and become professionals.

Yeah, so I obviously fucked that last part up.

But because I followed my dream, I can pay for my niece to go to college. I'm funding the educations of family members here in America and back in the Philippines. I'm doing what my mom taught me.

I can help make their dreams come true the same way my mom helped me make my dream come true—even if it wasn't exactly the dream she wanted me to have.

I'm not taking any of this money with me when I die. What should I do with it now? Hoard it? Invest it in the stock market? No, I'm gonna invest it in my family's next generation. I'm gonna open doors for them that weren't opened for us when we got to this country.

So maybe, just maybe, they'll have to sacrifice a little less, and be able to do a little more.

∽

JUST A FEW WEEKS AGO, I had lunch with my cousin Mona and my auntie Evelyn, my family's queen of nicknames, the woman who first called me "Jo Koy." Auntie Evelyn wanted me to take her out to her favorite restaurant, Long John Silver's. It was a splurge, but I wanted to treat her.

We got to the restaurant, and I started thinking.

"Auntie, people always ask me where I got 'Jo Koy' from, but I never have a great answer. How did you come up with that name?"

She looked at me.

"*I* don't you call you 'Jo Koy,'" she said. "*You* call you 'Jo Koy.' *You* made that up!"

What?

"But thirty years ago, when I was with you and Mona . . . You said 'Jo Koy, eat!' You said that!"

"No," she said, shaking her head. "I called you 'Jo *Ko.*' I called you '*my* Jo.'"

I couldn't believe it. "My" in Tagalog is "ko." Put them together and you've got "Jo Ko." All those years ago, *that's* what she said?

My Jo. I may have misheard her way back then, but something about that name felt right.

My Jo. In a way, I am hers. In a way, everything I am, everything I've accomplished, rests not just on my aunt, but on everyone who's been there for me, caring for me, nurturing me, surrounding me with their love, all through my life.

My family—my mom, my dad, Fred, my sisters and brother, my son and his mom. My friends—on military bases across the globe, in Tacoma, in Vegas and LA. Even my fans—in America, my home, in the Philippines, my heritage, and all over the world.

I've been "My Jo" to all of them for all this time. I've felt the power of their connections, pushing me forward, picking me up whenever I fall. I've felt their energy invigorating me. I've felt their laughter sustaining me. And you know what?

I really am theirs. My heart belongs to them.

In the restaurant, my auntie Evelyn, Mona, and I stared at each other in shock.

"Shit," I said. "We gotta print up some new T-shirts for the tour."

ACKNOWLEDGMENTS

This book is about everything you don't get to see onstage. All the blood, sweat, and tears behind my journey from being a funny, mixed-up kid who didn't know how he fit into this country to being the comedian—and man—I am today. And I want to thank all the people who helped make that journey possible, because without your support I wouldn't be here now.

Thank you so much to my entire family. I talk a lot in my act, and in this book, about our complicated relationships. And it's true—they are complicated. But that complexity is simply a sign of their depth. My love, my respect, my gratitude for all of you goes deeper than you'll ever know.

I wouldn't be the person I am without my mom. She sacrificed so much for me growing up, in ways I'll probably never fully understand. Thank you.

I've written a lot about my dad and the mistakes of the past here. But I'm grateful we have the relationship we have today. Dad, thank you for believing in my comedy dream.

In many important ways, Fred was the dad I needed back in high school. Thank you, Fred, for being such a source of stability in my life, for hanging out and watching sports with me, and for not getting too mad when I wrecked your car at prom.

I want to thank my brother and sisters. Robert, you'll always be my big brother. I love you. Rowena, you were the first one to really make it in the entertainment game. I love you, and thank you for inspiring me to raise my own game. Gemma, you're my right hand. I love you, I trust you, and none of this—including this book—would be possible without you.

Little Joe, you know how much you mean to me. I'd write more, but I already dedicated the whole book to you. Come on, how much more do you want?

Through all our ups and downs, Little Joe's mom, Angie, has been one of my best friends. It's so cool that my son's mommy is such a special part of both his life and mine. Angie, I love you, and I got you.

To my cousin Mona—what more can I say, I love you.

I'd like to thank all my aunts. Auntie Evelyn, thank you for giving me my name—and then telling me I got it wrong thirty years later. Auntie Bel, thank you for always being the first to have the new stuff, and for always taking care of me. Auntie Lynn, not only were you my favorite aunt, but you were also the best uncle. Rest in paradise.

After I broke my leg and was in the hospital, I could always count on my uncle Charlie Hibbard to come visit me. I felt so loved. I'll always remember our conversations, and I know where I got my humor from. Rest in paradise.

Uncle Jay, you're like a big brother to me. Seeing you live your best life in your younger days helps me live my best life today. Thank you—and I'm sorry I stole the chrome tire valve caps off your car when I was a kid. But man, my bike looked good.

Gino Perez, you're one of the dopest skaters and one of the dopest artists ever, and I'll always cherish "From the Ghetto to the Getty." But most important, thank you for being there for my son when I was on the road. He loves you, I love you, and you'll always be family.

Shoutout to Brian Terry, who finally gave me his "I ♥ NY" sweatshirt and who also taught me how to grab a basketball rim. You might not know it, but I looked up to you like a big brother. You're the dude. Little things mean a lot.

To all my nieces and nephews—your uncle Jo's got your back. See you in Hawaii soon.

My friends in the comedy and entertainment business have been there for me for years, inspiring me, guiding me, and pushing me to be the best I can be. You might not know it, but you all mean the world to me.

Thank you to Eddie Murphy for lighting that flame. I watched *Delirious* when I was a kid and knew I wanted to be a comic, just like you. I also knew I had to steal my mom's credit card so I could buy tickets to see *Raw* live in concert a few years later. You blazed a trail for me in more ways than one.

To the entire crew at Dada Supreme—you guys were trailblazers, true originals. To see a company founded by Black men in the nineties that went from almost nothing to competing with Nike, that was an inspiration not just to me but to all of us trying to come up. We'd wonder "Can I do it?" then we'd spot Dada in the stores and realize the answer was yes.

Lantz Simpson, you made my show happen. Not just because of the money, but because you believed in me. You said yes before anyone else would. I'll never forget it. Carlos Parrott, no one hustles harder than you. Thank you for being my friend and for motivating me to hustle just as hard as you. Dwayne Lewis, when I first met you I was just checking you into a hotel. But you took the time to talk to me and encourage me, and you gave me the opportunity to make my show a reality.

Thank you to my friend Aristan for being a true inspiration.

Shoutout to Chen Young, my mom's optometrist. We were two guys in Vegas living the dream, and here we are thirty years later. Thank you for being one of my best friends—and for still charging me for my glasses.

Thank you to Paul Ogata, my mom's mechanic, for all the shows he sponsored. Paul, you helped my career in ways you'll never understand. You're the reason I pay it forward.

A big thank-you to the Style Elements Crew, Quali-D, Remind, and Crumbs, and to all the other crews that supported me and my show—Havik Koro, Marlon, Moy, Lil John, and Boy.

Jay Lamont was my headliner on my first big show in Vegas. Thanks for crushing it that night. I'll always remember.

JB Smoove, you are legitimately a beast. I'm proud to say that I got to book you first in Vegas, but I'm even prouder to say we've been friends for over twenty-two years. To this day, I remember you telling me when I was opening for you on the road, "Joseph, stop eating that fast food. It'll kill you!" Then you went and bought me a nice, healthy sandwich. I love you, man.

Michael Blackson is another one of those headliners I got to book before most people understood how great he was. He's been crushing it ever since. I love you, mooda-sucka.

Joey "J Dub" Wells—I still have your Dave Hollister CD. Thank you for killing it in Vegas.

Honest John Basinger—thank you, thank you, thank you. You opened so many doors for me. I owe you big time.

Rudy Rush helped get me on *Showtime at the Apollo*, which was a huge dream of mine. Thank you, man.

Corey Holcomb, you're the real one, man. When I moved to LA, you were the first one to take me under your wing, and I still take your advice with me wherever I go. I love you, brah.

Ralphie May, I love you and miss you so much. Thank you for believing in me when I felt like no one else did. I still brag about you to this day.

Joe Torry, I still remember the advice you gave me about not being afraid of the silence. I took it to heart, and I use it to this day. Thank you.

Gabriel Iglesias, you inspired me to aim high, you showed me what's possible. Thanks for being there for me. Now let's go knock down some doors together.

Cedric the Entertainer—you are what your name says you are, the consummate entertainer. Thank you for showing me that a headliner always has to work for his audience.

A big thanks to Adam Carolla for always believing in me, promoting me, and sharing me with his audience. Adam, you're a huge part of my career, but that still doesn't mean you can eat a thousand dollars of meat at my restaurant. Please, pay me back. I love you.

Rob Schneider, you were the first half-Filipino half-white guy to inspire this half-Filipino half-white guy. Thank you for crushing it and opening the door for guys like me.

Wanya Morris, you helped inspire me to be who I am today and now we're brothers till the end. Thank you for sharing that magical night at the Forum with me. Let's rise together. Love you, my guy!

Tisha Campbell—there's nothing cooler than being someone's biggest fan and finding out they're your fan, too. I'm so happy I can call someone so smart and talented my friend. Thank you for being in my life.

Thank you to Jay Leno for not only letting me appear on his show, but also waving me over to talk at his desk when I thought my time was up. Jay, you changed me life. I went back to work at

Nordstrom Rack the next day, and every other customer said, "You killed it on *The Tonight Show.* Can I please get this in a size 8?"

Jon Lovitz, I still remember when you called me on the phone about taking me on the road. You were my idol, and you still are. I'll never forget when you told me before my spot on *The Tonight Show* to acknowledge both Jay *and* his band, because it wasn't a one-man operation, it was *The Tonight SHOW.* To this day, because of you, I understand how important it is to appreciate everyone in my life, not just the "headliners." Thank you for noticing this young kid and taking him out of Nordstrom Rack.

When we got started in the business, Tiffany Haddish and I had nothing except some jokes and some stage time, and we were happy. We're even happier today. It's amazing to realize that my best friend is now one of the coolest, biggest stars in Hollywood. No one deserves it more. Thank you for always having my back and for always keeping it real. I love you. Let's keep rising.

Chelsea Handler believed in me from day one. Thank you for creating an incredible show that gave me and other comics a chance to shine under your bright light.

Bobby Lee, thank you for kicking doors down and leaving them open for comics like me. I'll always remember doing that MTV audition with you years ago. I wasn't taking it seriously, I said all I cared about was the money I made off touring, and you let me have it, man. You told me that making it in this business is about more than money—it's about passion, about determination and commitment. "You don't fucking get it!" you shouted. And you know what? You were right—I didn't. But your words lit a fire in me. To this day, if I get an audition, I hear you yelling at me, telling me to be better—and I love you for it. You've taught me so much, you're a true friend, and I'm forever grateful.

Thank you to Jamie Masada for everything you've done for both me and the entire comedy community. The Laugh Factory stage is still the best stage in my heart. Thank you for making me talk about my mom.

A huge shoutout to Bob Read and Ross Mark, who took a kid out of the shoe store and put him on one of the greatest comedy shows of all time. Thank you, guys.

Huge thanks to Kevin Kearney for giving me my first paid comedy-club gig at Catch a Rising Star.

Erin von Schonfeldt—being onstage at the Improv was my childhood dream. Thank you for making that dream a reality. You were always there for me, and I'll always be there for you.

Thank you to Steve Schirripa for taking an eighteen-year-old kid's phone call, giving him great advice—and telling him to please, stop calling.

Bob Sumner gave me a chance to go onstage, even if he didn't want to turn down the houselights. Thanks for the opportunity.

Tom Werner and Mike Clement believed in me before anyone else in the TV game. We didn't make it happen, but I'll always cherish the support you gave me.

To Paul Meloche and Mike Bernal at Icon Concerts—we had a dream, we had a vision, and we made it happen together. I appreciate you both so much. Let's keep dreaming.

Thank you to Kaity McQuade, my hardworking publicist, and to my lawyer, Danny F. Miller, who always has my back. I love you both.

Big shoutout to my assistant, Jacob Pulley. I wouldn't cut the hair of just any assistant. I'm so happy I finally convinced you . . . that you're bald. #nomorecombover Let's keep crushing this social media game together. Thank you for everything. You're a genius.

A heartfelt thanks to my amazing editor at Dey Street, Carrie Thornton. I'm so blessed I was able to work with you. Thank you for not only giving me the opportunity to tell my story, but for also being such a personal part of my book. I've loved talking to you and getting to know you, and you're not just my editor—you're my friend. We got pictures to prove it. Thank you as well to Chris Farah. From our first meeting over coffee talking about writing a book together, we've laughed, we've cried, we've watched your baby being born. You're more than my writing partner, you're my friend for life. Let's write some more books!

Huge thank you to everyone at Netflix. Robbie Praw, you've believed and invested in me from the start, from my first spot on Just for Laughs to all my specials. I'll treasure our relationship for the rest of my life. Thank you, and I love you. JoAnn Grigioni and Neil Sheridan, the Super Duo—I know I say this all the time, but I really, really love you. Thank you for being a part of the biggest specials of my career. Let's make some more. Plus, there's more gifts waiting for you. And to Rob Guillermo, thank you so much for helping to make me and my specials part of the Netflix family. I couldn't be prouder.

A giant thanks to Michelle Caputo and Shannon Hartman at Art & Industry, the visionary producer and director who helped make my *Live from Seattle* and *Comin' in Hot* specials happen. What can I say? You two killed it. They're my favorite specials of all time, and I'm so happy I made them with you. Thank you for being the best at what you do.

Melvin Mar, you're a visionary. You created a show that made an entire generation proud. I look forward to creating another show with you that'll make a whole new generation proud. It's been a blessing working with you, and I deeply appreciate you.

Dan Lin, you've already accomplished so much that's so incredibly special. It's such an honor for me to accomplish something with you. You're a genius and a leader, but most important you're my friend. Thank you.

To Holly Bario, Jeb Brody, Steven Spielberg, and everyone at Amblin Entertainment—I still remember when I found out Steven loved my special. Talk about a dream come true! Thank you for everything you do and everything you create. You're icons, and I'm still in awe that I'm about to create something with you. I love you from the bottom of my heart.

A big thanks to my team at CAA. Frank Jung, I still remember our conversation outside the Improv. You weren't even my agent yet, but you believed in me back then and you still believe in me now. You're more than an agent to me, you're my brother for life. Thank you for being a real one since the beginning. I love you. Matt Blake, when I was about to leave, you told me that would be the biggest mistake, and you showed me what the future could be. Thank God I didn't leave, because everything you promised came true. I can't wait to keep building our future together. Love you, Matt. And to the rest of the crew—Rosanna Bilow, Cait Hoyt, Anthony Mattero, Ari Levin, Marlene Tsuchii, Josh Pearl, and Steve Smooke—thank you so much for your incredible work and for taking me to the next level. I love you guys.

Joe Meloche—you're my best friend, and I thank God you came into my life. You know someone truly believes in you when they're willing to risk it all. Thank you for taking those risks with me, and I love sharing the rewards. You're more than my manager, you're my brother. We also eat lots of food together.

And finally, I want to give the biggest thanks of all to my fans. This is going to sound cheesy, but I honestly don't feel like I can call you fans—you're more like my family. Man, I still remember one of my biggest fans of all, Amir, feeding me some of the best

Filipino food of my life at his house in Illinois all those years ago. The love is real, and it's mutual.

I feel like my fan-family and I have been on this journey together for the last thirty years. It hasn't just been me, it's been all of us. We've laughed together, we've grown together, we've learned from each other. Thank you so much for standing by me. I love you all, and I hope our journey never ends.

ABOUT THE AUTHOR

Jo Koy is a comedian, actor, writer, and podcast host who sells out arenas around the world by telling real stories about his life, his family, and finding his way in the entertainment industry. He has multiple hit comedy specials on Netflix, and his unique brand of humor has been featured on Comedy Central, *The Tonight Show*, and *Chelsea Lately*. In 2018, Jo received the "Stand-Up Comedian of the Year" award at the legendary Just for Laughs Comedy Festival in Montreal, and the previous year he reached number-one on the Billboard Charts for his standup album, *Live From Seattle*. In 2019 in Honolulu, Jo broke the record for the most tickets sold by a single artist at 23,000 with his eleven sold-out shows at the Neal S. Blaisdell Concert Hall, inspiring the mayor to proclaim November 24 "Jo Koy Day." Jo currently lives in Los Angeles with his son, Joseph, who inspires him to be a better performer, father, and man every single day.